ESCAPE TO SHANGHAI

ESCAPE TO SHANGHAI

A JEWISH COMMUNITY IN CHINA

JAMES R. ROSS

THE FREE PRESS
A Division of Macmillan, Inc.
NEW YORK

Maxwell Macmillan Canada
TORONTO

Maxwell Macmillan International
NEW YORK OXFORD SINGAPORE SYDNEY

The Free Press
A Division of Macmillan, Inc.
866 Third Avenue, New York, N.Y. 10022

Maxwell Macmillan Canada, Inc.
1200 Eglinton Avenue East
Suite 200
Don Mills, Ontario M3C 3N1

Macmillan, Inc. is part of the Maxwell Communication Group of Companies.

Printed in the United States of America

printing number

1   2   3   4   5   6   7   8   9   10

Library of Congress Cataloging-in-Publication Data

Ross, James R. (James Rodman)
    Escape to Shanghai : a Jewish community in China / James R. Ross.
        p. cm.
    Includes bibliographical references and index.
    ISBN 0–02–927375–7
    1. Jews—China—Shanghai—History—20th century. 2. Refuges,
Jewish—China—Shanghai—History—20th century. 3. Refugees.,
Jewish—China—Shanghai—Biography. 4. Shanghai (China)—Biography.
5. Shanghai (China)—Ethnic relations.   I. Title.
DS135.C5R67   1994
951'.132004924—dc20   93–21337
                                                              CIP

In memory of my father, Dr. Maurice Ross,
a man who never stopped seeking truth
and knowledge and who dedicated his life
to comforting and healing.

Contents

PART IV: GHETTO (1943–1944)

PART V: EXODUS (1945–1950)

Author's Note

In December 1990, I visited Fred Fields in Hallandale, Florida, only a few miles from my mother's home. It was the first time I had met a Jewish refugee from Shanghai. A few weeks earlier, I had read an old newspaper article about a 1985 refugee reunion in the Catskills, and I telephoned Trixie Wachsner of Los Angeles, who was one of the organizers. She gave me the names and addresses of several other refugees, including Fred, and I arranged to talk with him and learn more about his story.

In those first few hours we spent together, Fred told me about escaping from Berlin as a nineteen-year-old in December 1938, just after *Kristallnacht*. He left his mother behind and, on his first trip out of Germany, boarded a ship in Genoa and traveled halfway around the world to Shanghai, an open port where he could enter without a visa. He reminisced about working at his uncle's German restaurant in Shanghai, writing about soccer and other sports for several newspapers, and learning English by sneaking into Nelson Eddy and Jeanette MacDonald movies in an air-conditioned theater. Fred also talked about the cruelty of the Japanese who controlled Shanghai, their decision to force all the Jews to live in a ghetto in 1943, and the tragic deaths of dozens of refugees in an American bombing raid just before the end of the war.

Fred had collected a treasure trove of material about Shanghai and the Jewish refugees, and he loaned me most of it. He also gave me three lists of the names and addresses of the hundreds of refugees who had attended the reunions in 1980, 1985, and 1988. That was the beginning of my adventure with the Shanghai Jewish refugees.

I was not a stranger to Shanghai or to Judaism. I had grown up in a Jewish home and received thorough religious training, although, like many American Jews, I often had wandered from my faith as I grew older. I knew Shanghai from my experience as a journalism professor there—I had spent two summers living in the city and teaching journalism at the Shanghai Foreign Languages Institute. Fred Fields' story—the story of the Shanghai Jewish refugees—brought together two powerful forces in my life.

For the next two years, I made my own voyage around the world, interviewing hundreds of refugees in Australia, Europe, Israel, and throughout the United States, tracking down letters and documents in a dozen archives, and walking the streets where the refugees grew up in Europe and where they lived in Shanghai. I felt as if I became part of their community, sharing in their stories, bringing together long-lost friends, and enjoying their warmth and generosity.

I attended Saturday morning services at a synagogue in San Francisco, surrounded by some of the Shanghai refugees who had founded the congregation after the war. I spent days at the Hakoah Club in Sydney, eating schnitzel and talking with the former soccer stars of Shanghai's Jewish teams. In Melbourne, I joined in one of the regular gatherings of refugees they call *schrei Abends* (yelling evenings); at Deveroli's Deli in St. Kilda, I met eighty-year-old Herman Natowic, who told me how he survived five months of torture and imprisonment in the notorious Japanese Bridge House. I attended Rosh Hashanah services at a synagogue in Berlin that had been destroyed during *Kristallnacht* and that is now officiated by a rabbi from Shanghai. I had dinner in Vienna at the home of Mary Steinhauser, a refugee who helps hold together the remnants of Jewish life there. In Tel Aviv, Kurt Maimann, who writes a newsletter for former refugees that circulates worldwide, introduced me to other refugees now living in Israel. Back in the United States, I talked with dozens of refugees at a reunion in Philadelphia. And when I returned to Shanghai, I found a few surviving relics of a once-thriving Jewish community.

There were once nearly 20,000 European Jewish refugees in Shanghai. Now, a half century after these events unfolded, many refugees have died. But among those who are still alive today there are thousands of different stories. This book recounts four of them: an Austrian doctor, a young man from East Prussia, a boy from Berlin, and a rabbi's daughter from Neukölln. This is not intended to be a definitive history of their community; it is simply part of a remarkable mosaic, told through the eyes of four survivors.

Most of the refugees I met now lead full and successful lives. Nearly all of them are past retirement age, but many are still working, well into their seventies and eighties. They continue to strive and to achieve; the upheaval that changed their lives seems to have left them all with something to prove, a need to show their energy, wit, and resilience to a world that more than once rejected them. Some have become well known, including author and MacArthur fellow Walter Abish, former Treasury Secretary W. Michael Blumenthal, hotelier Henri Lewin, artist Peter Max, engineering professor Peter Stein, educational psychologist Sigmund Tobias, and constitutional scholar Laurence Tribe, who was born in Shanghai in 1941.

Even those refugees who now appear sullen and bitter become animated when talk turns to Shanghai. Despite painful memories of poverty and disease, most recall their Shanghai days with a sense of wonder. It was the defining experience of their lives, a time when they learned to see themselves as survivors instead of victims.

For most refugees, the memories of Shanghai have faded. But they have left a legacy of a vibrant Jewish community in the strangest of places and the most difficult of times. Their story has taught me the importance of preserving Jewish history and has renewed my faith in Judaism. I hope it also serves as a small reminder of what the rest of the world lost fifty years ago when it denied refuge to them—and to the millions of others who did not survive.

Prologue

Shanghai is a city of extremes. Its weather varies from long, tropical summers, when the air is uncomfortably thick with humidity and pollution, to icy winters, with temperatures dipping well below freezing through March and early April. It rains almost constantly in the spring and again in the fall, when typhoons often flood the streets—most of the city was built on swampland. The only constant is a gray, dreary sky.

This is the city that became the refuge for 20,000 European Jewish refugees a half century ago. Much of Shanghai remains as it was when they first arrived. Its streets are still a crush of humanity, an endless flow of bicycles, pedestrians, pedicabs, cars, and twisting trolley buses that overwhelms most Western visitors. The traffic tangles chaotically at each interesection, competing for every angle amid a cacophony of horns, bells, and Shanghai-dialect curses. The frequent collisions add to the turmoil, as dozens of people push for a better view of a fallen bicyclist or pedestrian and offer their views on who was at fault.

Crowds seem to gather at almost any provocation. Despite their constant presence in Shanghai, foreigners are a subject of perpetual curiosity. Westerners who stop to sit on park benches or wait on a street corner often are surrounded by dozens of friendly, staring spectators, some of whom invariably try to practice their English.

Yet the historical separation between the Chinese and foreigners remains, long after the foreign enclaves established in the nineteenth century have lost their legal status. Today in Shanghai, as in the rest of China, most foreigners avoid the noise and crowds—and pay, by Chinese standards, exorbitant prices—by staying in luxury hotels, shopping in so-called friendship stores, and eating in separate sections of restaurants set aside for foreigners. Few visitors have much interaction with the native Chinese, other than hotel employees, tour guides, taxi drivers, and waiters and waitresses. The official Chinese view is that this system provides comfort for the foreigners; it also generates additional foreign revenues. And, in a nation long suspicious of outsiders, it insulates most Chinese from close contact with foreigners.

Other features of the city also have changed only slightly in the past fifty years. The Bund, facing Shanghai's busy Whangpoo* River harbor, looks much as it did in the 1920s and 1930s, when wealthy Western financiers built a mile-long row of banks, trading houses, and hotels, decorated with neoclassical domes, towers, columns, and statues. The buildings are now owned by Chinese firms but are a reminder of the former foreign dominance of the city. Remnants of Western architecture can be found in other parts of the city as well. Many of the mansions built by wealthy foreigners in the former French Concession, topped by red-tile roofs and surrounded by high walls, now house schools and government agencies.

In the older sections of the city, not far from the waterfront, there also is little evidence of change. Large families live in crowded, crumbling lane houses with few modern conveniences, other than television sets and radios. In the warmer months, foreigners who speed by in air-conditioned

---

* All Chinese words in this book are romanized under the Wade-Giles system, which was in use at the time the refugees lived in Shanghai. It has since been supplanted by the pinyin system.

tour buses and taxicabs gawk at groups of Chinese in nightgowns, T-shirts, and boxer shorts, escaping the heat of their houses to cook, play cards, do their laundry, and take afternoon naps on the streets and sidewalks.

But elsewhere Shanghai is undergoing rapid development, spurred by the country's new economic policies. Modern hotels and office buildings are rising in every corner of the city, and a new subway system is being built beneath it. Even desolate Putong, the site of prewar foreign tobacco factories and wartime camps where the Japanese interned prisoners, has been declared a special economic zone, and dozens of skyscrapers are under construction there. Throughout the city, there are five-star hotels topped by revolving restaurants and shops selling luxury items from Paris, London, and New York. As it was fifty years ago, Shanghai is a place where foreigners are both welcomed and isolated.

Shanghai was the birthplace of both Chinese communism and Western modernization in China. It has been the home for much of China's working class and many of its finest artists, writers, and scholars. After World War I, it was the world's most cosmopolitan—and corrupt—city. Its very name connotes deceit.

It had been a small trading port until the middle of the nineteenth century. Western trade in China had been limited to Canton and always had been practiced on Chinese terms. The foreigners exported Hangchow's tea and Soochow's silk and imported only a few products—the balance of trade was heavily in China's favor. But in the 1830s, the East India Company built up a powerful demand for its Indian opium in China. In 1839, Britain demanded full diplomatic recognition and access to trade.[1] The Chinese emperor, Tao-kuang, dismissed the demand and dealt with the British threat in the same way China had handled foreigners for thousands of years. He sent an official to seize and destroy Britain's opium stock in Canton, then sent a general to battle with the British. And when his tiny navy was overwhelmed by British gunboats in Shanghai and Nanking, the emperor compromised by signing a treaty, as he had done with other foreign barbarians in the past.[2]

The treaty opened five ports, including Shanghai, to foreign trade and gave the emperor foreign allies—as well as opium revenue—to support his crumbling dynasty. Two years later, in 1844, the Americans, benefiting from Britain's victory, signed a treaty that established extraterritoriality.[3] It meant that foreigners in the treaty ports were exempt from Chinese laws; they lived by their own rules.

Both the Chinese and foreigners now began to profit from Shanghai's economic potential. It was easily accessible to Japan and the West by sea and its Whangpoo River was a natural harbor, deep and wide and located at the southern tip of the heavily-populated Yangtze River estuary. By the end of the 1840s, Shanghai had become one of the world's great ports, handling even more tonnage than London.[4]

In 1854, the foreign communities established their own government, headed by the Shanghai Municipal Council, and a police force. The council was elected by those foreigners who held land and paid taxes in the settlement. At first, the settlements were divided into three concessions—French, British, and American—but the Americans and British combined their territory in 1863 to form the International Settlement. In 1895, after humiliating the Chinese navy in the Sino-Japanese war, the Japanese also were granted treaty rights in the settlement.[5]

The settlement was on both sides of Soochow Creek, from Jessfield Park in the west to the Yangtzepoo Creek in the east. Its streets had American names like Broadway and British ones like Alcock and Muirhead, in honor of the early British settlers of Shanghai. The foreign-named streets intersected with Chinese ones. Most north–south streets in Shanghai are named after Chinese provinces, like Szechuen and Yunnan; the east–west streets after cities, like Peking and Nanking.

The smaller French Concession remained apart, with its own government and police force, covering the land south of the International Settlement and surrounding the original walled

Chinese city.[6] Its streets took on names like Rue Lafayette and Avenue Edward VII.

The foreigners built their own hotels, clubs, restaurants, banks, schools, hospitals, an electric plant, warehouses, factories, and parks. They published newspapers, had their own postal service, and controlled the customs office.[7] Shanghai offered China's most elegant shops and some of the world's finest hotels and restaurants. It also was the favorite destination for the world's most notorious swindlers, spies, and scoundrels—no visa was required to enter the city.

The British and a small community of Sephardic Jews, most of whom were British subjects, dominated that foreign society. But new groups of foreigners continued to find their own niches in the International Settlement and French Concession. The Japanese moved into the northern part of the settlement and ran factories owned by Mitsui and Mitsubishi. After the Russian Revolution, thousands of White Russians who had fled from the Bolsheviks moved into the French Concession and brought Russian music, ballet, and poetry—as well as prostitutes, low-paid laborers, spies, and shady nightclub owners—to the city. In the 1930s, Russian Jewish exiles who had settled in Manchuria began moving to Shanghai as the Japanese took control of northern China. The foreign community also included Americans, Italians, Latvians, Hungarians, Portuguese, Finns, and the turbaned Sikhs who directed traffic for the municipal police.

The number of foreign residents in Shanghai, which never surpassed 100,000, was far less than the Chinese population in the international area. Chinese living in the foreign community could not be arrested without approval of a foreign consul, and Chinese troops were denied authority to enter the settlements.[8] Many Chinese worked as compradores or domestic help, but the foreigners remained insulated within their own societies. The Chinese had no representatives in the settlement government until 1927, and then only in an advisory role.[9]

Western influence in Shanghai declined steadily in the 1920s and 1930s, yielding first to the antiforeign Chinese labor movement and then to the Chinese Nationalists. In February

1930, the British and Americans agreed to grant the Chinese control of the court system in the International Settlement.[10] But it was another foreign power, Japan, that finally destroyed the independence of the Western community.

In January 1932, Japanese planes bombed the Chapei section of Shanghai, just north of the International Settlement, killing hundreds of civilians. Chinese troops withstood the assault of three Japanese divisions.[11] Five years later, the Japanese again moved on Shanghai. Most of the initial damage was done in August 1937, when Chinese planes accidentally bombed their own civilians, killing hundreds. In the battle that followed, as many as 250,000 Chinese and more than 40,000 Japanese were killed or wounded.[12] The heaviest fighting was in Hongkew, northeast of Soochow Creek. By November, the Japanese had defeated the Chinese forces. But the loss of Shanghai was only a prelude to one of the worst massacres in modern history. The Japanese moved north to Nanking and, after the Chinese forces withdrew, their soldiers brutally raped and murdered tens of thousands of defenseless civilians in seven weeks of inhuman fury.[13]

Shanghai, and about half of the International Settlement, was now firmly controlled by the Japanese. The other half of the settlement, crowded with four million Chinese refugees,[14] maintained a tenuous and uneasy independence. British, American, and other foreign troops patrolled opposite Japanese soldiers. Much of the city was in ruins; entire streets in Hongkew, one of the poorest sections of the city, had been turned into rubble and the lanes were filled with corpses.[15]

In the years that followed, as nations throughout the world continued to turn away Europe's Jewish refugees, the city the Western powers had forced open a century earlier became the Jews' only refuge. It had little else to offer them; most of the refugees were directed to Hongkew.

I
ARRIVAL
(1938–1939)

1

Didner

Dr. Sam Didner stood on the bow of the pilot's boat as it motored through the gray, murky Whangpoo River and neared the *Conte Rosso*. The Italian ocean liner in front of him was almost as long as two soccer fields and loomed high above the small boat. Plumes of smoke poured from the liner's two huge stacks, blown toward shore by the stiff, cold breeze in late December 1938. Didner squinted through the smoke and the morning haze. He could see the outlines of some of the refugees, leaning against the rail on the upper deck. A few waved their hats and handkerchiefs at the approaching boat.

When the pilot's boat reached the ship, the *Conte Rosso*'s crew lowered a ladder and Didner, along with two nurses, followed the harbor pilot aboard. The pilot would guide the passenger liner the last few miles to Shanghai, past the cargo ships and British, American, and Japanese cruisers anchored there. Didner and the nurses were aboard as medical representatives of one of the refugee relief committees. They planned to immunize the refugees for smallpox, one of the dozens of deadly diseases that awaited them in Shanghai.

Before Didner stepped onto the deck, several refugees crowded toward him. He noted they looked healthy and well fed—the food on the Lloyd Triestino liners was rich and plentiful—but their clothes were rumpled. Many had been wearing the same clothes for the entire thirty-day voyage. Didner could tell from their hefty builds and pale skin that they were mostly Germans and Austrians. The men wore homburgs, porkpies, or berets and double-breasted, wool herringbone coats. A few women sported feathered hats and coats with fur collars. The children, scurrying by as they played tag on the deck, wore pulldown woolen caps and sailor suits.

Didner, in his starched white lab coat and large black bowtie, smiled and gently pushed his way through the waiting group. But one of the older refugees blocked his path. His face was deeply lined and he smiled darkly. He spoke in a German dialect that sounded odd to Didner.

"So, Herr Doctor, what do they have for us here in Shanghai?" the man asked. His voice wavered with anxiety. "Is it true there is only dirt and disease and people are sleeping and dying all over the streets?"

Didner smiled again. He had wondered the same thing when he arrived here less than two weeks ago, thinking then that he would end up shoveling coal for a living. He tried to reassure the man.

"Do not worry, my friend. We have a committee here to help you with housing and food," Didner replied. He spoke formally, as one might expect of an Austrian doctor. But his tone was gentle. He spoke loudly enough so that others could hear him. "You must be careful about what you eat here and you must not drink the water. But you will be well taken care of."

"Now tell me," Didner said more quietly, with an impish smile, "what language is it that you're speaking?"

The older man laughed. "It's German, of course. I am from Berlin. So where do you come from that you speak German so strangely?"

"I am Austrian," Didner replied. "I came here on the *Conte Biancamano* a short time ago."

It had been just twelve days, but Didner had already settled in. He had found a job as medical director of the new

Emigrants' Hospital and a room in the hospital to sleep in. For the past week, he had been buying medical equipment, hiring nurses, and setting up the hospital, the former British Old Women's Home on Washing Road, to treat the steady influx of refugees coming to Shanghai. The home had once served as a dormitory for sixty to seventy refugees, but now it was needed for medical care, because few of the refugees could afford the fees at Shanghai General Hospital.

The visit to the *Conte Rosso* was one of Didner's first official tasks as medical director. It took him and the nurses about an hour to organize the 259[1] refugees and vaccinate them with a simple scratch on the skin. By then, the *Conte Rosso* had anchored in the harbor and Kurt Marx, secretary of the Relief Society for German and Austrian Jews, had come aboard to hand out an announcement to the passengers. It read:

INSTRUCTION SHEET

In the interest of the newly-arrived refugees and those Jews already settled in Shanghai, we recommend that the following directions be taken note of and observed. Otherwise, mistakes cannot be avoided and these could be harmful to the person concerned and to the general public.

The orders given by the assistants on the ships are to be followed without fail. Otherwise, it is impossible to facilitate an orderly completion of the landing and customs formalities.

It is forbidden to give information to unknown persons, especially to reporters . . .

Political discussions are strictly forbidden.

Due to military reasons, it is forbidden to take photos in Hongkew; the carrying of photo-cameras is to be refrained from.

Conspicuous conduct on the street, loud conversation, loitering in hotel lobbies and begging is to be refrained from absolutely. . . . It is forbidden to enter nightclubs and bars and to participate in gambling of any kind, including slot machines . . .

It is compulsory for those who receive monetary assistance to participate in English language courses. We warn of pickpockets. Watch your handbags.

We repeat that these instructions, even if they are presented as prohibitions, are for the benefit of the newcomers and unavoidable and necessary. Cooperation between the committees and the newcomers makes execution of these measures easier.[2]

When he was done with the vaccinations, Didner helped other representatives from the relief committees lead the refugees off the ship to a ferry that brought them to the customs shed. At the dock, dozens of coolies, dressed only in torn, filthy pants and bamboo hats, circled around the passengers, grabbing for their luggage and racing with it toward customs. The first refugees already were lining up at the shed, a large wooden shack where uniformed British inspectors carefully searched their small, tattered suitcases. A few had to pay a small duty, but all were allowed to enter the city. With the passport office closed since the Japanese had taken over most of the city, even those without valid passports were admitted. The international community's unusual legal status had made Shanghai an open port. Now it was the only place in the world that would take in these refugees.

A row of trucks lined up outside to take the refugees to their new home. The trucks, with open wooden slats on the sides, seemed more suited to carrying cattle than people. Didner had his own transportation. He jumped on his bicycle—a sturdy old Brennerabor he had bought just after he arrived—and headed back to the hospital in Hongkew.

Didner pedaled along the Bund, Shanghai's waterfront thoroughfare, as trucks and buses blared their horns and swerved among the crowds of rickshaw drivers, pedestrians, and bicyclists. He remained awed by the magnificent row of hotels, banks, and office buildings. Sassoon House, the Bank of China, the Yokohama Specie Bank, the Ewo (Jardine Matheson & Co.) Building, and other massive edifices towered over him. Just past the Ewo Building, Didner swung toward Soochow Creek, a tributary of the Whangpoo that separated Hongkew from the rest of the International Settlement.

As he passed over the sampans on the creek below, Didner could smell rice and vegetables cooking as families who lived on the water prepared their lunches. The creek had become home to hundreds of Chinese refugees trying to escape the war with Japan. It also smelled like Shanghai's sewer. Everything from corpses to watermelon rinds floated to the surface and gave off a foul, pungent odor.

Didner entered Hongkew on the Garden Bridge, a two-lane crossing with two long iron trestles overhead. A Scottish sentry patrolled the western end of the bridge, still controlled by the Western powers of the International Settlement. The eastern end belonged to the Japanese, who had occupied Hongkew since the summer of 1937. Two Japanese soldiers there quickly looked over Didner and then sent him on his way. As he stopped on the bridge, he could see the imposing twenty-two-story Broadway Mansions and the row of foreign consulates just past it. The Nazi swastika flag flew prominently, not far from the Soviet hammer and sickle. Didner headed east into Hongkew.

In an hour or so, the first group of new refugees would take this same route. But after crossing the bridge, the truck would swing west along the north side of the creek and up North Soochow Road, into the International Settlement. There the refugess would pass factories reduced to burned-out shells and houses and shops that had been blown into piles of dirt and scorched bricks. Only a few buildings remained standing amid the rubble. It was an eerie landscape of wartime desolation.

The refugees were headed for the Embankment Building, a broad, nine-story luxury office building next to the main post office constructed less than ten years earlier by an enormously wealthy Sephardic Jew, Sir Victor Sassoon. It had escaped damage in the intensive bombing and shelling, and foreign businessmen continued to occupy offices there. But Sassoon recently had turned over the first floor to the relief committees to house and feed the refugees. Now, with the new arrivals from the *Conte Rosso* and hundreds more on the way, the first floor of the Embankment Building was nearly filled to capacity.

As Didner bicycled east on Broadway, he thought about what was awaiting the refugees and wondered how they would adapt to Shanghai. The refugees' arrival also reminded him of home and of the family he had left behind.

Like most Austrians, Didner came from a family of immigrants. Both his parents, Zallel Leib (Leo) and Hedwig, came from Przeworsk, Poland, and had emigrated to Graz in the 1890s. Shortly before Samuel was born, Hedwig returned to her mother's home. Samuel was the youngest of eight children, born in Przeworsk on November 10, 1905. When the new year began, his mother returned to Graz to raise him.

Graz was the ancient capital of Styria, in southern Austria, a city of 150,000 at the eastern end of the Alps. Its musicians and actors made Graz a cultural capital second only to Vienna; its doctors and scientists, including Fritz Pregl, who won the Nobel Prize in chemistry in 1923, were among the best in the world. Graz also had a quiet charm. A gentle river, the Mur, divides the city, crossed by seven bridges; broad, green parks and cathedrals dominate both river banks. The Humboldt district, north of the Stadt Park, was a popular retirement area for Austrian civil servants and officers. Graz also was headquarters for the Third Army Corps.[3]

Graz had been one of the first places where Jews settled in Austria, beginning in 1166, only thirty years after the city was founded.[4] Most of the small Jewish community eventually emigrated to Hungary during the various waves of pogroms, but by the middle of the nineteenth century, under the relatively benevolent rule of Emperor Franz Josef, Jews were allowed to return there.[5]

The Jews of Graz completed a Jewish primary school in 1892 and, in 1895, Franz Josef came to consecrate a new synagogue. By the time Samuel was born, there were about 2,000 Jews in Graz, the second-largest Jewish community in Austria.[6]

Samuel grew up in a kosher home and went to synagogue on holidays. He studied Jewish history and learned some Hebrew at the Jewish primary school. Like many of his acculturated Jewish schoolmates, he was not particularly religious; he didn't eat kosher food when he was away from home. Yet he felt strongly about his Jewishness. He dated non-Jewish girls but never considered marrying one. At the time, about two-thirds of the Jews who were married in Graz wedded non-

Jews, although half of the non-Jewish partners converted to Judaism.[7]

Samuel's father, Leo, was a shadow figure in his youth, suffering from heart trouble and only occasionally working in the family's copper and bronze business. The youngest boy's early interest in medicine—he knew he wanted to be a doctor at age ten—may have stemmed from the hours he spent helping take care of his father. Isak, the oldest son, ran the business and supported the family. The Didners lived comfortably. They owned two apartment houses as well as their own home in the northeastern part of the city, not far from Karl Franz University.

Samuel did well in primary school and his parents sent him to Gymnasium to study Latin and prepare for college. He was a bright student, but lazy, and he found he could succeed by coasting through most of the school year and then studying day and night for final examinations. That left him time for recreational reading. But the Gymnasium was extremely strict—Samuel was once nearly thrown out of school for sneaking in one of his favorite books, an American cowboy and Indian story.

Samuel also loved sports, even though he was small for his age. He joined his Jewish classmates in the Hakoah Sports Club, where he learned to play soccer and box. His best friends were soccer players and they often spent their afternoons walking and playing in the Stadt Park.

The park wasn't a safe place for Jewish boys. The sons of the army officers posted in Graz, some of whom were early supporters of the Nazis in Germany, regularly beat up Jewish kids. But Samuel was always safe when he walked with Moses Berger. Everyone seemed afraid to challenge Moses, a short, stocky boy with spiky hair. Samuel developed a reputation of his own as well. He once fought the champion of southern Austria to a three-round draw after being knocked down five times in the first two rounds. The young toughs respected the Jewish kids who could defend themselves.

Didner remained in Graz to attend university, matriculating at Karl Franz, the state-run school that had been founded in 1573 as a Jesuit seminary.[8] In college, he encountered a different kind of anti-Semitism, far more hateful and violent than he had seen in his younger days. Jews made up an unusually high proportion of students and faculty at Austrian universities—up to one-third of university students were Jewish, although Jews made up only about three percent of the total Austrian population. The Jews had flocked to Austria's universities not only because of their traditional love of learning but also because they could qualify for employment outside of the civil service, which was virtually off limits to them.

In the postwar depression, non-Jewish students and faculty focused their anger on the Jews, demanding limits on their enrollment. Anti-Semitic rallies and attacks on Jewish students and teachers were routine parts of university life.[9] The year Didner enrolled, rioting students at Karl Franz had disrupted classes for a day and beaten Jewish professors and students while university administrators refused to intervene. But not all Jews were targeted. Most of the fury was directed at the Orthodox Eastern European Jews. Didner, who looked as Austrian as any of his classmates, attended school that day and was left alone.

After six years at the university, Didner was ready to begin his medical training. Many Austrian Jews were then pursuing careers, like law and medicine, in which they could work independently. Medicine had one other attraction for a people with a history of uncertain futures: It could be practiced anywhere in world.[10]

Didner moved to Vienna to serve a rotating residency at the Allgemeines Krankenhaus, a 5,000-bed general hospital affiliated with the University of Vienna Medical School, the most renowned medical institution in the world. The medical school had been founded in the middle of the eighteenth century. Its faculty excelled at diagnosis and produced pioneers in almost every field of medicine, including dermatology, urology, and anesthesia. Patients came from all over the world for treatment. Sigmund Freud received his medical training at the school and later taught there.[11]

Vienna was a center of culture and intellect in other fields as well. And many of its most brilliant minds—Wittgenstein in philosophy; Schoenberg and Mahler in music; Schnitzler, von Hofmannsthal, and Zweig in literature; Freud and Adler in psychology—had Jewish origins.[12] Although Jews made up less than ten percent of Vienna's population, they dominated its schools, salons, theaters, newspapers, and opera houses. More than half of Didner's medical professors were Jewish.[13]

Despite this Jewish presence—at the time, Vienna had the sixth-largest Jewish population in the world[14]—Didner found even less sense of Jewish identity than he had found in Graz's small Jewish community. An increasing rate of conversions and intermarriage, combined with a low birthrate, seemed to foreshadow that Viennese Jews would be totally assimilated into Austria within a generation. The Jewish immigrants from Galicia, most of them ardent Zionists, provided the only counterweight to that trend.

But the assimilation was in some ways only cursory. Although many Austrian Jews had stopped practicing their religion, they maintained traditional Jewish values. Some had seen their relative freedom from government persecution as an opportunity leave the *shtetl* and replace their study of Talmud with the study of science, philosophy, literature, and music.[15] What they discovered instead was a new ghetto, a Jewish cultural and intellectual enclave set apart from the rest of Austrian society. And within that enclave, few Jews were able to recognize that Austrian anti-Semitism remained just below the surface, like some bubbling swamp whose monsters burst forth in times of crisis.[16]

Didner was a resident for six years, forced to work his hardest for pro-Nazi professors who openly berated Jewish students. Physical violence against Jews occurred regularly. Didner was working in the hospital emergency room during one of the anti-Jewish riots, in the summer of 1931, and was surprised to see only Nazis being brought in with cuts and broken bones. But Didner did recognize one Jew as he sutured a small cut on his hand. He was the national wrestling champion. The Jewish students had anticipated the attack that day and recruited boxers and wrestlers from the Hakoah Club to fight for them.

Despite the attacks on Jews and the Nazis' rise to power in

neighboring Germany, Didner and most Austrian Jews remained hopeful about their future. The Christian Social chancellor who took power in 1932, Engelbert Dollfuss, was one of the few recent Austrian leaders who had refused to incite anti-Semitism. He won support among the Jews by taking steps to protect them against violence at the universities and by outlawing job and housing discrimination. Dollfuss was an ardent opponent of the Nazis and, in June 1933, he outlawed the Austrian Nazi Party.[17] But the Nazis continued to function illegally, and discrimination against Jews remained widespread. The Austrians called it "rubber-soled anti-Semitism," more silent, but just as virulent, as the sickness in Germany.[18]

The discrimination was particularly hard on Jewish physicians in Vienna, who had so thoroughly dominated their profession. After the Socialist uprising early in 1934, many Jewish physicians were fired from municipal hospitals; it became impossible for a Jewish doctor to find a job at a federal hospital or public health facility.[19] For Didner, this meant that he would have to try to find work outside Vienna. In his final years as a resident, he trained to be a country doctor, studying all the specialities, including a year of dentistry.

Just before completing his residency, Didner met with Dr. Hermann, the president of the Medical Society of Lower Austria. The society helped find positions for newly licensed physicians. Dr. Hermann seemed stiff, but he smiled politely after examining Didner's transcript and recommendations and assured him he could find him a good practice. He took Didner's records, excused himself, and left his office. But in a few minutes, he burst back into the room, waving the documents and screaming.

"Why did you not tell me your first name is Samuel?" Dr. Hermann spit out the words as his huge head continued to turn red. "This means you are a Jew!"

Didner, taken aback by the doctor's anger, simply nodded.

"Get out of here! Get out of here!" he yelled. "I have no jobs for you!"

Didner learned later that Hermann, who signed his letters

"Heil Hitler," was one of the many secret members of the outlawed Nazi Party.

So he found a job on his own, in a small community called Obersiebenbrunn fifteen miles east of Vienna. It was a town of good, hard working people, many of them farmers, who didn't seem to know or care that he was Jewish. His only competition was another secret Nazi, a Dr. Urschitz, who was the community physician and had been practicing there for years.

Urschitz made no secret of his hate for Didner. Not long after Didner arrived, Urschitz began writing complaints to the medical association, claiming that Didner was unethical, taking patients away from him and charging them less. Didner answered all the complaints promptly and thoroughly; the medical association determined that Urschitz's charges were frivolous and found that Didner had acted ethically. But another confrontation with Urschitz had greater consequences.

In the winter of 1936–1937, a powerful influenza epidemic struck Europe, killing hundreds of people throughout Austria. Infants were particularly vulnerable to contracting pneumonia and dying from a buildup of pus in their lungs. In Obersiebenbrunn, two young girls were among the first to contract the disease. One was Didner's patient; the other was Urschitz's daughter.

Urschitz struggled to save his daughter's life, trying every cure then known to medicine. He even brought in Dr. Kupperman, a noted professor of pediatrics at the University of Vienna Medical School, to supervise his daughter's treatment. But there seemed to be no antidote (antibiotics were not yet available) and, after weeks of suffering, his daughter died.

At the same time, Didner was in a desperate fight to rescue his own patient, who also was near death. The girl was from a working-class family, a classmate of Urschitz's daughter. Didner recognized that the prescribed treatments for influenza would not save this girl. But his rigorous training at medical school had taught him more than medical protocols. His teachers had encouraged him to be innovative and, in life-threatening cases, to use treatments that did not always follow the rules. One winter during his residency, while working at a tuberculosis clinic near Salzburg to earn extra money, he had been intrigued when the doctors there took some of the patients outside into the cold during the day. So, although it was the middle of winter, he advised the girl's parents to bundle her up to the neck in blankets and take her outdoors, protected from the wind but exposed to the sun. Some of the farmers' wives began to whisper that their new doctor seemed to be losing his mind. But, after a few days, the exposure to the cold had its intended effect. Instead of wasting away in a warm room, the girl built up an appetite and began to eat heartily. The food strengthened her and, within a week, she recovered.

Didner's practice grew quickly after that and he began to feel there was a future for him in Obersiebenbrunn. But as his career blossomed, the political situtation continued to worsen.

Hitler was solidifying his control in Germany and whipping up support for annexing his native Austria. The pressure forced crippling concessions from Austrian Chancellor Kurt von Schuschnigg, who had succeeded Dollfuss after he was assassinated by Austrian Nazis. On March 9, 1938, Schuschnigg inspired one final moment of hope when he called for a plebiscite on Austrian independence.[20] His supporters celebrated and painted Dollfuss crosses on the sidewalks. Three days later, an enraged Hitler sent thousands of German troops across the border to annex Austria. The troops were greeted by mass rallies of enthusiastic Austrians and, on March 14, Hitler paraded triumphantly through Vienna. A month later, Hitler held his own plebiscite and, with the encouragement of the Austrian Catholic Church, 99.7 percent of the Austrian people voted in favor of the German annexation.[21]

The German takeover unleashed the vicious Austrian anti-Semitism that had been bubbling below the surface. Jewish shopkeepers and passersby in Vienna were ordered to their hands and knees to scrub the Dollfuss crosses from the sidewalks;[22] Jewish children were forced to paint *Jud* across the windows of their families' stores; gangs looted Jewish shops, department stores, and homes, stealing money, jewels, and other valuables.[23]

On April 1, the first Jewish prisoners were sent to the

Dachau concentration camp outside of Munich. They were told they would be released if they would immediately emigrate from Austria.[24]

Within weeks, most Austrian Jews had lost their jobs and many had been thrown out of their homes. Jews were banned from swimming pools, concerts, and most restaurants. Hundreds committed suicide.[25] Austrian anti-Semitism was so ruthless that it became a model for the Germans.[26] In just a few months, the Austrians had done more to rid their country of the Jews than the Germans had accomplished in five years of Nazi rule.[27]

Didner had stayed away from Vienna when his sister Ala visited in March, frightened by the torchlight parades of Nazis through Obersiebenbrunn on the night Hitler had come to the capital. Although they smashed windows of some Jewish stores, they left Didner's apartment alone. But he had his first close call with the Nazis in April when a group of army officers came to visit him. One of them was a patient, but Didner barely recognized him in his SA uniform, bedecked with Nazi swastikas. He brushed by Didner's secretary and stepped into his office, carrying a bill. The other five or six soldiers stood by the door to watch.

"I paid you last month," the soldier said, "but you sent me a second bill." He sounded more hurt than threatening, although Didner knew that, under the circumstances, he easily could have refused to pay. Didner tried not to smile.

"I probably made a mistake," Didner replied. "I've never been very good at bookkeeping." The soldier nodded and, despite the intimidating contingent of Nazis waiting for him, left without another word.

The local soldiers from Obersiebenbrunn continued to surprise Didner with their decency. A few weeks later, another SA officer stopped Didner as he rode his motorcycle back from Vienna after visiting a friend. He gently warned Didner about the dangers of being arrested in Vienna and suggested he should not return there. Didner appreciated the advice but didn't follow it. When he drove past the same checkpoint a few days later, the same officer took him to the police station and confiscated his motorcycle.

Didner had yet to feel directly threatened. But he had to concede defeat that summer when the Nazis canceled the licenses of all Jewish doctors.[28] He now had no way to make a living and would have to close his practice in Obersiebenbrunn. It also meant he would have to leave Austria.

Didner sent his patients their final bills, even though he knew they were free to ignore them. He also knew the fall harvest was still weeks away and few of the farmers would have money to pay him. But he hoped to collect enough to live in Vienna for a few weeks until he could emigrate. To his surprise, nearly every one of his patients not only paid him but also came to wish him luck.

Didner moved to a small apartment in Vienna on Wiedner Hauptstrasse, the busy street that runs between the Wieden and Margareten districts to the central market. He spent the next two months visiting consulates in the center of the city and searching for a way to get out. The Nazi attacks on Jews continued, and thousands more were arrested and sent to Dachau. Adolf Eichmann was put in charge of Jewish matters and orchestrated the campaign to force Jews to emigrate. But, like thousands of other Austrian Jews, Didner could find no country that would take him.

He tried the United States first. Didner had a distant cousin in Chicago and, with the help of a friend, applied for a visa at the U.S. consulate near St. Stephen's Cathedral. (That summer, at an international refugee conference, the United States had pledged to accept its full German-Austrian refugee quota, about 27,000 people, for the first time.[29]) But the consulate advised him that since he had been born in Poland, Didner fell under the much smaller Polish quota. It would take at least a year, they told him, before his quota number would come up. Didner knew he didn't have that much time.

In the Viennese cafes where Jews were still allowed to go, Didner heard talk of other plans to emigrate. Some had attempted illegal crossings into Czechoslovakia and had been sent back; others secretly planned to leave as tourists for other countries in Europe. But by October, even the Swiss border was closed to Jewish emigrants. A few talked about plans to settle in a Jewish farming community in Argentina or of settlements in Cuba and the Dominican Republic. To Didner, these schemes seemed far-fetched.

For a time, Didner considered emigrating to Palestine. His sister Amalia had been an ardent Zionist for years and she and two of his brothers, Sigmund and Max, already had emigrated to join the struggle to build a Jewish state. Didner did not share in their dream—he considered the "blue white" Zionist organization in Graz and Vienna to be arrogant and dictatorial—but he was running out of options. At the British consulate, also near the cathedral, he learned, however, that the British, under Arab pressure, had sharply reduced the quota of Jewish immigrants to Palestine.[30] Only a few hundred Jews would be allowed to go there legally.

One other country came up in the discussions in the cafes, but no one had anything good to say about it. China, they said, was a terrible place to live and thousands of miles away. The place was so terrible, in fact, that they didn't turn anyone away. Didner was intrigued. Perhaps, he thought, this will be my last resort; at any rate, it doesn't hurt to be on the safe side. So he visited the Chinese consulate and, as the storytellers in the cafes had predicted, he was told he would be welcome in Shanghai. Although he didn't need a visa, he got one anyway.

The next day, Didner visited the Jewish community offices on Seitenstettengasse to fill out emigration forms. He spent the whole day in line, getting clearances from the police and other authorities and turning over his remaining funds before receiving a temporary passport.[31] He would be allowed to take ten reichsmarks with him out of the country. With the help of the Jewish community office, he purchased a second-class ticket on a ship leaving from Italy for Shanghai on November 17.

A week before he was scheduled to leave, Didner celebrated his thirty-second birthday alone in his apartment. He was unaware that the evening before, the Nazis had orchestrated the pogrom they called *Kristallnacht*, blowing up and burning nearly every synagogue and prayer house in Vienna, plundering thousands of Jewish shops, and throwing Jews out of their homes and apartments. More than 6,500 Jews were arrested and herded into public buildings, including the historic Spanish Riding School.[32]

Didner was spared from the attack, probably because he had recently moved to Vienna and lived outside the predominantly Jewish area. But on November 11, he returned home to find a note under his door summoning him to appear at the neighborhood police station. He went promptly to the station, presented his letter, and was ushered in to see a burly police sergeant. The sergeant was polite but brief.

"Dr. Didner, I am advised that you are a Jew. I think it would be wise if you left the country. Do you perhaps have any plans to leave?"

Didner showed him his passport and his ticket for Shanghai.

"That's good," the sergeant said. "You are free to go."

As he walked out of the police station, Didner recognized how lucky he had been. A row of buses, loaded with Jewish prisoners, was lined up outside. Jews who could not prove they were about to leave Austria were being taken to Dachau.

Didner began his train trip to Italy the next day, stopping on the way to pay one last visit his family in Graz. His father had died the year before and his mother and four of his siblings were still living there. When he arrived, he found his family had been thrown out of their house during the pogrom and most of their possessions had been destroyed or stolen. They were huddled in the basement of one of the apartment buildings they once owned. His mother wished him a tearful goodbye and urged him to leave town as quickly as possible before he was arrested.

Didner took the train south through the Brenner Pass to Genoa, his first trip out of Austria. On November 17, he boarded the *Conte Biancamano*, a giant cruise liner that carried 562 passengers, and sailed to Shanghai. It was a choppy voyage and he was seasick for most of the trip. When he tried to treat two girls who also were ill, he fell over backward in the middle of their cabin. He was even more seasick than they were.

Didner had been in Shanghai only a few hours when he found his way to the offices of the International Committee for European Refugees (known as the IC) on Kiuking Road. The relief committee representatives at the harbor had told the refugees not to look for work without the permission of Paul Komor, head of the IC, and Didner wanted to be among the first to see him.

Komor was a tall, thin Hungarian in his mid-forties with a kindly, almost saintly appearance. When Didner was ushered into his office, he handed Komor his credentials, told him about his medical training in Vienna, and said he was eager to work. Komor told Didner he was in luck. The IC planned to convert the small dormitory on Washing Road into a hospital for refugees and needed someone to set it up and to inoculate the incoming refugees. The pay was minimal, Komor said—all employees of the IC were paid the same small wage, about twenty dollars a month—but there would be plenty to do. Could he interest Didner in serving as medical director? Didner smiled and reached out to shake Komor's hand.

For the next ten days, Didner worked long hours hiring his staff—mostly nurses from Austria who also were refugees—and searching for medical equipment and supplies. The facility would be called the Emigrants' Hospital. It had about sixty beds and a dispensary on the veranda. Didner, along with two other doctors and five nurses, began to prepare for the influx of three hundred refugees at the end of the month, when the *Conte Rosso* and SS *Pottsdam* were expected to arrive.

But the night before the hospital was scheduled to open, Didner decided to celebrate his new job at a party sponsored by a rich Russian Jew who lived in the French Concession. It was a loud, smoky party with a jazz band playing songs he didn't recognize. Didner felt woozy from his first drink. Then he heard the band play something familiar. A Russian Jewish girl, in a black dress slit down the side, mouthed the lyrics—"B'mir bis du schön" (You're my one and only)—and jumped up on a table just in front of Didner as she danced the jitterbug. This, to an Austrian whose idea of dancing was limited to proper waltzes, was more intoxicating than the alcohol. But the feelings of excitement soon evaporated into melancholy. It was never easy for Didner to relax; liquor always seemed to make him depressed.

2

Levin

Horst Levin settled back into the soft red leather couch and sipped slowly on his Scotch. For a few moments, he studied his surroundings, from the oriental rug at his feet to the brass frames on the movie posters that lined the office walls. Through the window to his left, on the second floor of the Embankment Building, Horst could see Broadway Mansions in the distance through the thick afternoon clouds. It was quite a thrill for a small-town German who had arrived as a refugee in Shanghai only a month ago, in February 1939, and had spent the past few weeks hustling for work and living in a tiny apartment in Hongkew. Levin was finding it hard to focus on the purpose of his visit.

This was his third trip to the Metro-Goldwyn-Mayer offices, and he had finally talked his way into the suite of M. Marcus, the garrulous American who was in charge. Marcus, with his thick white hair and tailored pinstriped suit, was as elegant as his surroundings. He seemed receptive, too, although Levin worried that he was more interested in drinking whiskey and talking about soccer and German music than about advertising in his newspaper. Marcus walked around his mahogany desk and refilled Levin's glass.

"I'm still not quite clear about one thing," Marcus said, momentarily returning to the reason for Levin's visit. "Why would German refugees be interested in American movies?"

Levin thought he had explained that earlier, but he tried again.

"This is how they are learning to speak English," Levin said. "The theaters are filled every day with new refugees. And for many of us, the movie theater is the only quiet place to get away from the crowds in Hongkew."

Marcus smiled. He had to be amused by the idea that European refugees in Shanghai could learn English from MGM productions like *The Good Earth*, a two-year-old movie about Chinese peasants, based on a novel by the daughter of an American missionary, Pearl Buck, and starring an Austrian-born actress, Luise Rainer. (*The Good Earth* was not the best way to promote the country, however—some of the refugees already had seen it on their sea voyage to Shanghai and were even more reluctant to come to China.)

"There are thousands of us here already and more coming every day," Levin said, trying to get Marcus's attention. "I think *Shanghai Woche*, for a very reasonable price, would bring you many new customers."

Levin sensed he really didn't know much about being an advertising salesman, but he'd been successful so far. He'd already sold small ads to the local distributors for Coca-Cola and Camel. A major account like MGM would give the paper enough revenue to survive for months and perhaps even hire typesetters who could read German. The Chinese printers worked hard, but every page proof Levin edited seemed to have a dozen new mistakes.

Marcus tilted his head back and finished off his third Scotch.

"Things are a bit tight now, you know, but I'll take a look at my budget. We should talk more, maybe play some chess. Perhaps dinner at my place next week? I'll have my secretary call you."

"Of course," Levin replied. He sensed that Marcus was lonely and mostly interested in his companionship, but he enjoyed talking with him. He also hoped their friendship would pay some dividends. He stood up, shook hands with Marcus, and headed out of the office.

On the way out of the building, Levin stopped to look at the refugee housing there. Walking down a long corridor on the first floor, Levin passed a row of rooms crowded with wooden cots, thirty or forty bunk beds pushed together in each of the small offices. Only a few refugees were there, taking afternoon naps. Clothes and blankets were hung off the sides of the beds, but there were no other furnishings in the rooms, not even tables or chairs. Although the building was only ten years old, there were holes in the ceiling and spiders and insects were crawling on the walls. Levin felt lucky that he had been able to afford the rent for his small apartment in Hongkew.

He headed out of the Embankment Building and up North Soochow Road. In the misty rain, most of the pedestrians were hidden under tattered, black umbrellas, and he dodged and shuffled to avoid the pointed spokes that threatened to poke him in the chest. Levin was tall and broad shouldered, and he felt like a giant among the smaller Chinese.

Levin crossed Soochow Creek on North Szechuen Road and walked into the main business district of the International Settlement. He was headed for some coffee and cake at Cafe Louis, the new restaurant on Bubbling Well Road recently opened by the Eisfelder family from Berlin. Jewish refugees had been in Shanghai only a few months, but, like the Eisfelders, they already were making their presence felt.

Most Jewish refugees arrived with little money and no connections; they started anew in Shanghai, near the bottom of the foreign community's well-established social and economic hierarchy. There were forty-six nationalities represented in Shanghai and each had its own niche.[1] At the top were the British, who comprised nearly forty percent of the 40,000 foreigners in the city in the early 1930s. They controlled the Municipal Council, police force, post office, and utilities in the International Settlement, the major trading houses on the Bund, and large factories throughout the city. They brought in hundreds of Sikhs to serve as policemen. The British established English clubs, schools, and colleges, played cricket and held bowling matches, and built a huge horse track in the center of Shanghai. On Sundays, nearly all of British society convened at the Shanghai Race Course to drink and bet on ponies. Even British customs like cross-country horse riding contests—the Paper Hunt Club was founded in 1864—were transplanted to Shanghai.[2]

The leaders of a small community of Sephardic Jews, originally from Baghdad, also were at the pinnacle of the foreign hierarchy. They owned much of Shanghai's real estate, built many of its hotels and offices, and controlled some of the major trading companies. The Sephardis adopted British manners and customs, although only a few of the most wealthy Jews were welcomed into British high society.

The Japanese population surpassed the British after 1910, and by 1930 Japanese made up about half of the foreign community.[3] They lived in the northern sections of the International Settlement and established major banks, factories, clubs, and restaurants. As Japanese troops took control of the rest of the city, the Japanese influence in the settlement also grew.

In the 1920s and 1930s, Russians were the fastest-growing group of foreigners in the city. There were more than 30,000 of them by the beginning of the war, the second-largest group of foreigners in the city after the Japanese. Most of the newcomers were White Russians who had fled from the Bolsheviks. There also was a large Russian Jewish community, many of whom had first settled in Manchuria and then migrated to Shanghai after the Japanese occupation. A few Russians were wealthy furriers and importers, but most were lower and middle class. The Russians worked in small shops, bars, and restaurants; some took menial jobs previously shunned by foreigners, working as rickshaw drivers and prostitutes.[4]

The first Jewish refugees from Europe came to Shanghai in 1933–1934. Most were doctors, and many of them settled in the interior of China.[5] Refugees who remained in Shanghai established businesses in the French Concession, where many of the Russian Jews lived. Bernard Cohn opened the first

Jewish refugee business in 1935 on Route Soeurs, selling bed linens and later manufacturing feather beds. With the influx that began in the fall of 1938, more refugee businesses sprang up. Fritz Strehlen and Hans Jabloner, two Austrians, opened the Fiaker Restaurant on Avenue Joffre. It came to be known as one of the finest Viennese-style restaurants in the world, attracting customers ranging from Nazi generals to Chinese gang leaders to British diplomats.

In the following months, refugees opened textile stores, clothing stores, a watchmaker's shop, and more restaurants, including the Barcelona, with less expensive Viennese cuisine, which began serving meals in January 1939. A new nightclub, the Black Cat, opened on Roi Albert Avenue, where comedian Herbert Zernik began his Shanghai career as a singer. New businesses began in the International Settlement, too. At about the time that Horst Levin arrived in February 1939, the Eisfelders founded Cafe Louis and made their own cakes and chocolates.

But as the number of European refugees grew from hundreds to thousands, few opportunities remained in the International Settlement and French Concession. Only a handful of the refugees had the wealth or professional and social standing to make contacts in the established foreign communities. New businesses were needed, however, in Hongkew, where most of the refugees lived. Among the earliest were Alex Fessler's European hair salon, Springer's Broadway Shoes, and Hans Schwarz's Quick restaurant, the first German-style restaurant in Hongkew. The Carioca Bar on Broadway began serving customers in January 1939. Amalie Leschnik had opened one of the first businesses on Wayside Road, a specialty shop for household goods, and, at about the same time, Alfred Flatow founded a butcher shop and grocery store at the corner of Wayside and Chusan roads, not far from Levin's apartment.[6]

A remarkable new community was beginning to take shape as the refugees moved in. It was beginning to seem a bit like the Europe Levin remembered.

Levin's family was from Loetzen, a small town on the Masurian Lakes in East Prussia, a 150-mile-wide island of German territory surrounded by Poland and Lithuania. His father's parents had come east from Bavaria after anti-Semitic laws were passed there, and they made a living as peddlers. His mother's parents, the Motulskys, were from Poland and had moved to East Prussia in the late 1800s to open a dry goods store in Fischhausen, near the Baltic Sea. Their business was so successful that the Motulsky family and their relatives eventually owned a chain of dry goods stores throughout East Prussia. They sent their four sons to college and provided large dowries for their two daughters. When Fred Levin married Betty Motulsky in 1913, they had enough money to start their own dry goods store in Loetzen.

Betty was forced to flee the next summer when Russian troops overran East Prussia; the Levin's first child, Ruth, was born during her flight north. Fred enlisted in the German army and joined forces led by Field Marshal Paul von Hindenburg, an aristocratic, sixty-seven-year-old general who had come back from retirement, wearing his old-fashioned blue uniform, to command the Eighth Army. The Germans defeated the Russians in the battles of Tannenberg and the Masurian Lakes in September, pushing the Russians out of East Prussia and inflicting more than 300,000 Russian casualties. The campaign ended in a stalemate, but Hindenburg became a German hero;[7] Fred, now a decorated war hero himself, moved back to Loetzen with Betty and Ruth.

Despite the continuing German defeats on the Western front, a relative calm had returned to East Prussia, and business in Loetzen thrived. The Levins sold bedding, linen, and household goods from their store facing the tree-lined town square. Almost everyone who passed through Loetzen stopped to admire the colorful displays in the Levins' plate-glass windows. In the summer of 1916, the store drew special attention. Fred's loyalty to Germany, and von Hindenburg's planned visit to East Prussia, had inspired him to drape German flags over and around a display of suitcases in his front window. A few days later, a military staff car stopped in the square and a uniformed lieutenant entered the store. He saluted Fred and informed him that von Hindenburg, who was waiting in the car outside, had dispatched him to commend Levin's patriotism. From then on, Fred called it the Hindenburg suitcase display. There was another special event for the Levins that summer. Their second child, a son, was born on June 3, 1916. His parents named him Horst.

Horst's father was a good businessman and adapted as the inflation that followed Germany's defeat made money almost worthless—in the early 1920s, it took a straw laundry basket full of paper money to buy a loaf of bread. Fred learned to barter, exchanging his cloth and leather goods for other commodities. In a few years, he had filled a large warehouse with saws, hammers, and machines.

The Levins were German patriots as well as observant, but liberal, Jews. Fred was vice-president of Loetzen's small Jewish congregation and Betty kept a kosher home—on Fridays, Horst often walked with their maid to a kosher butcher where they had their chickens killed. Both children attended religious classes on Saturdays.

Horst was an indifferent student, although bright enough to pass the examinations to enter Gymnasium. He was the only Jew in his class but was one of the regular guys, playing soccer and water polo and winning medals as a swimmer and cross-country skier. He did well in languages, learning how to read Latin and speak English. Horst also entertained his friends by playing the piano in his parents' living room. His best friend, the son of an army officer, lived across the square and they visited each others' houses nearly every day.

As inflation and unemployment skyrocketed in the early 1930s and the Nazis preyed on the growing fear and anger, Horst began to feel more isolated. Jews once again took the blame for Germany's troubles. Horst's teachers, many of whom were Nazis, often singled him out for criticism. The coach of the swim and water polo teams told him he could no longer come to practice. And one by one, his classmates began to shun him. One day, when Horst visited his best friend's house, the boy greeted him wearing a black Hitler Youth uniform. He told Horst he couldn't see him anymore.

Horst finished school in 1933—by then he was barred from

attending university because he was Jewish—and he couldn't attend his own graduation ceremony. The school mailed him his certificate.

His father's business suffered, too, as neighbors and former friends stopped shopping in his store after local Nazis organized an anti-Jewish boycott in March 1933. On April 1, when Hitler called for a nationwide one-day boycott of Jewish businesses, no one dared to pass the SA and SS guards who stood in front of the store. After the official boycott ended, however, a few loyal customers secretly sent orders and money to a post office box and the Levins delivered goods by messenger.

Despite these setbacks, Fred Levin remained a loyal German and continued to hope that Hitler, like dozens of leaders before him, would soon lose his power. He was encouraged that the first Nazi anti-Jewish laws—in deference to his hero and then German president, von Hindenburg—had exempted Jews who had fought for Germany in the world war.[8] His optimism was so great, in fact, that in 1934, he sent his son to a friend's dry goods business in Allenstein, about sixty miles away, to serve as an apprentice.

But after a year of relative quiet, the situation in Loetzen deteriorated. A former friend from his hunting lodge had been urging Fred for months to sell him his business. Fred resisted, even when a new boycott began that summer. But when the local police put Fred in jail on a trumped-up charge, he knew it was time to quit. His former friend arranged for his release from jail, then made what he called a generous offer: He would take over the business and the goods in the warehouse and rescue Fred from the pressures of the police and the Nazis. He offered less than ten percent of what the business was worth. Fred knew he had no choice; he took the money and prepared to move his family to Berlin. There, he hoped, they would find safety in the large Jewish community and, if necessary, make plans to leave the country.

The Levins' relatives throughout East Prussia were facing similar pressures, and most were forced to liquidate their stores. After he finished his apprenticeship, Horst spent six months with one of his uncles in the coastal town of Pillau. His uncle, too, had been sent to jail and had agreed to sell his two stores for a fraction of their worth. He planned to use the money to take his family out of Germany. But the exorbitant Nazi taxes on Jews who left the country meant that he would have to turn over at least half of his assets. Horst's uncle decided to become a smuggler.

Horst, his cousin, and his uncle spent a week carefully sewing packets of cash into terrycloth robes. Then the three of them traveled by boat across the Bay of Danzig to Zoppot, a Polish summer resort near Gdansk. There they deposited the money in several Polish banks, safe from German taxes on Jews.

A week later, Horst headed for Berlin. His family had sold all of their furniture and household goods in Loetzen and settled in the middle of the city. Fred had invested their money in a restaurant, the Cafe Hansa, located just outside the English Gardens in the center of a large Jewish population. It had its own bakery, served kosher food, and was one of a handful of restaurants that was allowed to serve Jews.

Berlin had been the birthplace of Jewish enlightenment, home to Moses Mendelssohn, Heinrich Heine, Joseph Meyerbeer, Albert Einstein, and August Wassermann.[9] But by the time the Levins arrived, the Berlin Jewish community was rapidly disintegrating. Most of the customers at the Cafe Hansa were unemployed, living on their savings or with the help of Jewish relief. They spent their days playing skat in the two card rooms and discussing plans to emigrate. Some even talked about Shanghai and read letters from their sons and daughters there. They wrote about living in crowded camps and suffering from dysentery and other diseases.

The Levins had talked about emigrating, too. Fred's twin brother had purchased a certificate to emigrate to Palestine and offered to take Horst with him. Horst had even signed up for a course in a vocational school to learn how to drive a tractor, but his father refused to let him attend. Fred insisted that the family should stay together. Because they would lose almost all of their assets if they left Germany, he remained reluctant to leave.

So Horst and his sister focused their energies on the restaurant business, learning the trade from the two old

Hungarian waiters who had worked there for decades. The children took on increasing responsibility as their parents' health suffered. Their forced departure from Loetzen and the difficulties of surviving in Berlin had taken a toll on Fred and Betty. Betty had become manic depressive and needed care, but the Germans had cut off welfare and health care assistance for Jews,[10] making it impossible for the Levins to find her a place in a sanitarium. Fred had suffered a series of heart attacks and was being treated at the Jewish Hospital, where he spent months recovering.

By early 1938, two years after the Levins had moved to Berlin, there were more than 350,000 Jews living in Germany; about 120,000 had left the country in the five years since the Nazis came to power. More than forty percent of the Jews who remained lived in Berlin, many of them, like the Levins, recent immigrants from smaller towns. The Jews had been forced to sell their businesses, fired from their jobs, and banned from virtually every social or political activity as the Nazis gradually increased the pressure on Jews to emigrate. In 1938, the Nazis took the final steps to completely exclude the Jews from German economic life, force them to leave, and turn over their remaining assets to the government.[11]

At the end of October, the Nazis rounded up about 18,000 Jews with Polish citizenship and deported them to Poland.[12] Even at this point, some German Jews found reasons for optimism. One Jewish world war veteran brought his son to Alexanderplatz station to witness the deportation, telling him he should be proud to be part of a nation that had the wisdom to send away "those kind of people."[13] Among the deportees were the parents of Herschel Grynszpan. When Grynszpan retaliated for his parents' deportation by assassinating a German official in Paris, it gave the Nazis the pretext they had been waiting for to organize the anti-Jewish November pogroms that swept Germany and Austria. Unlike Sam Didner in Vienna, the Levins did not escape the pogroms.

Fred had returned home from the hospital on November 8, against his doctor's advice. The doctor had sent Horst a note, telling him his father needed constant care. The day Fred came home, the local police commissioner, an old Social Democrat who often stopped by the restaurant after hours for beer and conversation, had warned him that the Nazis were planning an action against the Jews. The next night, Fred, Betty, Ruth, Horst, the two Hungarian waiters, and a visiting relative from East Prussia hid in the basement. Before dawn, Horst heard a mob yelling anti-Jewish slogans on the street. He sat up in bed and listened, terrified and half asleep, as he heard glass shattering on the floor overhead. The sound of the heavy SA and SS boots echoed above him; he could hear chairs and tables being smashed and the ovens being tipped over. Horst wanted to fight back, but he knew it was hopeless. He sat awake the rest of the night, feeling angry, afraid, and helpless.

In the morning, Horst climbed upstairs to survey the ruins of the cafe. Virtually everything had been demolished. The plates and cups all had been broken, and most of the food in the freezer had been stolen. As Horst combed through the wreckage, a local policeman stopped by and suggested that Horst should board up the front door and windows and submit a claim to their insurance company. Horst walked to a nearby carpenter's shop, past the wreckage of other small Jewish shops, to arrange for the work. But while he was there, one of the waiters ran to get him. Horst's father, who had gotten out of bed to look at the damage, had been arrested.

Horst feared for his father's life, knowing he was in no condition to withstand imprisonment and questioning. He ran to the police station and went to see his father's friend, the police commissioner. But the commissioner could offer no assistance. He told Horst his father was being held by the Gestapo and directed him to their office; he warned Horst that he would be putting himself in danger by going there.

Horst was too upset to hesitate. He raced down a long corridor to an office with the word Gestapo on the outside and pushed the door open without knocking. Inside, behind a desk, sat a tall, menacing Nazi in his black uniform. Horst, energized by his adrenaline, was nearly in a frenzy. He directed his fear and hate at this impassive soldier.

"You must release my father, Fred Levin! He is a sick man

who belongs in the hospital!" Horst, normally low-key and soft spoken, was screaming, making little sense to the man behind the desk.

"I have a letter from his doctor! It says he must be under constant care! You must release him now!"

The Gestapo official smirked. He stood up to his full six-foot-five height, towering over Horst.

"Don't worry, young man," he said. "We are simply asking your father a few questions. We will send him home soon."

"No! You must let him go right away!" Horst was yelling hysterically, out of control. "You must promise me you will let him go now!"

"Come, young terrier," the Nazi said. "I will take you to see him."

He led Horst down another long corridor. At the end of it, he unlocked a door and, as Horst rushed past him, kicked him down a flight of stairs.

"Here's another Jew!" the Nazi bellowed from the top of the stairs.

Horst tumbled to the bottom, then fumbled to find his glasses. He was in a courtyard, surrounded by hundreds of Berlin Jews who had been arrested the night before. They were among the 30,000 Jews in Germany and Austria who were arrested during the November 9–10 progrom the Nazis had called *Kristallnacht*, the night of glass. Nearly a hundred Jews were murdered, more than 1,000 synagogues were set on fire or blown up by hand grenades, and 7,500 businesses had been demolished.[14]

That evening, Horst was pushed onto a covered truck with dozens of others for the two-hour ride to Sachsenhausen. There he joined thousands of other prisoners, most of them Jews, who were herded into the camp's floodlit central square and forced to stand for hours in the cold, surrounded by armed SS guards and barking Dobermans. They were warned to stand at attention and not to move. But with no food or water, some of the prisoners collapsed. When two older men pleaded for permission to urinate, an SS guard pointed them to a latrine then sent his dogs to attack them.

In the morning, Horst turned in his clothes and the three

reichsmarks he had in his trousers. His head was shaved, and he was given a blue-striped work uniform and a blanket and crowded into a huge barracks with about five-hundred other inmates. The building was designed to sleep about half that many. Horst recognized some of the prisoners as former customers of the Cafe Hansa, but was too fearful to talk to them. At night, searchlights flashed through the windows and rifle shots echoed in the yard.

Each morning the inmates marched one mile to a construction site. On nearly every march, one or two of the older men collapsed or fell behind and were pounded by a rain of blows from the guards' rifle butts. Any prisoner who stopped to help also was beaten. Horst learned to keep to the middle of the formation, away from the guards.

They worked for ten or twelve hours a day, excavating foundations and pouring concrete. A chain of workers hauled the 110-pound cement bags from the building site to a shed that held the mixing machines, fifty to sixty yards away. Most of the men had been merchants or professionals; few were strong enough for the hard labor. Many of the bags broke before they reached the shed. Even Horst, young, healthy, and athletic, didn't have the strength to lift the bags.

Each time he dragged a bag to the shed, he chatted briefly with the *capo*, an older inmate from Berlin. Horst was affable and the *capo* seemed to like him. He decided to try to charm him with cigarettes and bought some from his small account at the camp store. The bribe worked. The *capo* offered Horst easier work if he would bring him cigarettes and candy every day.

From then on, Horst's job was to push a wheelbarrow and collect the broken bags, then shovel the cement into the machines. He spent most of his time inside the shed, out of the icy cold. It was easy work but still strenuous enough that Horst lost weight—lunches consisted of only thin soup and bread. Each night, when they stood for a head count, a few more names went unanswered. But in January, the guards announced at the morning roll call that some of the prisoners were going to be released.

One morning that month, on the march to the work site, Horst saw a man behind him fall to the ground. Without thinking, he tried to lift him back up as the column of men walked around them. A guard yelled at Horst to leave him, then suddenly struck Horst's head with his rifle, knocking off his glasses. The frame was broken and the right lens shattered, but Horst gathered up the pieces. He scrambled to his feet and rejoined the march. His poor eyesight now threatened his survival. He could barely see well enough to find the broken cement bags. That night in the barracks, Horst stayed up most of the night trying to tie the glasses together with string. He fashioned an awkward jumble of glass, metal and string that at least let him see out of his left eye.

The next day, Horst applied for permission to order a new pair at the medical clinic. The clerk there laughed at Horst's mangled glasses and agreed to order a new pair.

"But I wouldn't worry too much," the clerk said offhandedly. "By the time your order comes back, you will be out." For the first time, Horst allowed himself to hope that he would be released.

A week later, at morning roll call, they read off the names of those to be released at the end of the week. Horst almost didn't recognize his name when it was called—"Horst Israel Levin." (As of January 1, 1939, a Nazi law required all Jews whose first names did not appear on list of "typically Jewish" names to add Sara or Israel to their first names.[15]) The clerk was wrong about one thing: Horst's new glasses arrived the day before he was released.

Before he left Sachsenhausen, a Gestapo officer lectured him about his good fortune in being released and warned him never to discuss his treatment there, regardless of where he went. The arm of the Gestapo, he said, is very long. Then Horst exchanged his prison uniform for the clothes he had worn the day of his arrest and walked to the train station.

Horst still had no idea why he was released or what had happened to his family. He took the train to Berlin and the elevated train to Hansaplatz, then walked through the neighborhood. He stopped on the way and spent his last pfennigs on a woolen cap, embarrassed by people staring at his bald head. Then he reached the corner where the cafe had been. He froze in disbelief.

The sun was gleaming off the front windows of the Cafe Hansa and customers were at the tables inside, smoking and chatting and playing cards. It was just as it had been before the November pogrom, as if nothing had happened. He hesitated to enter the front door, still unsure if he would find his family there. Horst walked to the delivery entrance on the side to ring the bell. His sister Ruth ran to greet him, hugging him tightly around the chest. His parents were right behind her, pecking him with kisses as Ruth held on.

Ruth, Fred, and Betty all started to talk at once. Horst learned that his impulsiveness had saved his father. The Nazis had a precise quota of people to be arrested from each district on November 9–10 and Horst had taken his father's place. The Gestapo man had kept his word and released Fred. But his family didn't know what had happened to Horst. After a week, they had received a notice from the Gestapo informing them Horst was in Sachsenhausen. It said they would release him if his family booked him passage out of the country. For weeks afterward, Ruth had lined up at the Jewish community (Hilfsverein) offices seeking help. Jews had been leaving by the thousands since November and there seemed to be no chance for Horst to get a visa.

But early in January, a customer at the cafe approached Ruth and offered to sell her a first-class ticket on a Lloyd Triestino liner, the *Conte Biancamano*, that would be leaving Genoa for Shanghai later that month. Horst wouldn't need a visa to travel there. The stories about China had frightened her, but this was the only way to save her brother. The Levins raised the money to buy the ticket, then notified the Gestapo. A week later, Horst returned home. He would have to leave for Genoa within ten days.

That night, the first in his own bed for almost three months, Horst couldn't sleep. He stayed awake thinking about his former comrades at Sachsenhausen. He had saved his father and survived his imprisonment, but he felt like a traitor—he had bribed his way into an easy job while others had worked themselves to death and had been released while others remained to die. A few times, he had tried to help the others, but there were so many other times when he watched helplessly as prisoners were humiliated, beaten or taken away to be shot. Horst knew it was unfair to judge himself; all that he had known about humanity and morality had been shattered by the horror of Sachsenhausen. Yet now that he was free, the feelings of guilt wouldn't disappear.

In a few days, Horst went to the police station and got his passport and exit visa with a J stamp identifying him as a Jew. It listed his official name as Horst Israel Levin. He was told he could take only ten reichsmarks out of the country. On January 25, 1939, Ruth, Fred, and Betty went to the train station to send him off. They held back their tears as Horst, only twenty-two years old, left them for the last time.

The train took most of the day to reach Munich, then crossed what had recently been the Austrian border. German soldiers boarded the train before the Italian border and inspected some of the passengers but left Horst alone. When they crossed the steep Brenner Pass into Italy, Horst felt at ease for the first time in months. Other than his brief smuggling voyage to Poland with his uncle, this was his first trip out of Germany and he saw it as a great adventure.

After a day in Genoa, he boarded the *Conte Biancamano*. It had just returned from bringing Sam Didner to Shanghai and now was crowded with more than eight-hundred passengers, nearly all of them Jewish refugees. Horst was one of the few traveling first class, and he slept in a luxurious cabin and ate in an elegant dining hall. In the one-month voyage, he regained the twenty-five pounds he had lost at Sachsenhausen, gorging himself on sausage, herring, veal, and sweetbreads. In the ports where the ship docked—Port Said, Aden, Bombay, Ceylon, Singapore, Manila, and Hong Kong—Horst searched for bakeries that sold dark German bread.

Horst also found a way to earn some money on the trip. His sister had been required to deposit several hundred reichsmarks with the Triestino office to purchase *bordgeld*, vouchers that could be used for gifts and drinks on the ship but that could not be redeemed at the end of the voyage. Horst made an arrangement with several wealthy businessmen on board to buy them alcohol and items from the gift shop and have them reimburse him in cash. By the time they reached

Shanghai, Horst had accumulated a large roll of dollars and pounds.

In Shanghai, on a dark, cold day—even colder than the winters in East Prussia—a representative from the committee greeted the ship and Sam Didner and his nurses inoculated the refugees. Horst stayed only one night in the Ward Road camp, one of the unheated, crowded barracks for refugees, and then used his cash to move into a small apartment on Chusan Road.

Horst was amazed by all the new sounds, sights, and smells in Shanghai, all so different from his native Germany. The smells of garlic and ginger—and the smell of raw sewage—were everywhere. There were crowds of Chinese on every corner, pushing onto buses, bicycling down the streets and lanes, and buying and selling raw meats and vegetables he had never seen before. The Shanghai dialect sounded more like yelling than speaking.

Horst spent his first days in Shanghai relaxing with his fellow refugees in the cafes and new restaurants they were opening in the French Concession and International Settlement. The German sausages and Austrian pastries were good and cheap, and many refugees and businessmen gathered there. In a small cafe owned by a Russian Jewish refugee, Horst practiced on a grand piano, the first time he had played since he had left Loetzen. He was good enough that the owner offered him lunch, dinner, and a Shanghai dollar (worth about sixteen cents in U.S. money) for a day's music. Horst played there regularly and met some people he had known in Berlin, including the editor and film critic Wolfgang Fischer, who had been a customer at the Cafe Hansa.

Fischer was talking about starting a weekly newspaper with some other German journalists. But he needed more advertising revenue than the small refugee businesses could provide. One evening, while he was on a dinner break, Fischer asked Horst, whose English was good, if he would be interested in trying to sell ads to the foreign business community. Horst would work on commission.

Horst was excited by the idea of joining a new enterprise and rubbing shoulders with the rich British and Americans in Shanghai. As he talked with Fischer, another refugee, old and somewhat disheveled, had taken his place at the piano. He played well, much better than Horst. It was time, Horst decided, to launch his newspaper career. He strolled over to the piano.

"I think you need this job more than I do," Horst told the piano player. "You're welcome to take it."

3

Heimann

Early in the morning, just before dawn, Gerhard Heimann woke to the voice of a man in the streets calling out strange words again and again—it sounded something like "*Moo-dong . . . moo-dong . . . aya wei*," and it kept getting closer. Some days, Gerd would get up early enough to run to the front door and catch a glimpse of the tiny Chinese man yelling, pulling a wooden cart, and stopping to grab the smelly wooden buckets from the women standing in front of their brick lane houses. The cart left a wet, brown trail behind as it wandered down the dirt path. When the "*moo-dong*" chant faded away, Gerd heard a whishing and rattling sound echo down the lane as the women scrubbed the now-empty buckets with horsehair bristles, pebbles, and cold water. The *moo-dong* man stopped at the Heimann's only once a month, but not to empty their bucket. He came to collect his *kamsha* (bribe). The Heimanns had an illegal toilet on the first floor and had to bribe the man to bypass their house.

Gerd's days that summer of 1939 were filled with excitement unlike anything he had experienced in his ten years growing up in Berlin. In the morning before school, he always would find Chinese men at mobile food stands on Seward Road, cooking and displaying their wares under broad umbrellas. Gerd often couldn't resist the yard-long rolls of yeast dough that the vendors twirled and fried in oil. When the weather got colder, he would sample the roasted chestnuts and sweet potatoes roasted over big drums filled with hot coals. He knew if he got caught eating street food his father would whack him hard with the long bamboo feather duster he had brought from Germany. But it was worth the risk.

After school, he might stop to watch the blacksmith, singing out a cadence of Chinese numbers as four shirtless men with heavy hammers struck the anvil in a smooth rhythm. Or he might stand for hours, watching men with long bamboo sticks, bows, and wooden mallets sort dirty bales of cotton into long, clean strands for weaving. Almost every day, Gerd saw old Herr Boldes, standing on a street corner selling matches, constantly calling out *"Die allerletzten"* (the very last ones). The Chinese peddlers also had learned to speak some German. A Chinese cobbler walked up and down the lanes yelling *"Schuhmacher! Schuhmacher!"* Another Chinese man, who could fix broken plates or bowls, deftly using string, glue, and clamps to make them look like new, would yell: *"Porzellan kaputte ganz macher."*

Later in the day, there were more Chinese men with food carts that they carried on bamboo poles. They brought steamed buns filled with pork or blue beans, hot noodle soup, and rotted cubes of tofu that tasted like cheese. There was German food, too, at the Wuerstelstand on the corner of Ward and Chusan roads.

Gerd hung out with a mischievous group of boys, including the dark-eyed Zimbalista brothers. Heini, who was Gerd's age, once bet the man who worked at the Wuerstelstand ten dollars that he could pee in his pocket without getting him wet. The old man couldn't resist the bet; Heini paid up after soaking the man's pants with urine. Then the brothers collected ten dollars from each of their friends. They all had wagered against Heini when he bet that he could pee in the old man's pocket.

In the afternoons, the boys played in Wayside Park, flying

high on the sturdy swings and trying to jump from one swing to the next. They also shot marbles together in the dirt; Gerd never went anywhere without his big pink "shooter." There were rough games, too—one was called "testicles grabbing" in German. And Gerd and his friends were known throughout Hongkew for reciting the endless verses of pun-filled German songs about promiscuous landladies and Viennese girls.

When he was by himself, Gerd loved riding around town on the whiproller scooter that his parents had brought from Berlin. There was so much to explore: the Chinese families who lived outside their homes in the summer heat, cooking their meals and sleeping on cots in the street; the row of shops that sold papier-mâché replicas of animals and furniture that were buried with the dead; and the long funeral processions, with everyone dressed in white, carrying a picture of the deceased, followed by the anguished cries of professional mourners and the twanging of stringed instruments.

He was entranced by all of Shanghai's odd and macabre sights and characters. Sometimes, he stared at the bodies of Chinese who had died from malnutrition or disease; he even found tiny babies, wrapped in straw mats, lying in the streets near his house or in empty lots nearby. Each day, another man pulling a wagon picked them up.

The Japanese soldiers and sailors, with their short stature, bandy legs, face masks, and funny backpacks, amused rather than frightened him. Most of the time he saw them, the soldiers were stumbling drunkenly down the streets, laughing and singing Japanese drinking songs.

One night a week, Gerd got a chance to wear his own uniform. Some Russians had formed a Shanghai branch of a Zionist group called Betar, and the refugee kids had their own chapter. They met on the top floor of the synagogue on Ward Road every week. Gerd didn't understand some of the songs about Palestine and the speeches about Joseph Trumpeldor and Zev Jabotinsky, the founder of Betar, but he marched proudly in his dark brown shirt with blue pockets and the blue kerchief tied around his neck. It didn't take long for him to assimilate the Zionist propaganda. His father had been upset when he first asked to join. After what had happened in

Germany, he said, he didn't want his son wearing a uniform that made him look like a Hitler Youth. So Gerd's mother bought the uniform secretly and stored it in a special place where his father wouldn't find it.

Gerd even liked his school lessons. His teacher was Mr. Katz, a short, bald man who taught English and math in the dining hall of the Kinchow Road camp, the block of buildings where his family first lived when they came to Shanghai. The big dining hall was nearly filled with children during school hours, and at recess they played tag around the archways and up on the second floor balcony. Mr. Katz spoke English almost all the time and Gerd was learning quickly. He and the other students sat on the floor, using the short dining room stools as desks. As Mr. Katz recited words in English, Gerd copied them on the gray sheets of paper inside the little blue exam books with Chinese characters on the outside. But the lessons ended for the day at lunch time, when the writing desks again became stools for the hundreds of refugees who came for their free meals in the dining room.

Gerd couldn't imagine a place with more mystery and adventure than Shanghai. He could never understand why his parents and the other old people complained so much about the heat, filth, and insects and talked so often about Berlin. His strongest memory of Germany was not so happy: he remembered how he had embarrassed his father on the first day of school.

Gerd's first school was on Dunckerstrasse, the Twenty-Ninth Deutsche Folkschule near the Prenzlauer train station in northeast Berlin. He and his father Gustav had walked there, just down the street from their house on Ahlbecker Strasse, for the first day of school in September 1935. It was a special occasion for a six-year-old. His father, who sold children's clothing, had given him a new suit of clothes—a dark sailor's suit with big white buttons and a scarf around his broad white shirt collar. With his right hand, he held onto the new leather school bag tied around his shoulder; with his left hand, he held a tall cardboard cone that was half his height. The cone was brimming with candy and sweets that he would devour when the school day was over. When they got to the school, Gerd joined his new schoolmates and sat at one of the small tables in the classroom. His father took the candy and lined up at the back, with all the other parents who were loaded down with packages of candy and other gifts. His father seemed very proud and kept nodding at Gerd and winking.

The principal entered the room, smiling and talking slowly. From now on, he said, each day when a teacher walked into the classroom, all the students had to greet her in a special way. They should stand up, click their heels together, salute with their right arms, and yell "Heil Hitler!" Gerd fidgeted in his seat and raised his hand to speak.

"That is all right for the others," Gerd told the principal, "but not for me."

The principal seemed surprised.

"Why not?" he asked.

"Because I am Jewish," Gerd said proudly. Gerd's father always had told him and his older brother, Benno, that they were different, that Jews didn't believe in the same things other people did. He thought his father would be pleased that he spoke out. But when he turned to look at him, his father's mouth had fallen open and his eyes seemed to bulge out.

The principal walked to Gerd's desk to look at him closely and studied his deep blue eyes and bright blond hair. He called Gerd's father over.

"The way this Jewish boy looks," he said, "overthrows all of the racial theories of Adolf Hitler."

After that first day, the teachers never asked Gerd to salute or to join in singing Nazi songs in class. Gerd's classmates didn't seem to mind that he was different and he made friends easily. But he continued to be outspoken. All of his teachers commented on his report cards that Gerd always was talking in the middle of class.

Gerd didn't see much of his parents once he was in school. They were away most of the time at weekly fairs all over Prussia selling children's clothing and ladies' undergarments. At Passover, his mother, Julie, came home to help his grandmother sell food for the holidays. The house was filled with boxes of round matzot and bags of meal that Gerd and Benno had to climb over and around. The two women divided the meal into smaller packages then delivered the flour and matzot by horse and wagon. Later in the winter, both his parents were at home to sell goods at the Christmas markets in Berlin. In the summer, they took Gerd and Benno with them to the fairs.

But in the fall of 1936, the Nazis began to restrict Jews from working as peddlers.[1] They refused to renew Gustav's license, despite the fact that he was a decorated German war veteran who had been held prisoner for most of the war by the Russian army. So Gustav began to look for a new job. For many years, he had been working weekends as a volunteer for Jewish community organizations. Soon after he lost his permit, the Jewish Reform Community offered him a job as superintendent of their five-story building and school on Nurnberger Strasse.

The new job meant the Heimanns would have to move, because the superintendent had to live in the building. The new apartment was luxurious compared with Ahlbecker Strasse. It was in an exclusive section in the middle of the city, at the corner of the Kurfurstendam and just south of the zoological gardens.

Gerd liked having his father at home all the time and loved riding the elevator up and down in their new building. Gustav spent most of his time in a loge in the lobby answering calls from tenants on the intercom and sending Gerd on errands. Each afternoon, Gerd would run to a nearby tavern to bring pitchers of beer for the attorneys, doctors, and musicians who lived in the building. Some were prominent Nazi officials; he made sure he was always polite to them, as his father had told him. All of them tipped him well. Gerd also made friends with a non-Jewish family who lived next door. On summer weekends, they took him to the beach, even though Jews were banned from going there. But no one could guess that the blue-eyed blond boy was a Jew.

Gerd also was sent to a new school, a few blocks away on Joachimstaler Strasse. It was run by the Jewish Reform Community and was smaller and more crowded than his first school. But he learned to speak some English and liked his teachers. Perhaps it was the sophisticated neighborhood, or perhaps it was because Gerd looked so Aryan, but Gerd never had to worry about being taunted or beaten up by other kids when he walked to school. The Nazis on the streets all seemed nice to him.

But everything changed one day in November when Gerd walked out of the apartment building on his way to school. As he turned the corner, he stopped suddenly in front of Mrs. Rutin's cigar store. The plate glass window had been smashed in. Instead of neatly arranged shelves and humidors, there was glass and tobacco strewn all over the inside of the store. Next door, the Kalisky's bedding store also was a shambles. A star of David and the word *Jud* were painted in white on the front of the store. Gerd was confused and scared. A gang of men was running toward him, carrying large wooden clubs and striking people on the street. He turned and ran back into the apartment building.

His father was working in the loge and Gerd ran to him. Gustav didn't try to assure Gerd, as he once had, that life in Germany would get better soon. Instead, he told Gerd about a special signal if there was trouble while he was away from the loge. If someone rang the bell in their apartment three times quickly, it meant they would all escape out the back. But the Nazis never came to arrest Gustav. The well-connected tenants in the building apparently protected the Heimanns.

Yet the Heimanns knew they would have to leave Germany soon. Benno, who was seventeen at the time, was in the most danger. Gustav, despite his lack of sympathy for Zionism, had sent Benno to a farm run by the Jewish community where they trained Jewish youths to go to Palestine. Benno learned how to clear fields and use a rifle. But just before Benno was scheduled to leave for Palestine, someone in the Jewish organization stole his permit. Gustav and Julie began to search for a place they all could go. Cousin Hans showed the way.

Hans was the only child of Sally Pape and one of Gustav's sisters, who had died in 1936. Hans and Uncle Sally, an avowed communist who somehow had avoided imprisonment, had moved close to the Heimanns after she died. Hans was five years older than Benno and also was in danger of being sent to a concentration camp. After the November pogroms, he and Sally developed a scheme to get him out of the country.

In mid-November, Hans went to the Hilfsverein, the Jewish relief society, and pleaded for their help. He told them he was guilty of *Rassenschande* (having sexual relations with an Aryan), a crime the Nazis would not forgive, and faced imprisonment or execution. The Hilfsverein officials believed his story and quickly found him passage to the only place open to Jewish refugees. He was to sail to Shanghai on December 31. Hans left Germany dressed like a rich tourist, with a blue blazer and white pants, carrying a tennis racquet and a small suitcase.

Hans planned to pull one last scam on the Germans. Before Hans left, Uncle Sally hired a goldsmith to melt down some gold they had saved and shape it into locks and fittings for the suitcase. (The Nazis would have taken the gold as part of the Reich flight tax.) No one questioned Hans on his trip out of Germany, except for one border guard who joked that, if he didn't know better, he might think the locks were made of gold. He let Hans pass through to Italy.

A few months later, Gerd's mother excitedly announced they had received a letter from Hans. The letter was on thin paper with a pretty stamp on the outside and Julie read it out loud. Hans wrote that it had taken him almost a month by ship to get to his new home. Shanghai was crowded, noisy, and dirty, he wrote, and very different from Germany. But the food was cheap—he could buy a dozen eggs for two cents and a goose for twenty cents—and he had a good job. He was the timekeeper at Sir Victor Sassoon's Cathay Hotel, in charge of purchasing for one of the most luxurious hotels in the world. Hans told his family to join him. Julie and Uncle Sally went to buy tickets the next day.

Gerd was excited about going, but it seemed to take forever to get ready. First his parents had to get all their papers and certificates, pay all their bills, and turn in some of their valuables. His father held onto his prized gold watch, but his mother gave up almost all of her jewels. Then they had to pack giant crates in their living room with all their household goods.

His mother carefully wrapped all their crystal, china, and silver and his father used the money they had left to buy pharmaceuticals he thought they might need in China, like quinine for malaria, and stuff them in the crates. He even found room for Gerd's scooter. Three customs officers were supposed to make sure the Heimanns didn't take any valuables with them, but Julie served them all a big lunch of sausages, cold cuts, and schnapps and they dozed off while the Heimanns finished packing.

The Heimanns and Uncle Sally left Berlin at the end of May 1939. The day they left, Gerd went from door to door in the apartment building, saying goodbye to his customers and neighbors. He didn't tell his father, but they all stuffed his pockets with reichsmarks, many more than the ten reichsmarks each emigrant was allowed to take.

The train trip took them across Germany and into Austria. Just before the Italian border, Gustav lost his nerve and threw his gold watch out the window. What he didn't know was that his young son, sleeping peacefully on the seat, was carrying enough money to get them all thrown in jail. But the German border guards didn't disturb Gerd's sleep and took only a quick look into their train compartment.

The train took the Heimanns to Milan, where some distant cousins brought them a basket of fruit, and then to Genoa. They had their first Italian food, a veal scallopini Gerd thought was the world's thinnest schnitzel. They stayed in Genoa for three days, hosted by the local Jewish community. Gerd explored the city while they waited to board their ship. When he got lost, he followed his parents' advice and stayed where he was. On the first day there, he stood under an overpass for what seemed like days until his parents found him.

On May 31, the Heimanns boarded the *Conte Biancamano*, the same ship that had taken Sam Didner to Shanghai in November and December and Horst Levin in January and February. It was the biggest thing Gerd had ever seen.

The ship was crowded to capacity, carrying almost nine hundred people. The captain made special provisions for the dozens of extra passengers pleading to get on board, moving the crew out of its normal sleeping area and turning their quarters over to the refugees. The Heimanns were among those who traveled in the crew's quarters, which the crew labeled fourth class. His mother, father, Benno, and Uncle Sally were in one cabin; Gerd was in another with three older ladies. Gerd slept on a bottom bunk and his legs were just long enough to kick the bunk above him. He nicknamed the poor woman who slept there *Oma Huppemal* (Grandmother Jump).

The ship's dining room was crowded during the first few days of the trip, with eleven people at each of the big round tables and a carafe of red wine for each of them. On the third day of the trip there was a near riot in the dining room when the waiters served Napoleons for dessert and the passengers grabbed wildly at them. Gerd's father told him to sit still, and he kept his hands on his knees as the pastries passed by. At other meals, some passengers hounded the captain, complaining about the conditions on board. A week into the voyage, the captain had seen and heard enough. He entered the dining room before dinner was served and gave a stern speech, reminding the passengers that many of them had begged to get on board and said they would sleep anywhere. He said he would no longer tolerate their grievances; those who were unhappy would be dropped off at the next port.

Seasickness put an end to the complaining. The next day, the *Biancamano* hit a storm and soon almost all the passengers were too sick to argue about anything. Gerd's mother insisted she wasn't sick, but she stayed in the cabin for the entire trip, she said, to make sure she didn't get sick. Gerd, Benno, Gustav, and Uncle Sally didn't mind the rough seas. They, as well as a wine dealer named Cohn, were often the only ones in the dining room during meals. There was still wine at every table, even the vacant ones, and Gerd watched in amazement as Mr. Cohn drained almost every decanter.

The boat now seemed less crowded and Gerd had the run of the ship. He had made friends with the crew, particularly a man named Enrico Lupe. Enrico had met one of Gerd's distant cousins, Lotte Engel, on an earlier voyage, and she had written to the Heimanns to ask for him when they boarded. Fourth-class passengers were supposed to remain on the lower deck, but Enrico became like an uncle to Gerd and took him everywhere, up and down the spiral staircases between decks, into the sailors' mess, even to the bridge. Enrico was in charge of distributing food to the ship, and he always made sure Gerd had enough sodas, candy, and fruit. When they stopped in port, Enrico let him serve the customs officers who came on board and Gerd earned more tip money.

When they stopped in Colombo, Gerd, Benno, and Gustav walked through the streets. Gustav attracted a big crowd when he lit a cigarette with his handsome German lighter. Several people tried to barter food, clothing, and strange money for the lighter, but Gustav shooed them away. Gerd traded a comb for a tropical helmet. In Singapore, after the three of them walked into a drug store and spoke to each other in German, a small man behind the counter spoke to them in Yiddish. He was an Indian Jew and he closed his shop to take the Heimanns home to meet his family. His wife served them tea and cakes, and the family gave them gifts and toys to bring to the other passengers. In Hong Kong, Gerd earned his first Shanghai dollar when he served drinks to businessmen who came on the ship. He ran to show the new money to his parents.

When they reached Shanghai at the end of June, Gerd was sorry the voyage was over but excited about seeing Hans and his new home. The harbor pilot's boat approached as they neared the Whangpoo River and, to Gerd's surprise, Hans was aboard, waving to him from the deck. Somehow, Hans had talked his way onto the boat. Once he was aboard the ship, Hans hugged Uncle Sally, Benno, and his mother and father and patted Gerd on the head. He warned them to hold onto the relief checks they had received before they left for Shanghai.[2] Someone from the Shanghai refugee committee had been collecting checks from incoming refugees, Hans said, and taking the money for himself.

When the ship reached the Shanghai and Hongkew wharf, Hans left with Uncle Sally and took him to his room at the hotel. The Heimanns would have to spend a few days in one of the refugee camps, Hans said, but after that they could use their checks to buy some property in Hongkew.

A few hours later, they rode one of the open-backed trucks to the Kinchow Road camp. When they first saw their new home in Shanghai, Gerd's parents fell silent. The camp was an old schoolhouse that was filled with metal and bamboo bunk beds. There were small bloodstains and crushed bugs all over the walls and a thick coat of dust on the floor. A man led the Heimanns to their corner of one of the big rooms, where two bunk beds were pushed together. He gave them each a thin gray blanket, spoon, tin cup, and dish. He told them it was warm enough so they wouldn't need their blankets and, if they wished, they could hang them up to close off the corner and give themselves some privacy. Children were running down the hallways, and unshaven old men in shaggy clothes roamed the building. A few feet away, an old woman was lying in her bed, coughing and spitting.

His mother sat at the edge of her bed and started to cry. His father put his arm around her and tried to comfort her, telling her softly that they would soon have their own place. But Gerd thought the camp looked like it would be fun. There were lots of kids around and a yard. He ran outside to play.

4

The Philanthropists

By the time Gerd Heimann and his family disembarked from the *Conte Biancamano* at the end of June 1939, nearly 10,000 European Jewish refugees had escaped to Shanghai in less than seven months. And thousands more would come that summer on dozens of European and Japanese ships. The *Biancamano* alone brought more than 3,000 refugees from Genoa to Shanghai—including Sam Didner, Howard Levin, and the Heimanns—on four voyages between December 1938 and June 1939. Other Lloyd Triestino liners—the *Victoria* from Genoa and the *Conte Rosso, Guilio Cesare,* and *Conte Verde* from Trieste—brought 4,200 more.[1] Despite warnings of deteriorating conditions in Shanghai, the refugees continued to flood in.

The Shanghai Municipal Council, the ruling body in the International Settlement, sounded the alarm before the end of 1938, when there were barely 1,000 Jewish refugees in Shanghai. The council sent a telegram to the American Jewish Joint Distribution Committee (JDC) on December 27, 1938:

MUNICIPAL COUNCIL OF INTERNATIONAL SETTLEMENT
SHANGHAI IS GRAVELY PERTURBED BY ABNORMAL
INFLUX OF JEWISH REFUGEES SHANGHAI IS ALREADY
FACING MOST SERIOUS REFUGEE PROBLEM DUE TO
SINOJAPANESE HOSTILITIES IT IS QUITE IMPOSSIBLE
TO ABSORB ANY LARGE NUMBER OF FOREIGN
REFUGEES COUNCIL EARNESTLY REQUESTS YOUR
ASSISTANCE IN PREVENTING ANY FURTHER REFUGEES
COMING TO SHANGHAI COUNCIL MAY BE COMPELLED
TO PREVENT FURTHER REFUGEES LANDING IN
INTERNATIONAL SETTLEMENT [2]

The JDC forwarded the municipal council's message to
Europe, where it had no noticeable impact on the thousands of
Jews increasingly desperate to get out. The Hilfsverein der
Juden in Deutschland replied in February, noting that it had
little power to stop the emigration to Shanghai. The German-
Jewish relief organization said it was convinced that Jews
would be better off in China than in Germany. "Of course we
do not deny that there is very great misery and unemployment
among the refugees in Shanghai," the Hilfsverein wrote, but
there seemed to be no choice. Other schemes for refugee
emigration were moving so slowly that they might come *too
late for a very great part of German Jewry"*(emphasis in the
original):

> Please trust us when we tell you that we are unable to diminish
> the emigration from Germany and that the only possibility to
> prevent our people from going to such places as Shanghai lies
> in the finding of some constructive opportunities for their
> emigration.[3]

As the JDC and other Jewish relief organizations were
receiving appeals from Europe, a Jewish committee in
Shanghai also was pleading for assistance. From the
beginning, refugee relief organizations in Shanghai were a
confusing patchwork of rival organizations. The first was
formed by German and Austrian Jews in 1934, shortly after
about eighty immigrants arrived that spring on the *Conte Verde*.
In July 1938, when the Jewish refugee community had reached
about two-hundred persons, a group of Czechs and Germans,

both Jews and non-Jews, formed the International Committee for European Refugees. It was headed by Paul Komor, a Hungarian gentile and unsuccessful businessman, and soon became known as the Komor Committee. Several prominent Sephardic and Russian Jews joined the committee and collected contributions from the leaders of the Sephardic community, including the Kadoories and Sir Victor Sassoon.[4]

The two committees agreed to merge in the fall of 1938, but disputes between the two groups continued. The new organization was called the Committee for the Assistance of European Jewish Refugees in Shanghai and it immediately called for help from international Jewish relief organizations, writing to the JDC on October 28, 1938 that the community had reached "the extreme limit of our resources":

> Impoverished as the local community has become as a result of the Sino-Japanese conflict it has nevertheless strained every effort to cope with the unparalleled situation. All who are in a position to contribute have been approached, canvassed and taxed to the hilt. Unfortunately, the vast majority of the Jewish community of Shanghai consists of Russian Jews who only arrived from Harbin as refugees a few years ago, and many are still receiving financial assistance from the various local charitable institutions.

The letter concluded with a lecture.

> Our problem is also essentially yours, and if there had been no restriction placed upon Jews entering the United States, European countries or the British Empire, this responsibility would have fallen upon your and their respective communities . . . our Committee represents the voice of the entire Jewish community of Shanghai which now appeals to world Jewry to do its duty in responding to our appeal for aid in order to bring succour and relief for these derelict souls who are arriving here in such large numbers.[5]

The JDC, which was focusing its relief efforts at the time on Jews who remained in Europe and those who had fled to Cuba and South America, didn't provide significant assistance to Shanghai until the following year. And perhaps the JDC was put off by the sermonizing, almost pompous tone of the appeal. So the Shanghai relief committee continued to rely on the charity of the prominent Sephardic Jews, the richest small Jewish community in the world and, in some ways, the most eccentric.

––––––––

The community had been founded in 1850 by the Sassoons, Sephardic Jews who had fled from Baghdad earlier in the nineteenth century. They had been among the first Jews to settle in Babylonia and the chief bankers for Baghdad's rulers, but they left for India when David Sassoon was kidnapped for ransom.[6]

David Sassoon founded an international trading company, exporting, among other goods, opium to China. David's son Elias set up offices in Hong Kong and Canton, eventually splitting off to establish his own firm, E.D. Sassoon & Co. After the British forced open the port of Shanghai, he set up an office there, too, and built warehouses along the Whangpoo River. The Sassoons hired only fellow Baghdadi Jews to help run their businesses; most of the rich Shanghai Sephardis got their starts working for a Sassoon.[7]

A majority of the Sephardic families were middle class or even poor, and worked in tobacco factories or as clerks. But the richest families—the Sassoons, Kadoories, Hardoons, Toegs, Ezras, and Abrahams—followed Jewish tradition by providing for their community. The Abraham family established the first synagogue in 1898; the Kadoories, with their strong interest in education, established the Shanghai Jewish School in 1902; the Ezra family in 1904 founded a Zionist newspaper, *Israel's Messenger*, that circulated worldwide. (The Ezras were among a handful of Zionists in the Sephardic community; the Sassoons and other community leaders were, at best, indifferent to Zionism.)[8]

Their philanthropy for their fellow Jews in China even extended to Kaifeng, the ancient Chinese capital where a Jewish community, originally from Persia or India, had been founded perhaps 1,000 years before the Sassoons came to Shanghai. In 1900, the Abrahams and Ezras established the

Rescue Society to visit Kaifeng.[9] They discovered that the Kaifeng Jews had almost completely assimilated into Chinese society. Unlike their persecuted ancestors from the Middle East, the Kaifeng Jews faced only curiosity, not discrimination, when they came to China. There was a remarkable similarity between Chinese and Jewish values. Both peoples revered education, had strict moral codes, and valued strong family ties. The Kaifeng Jews intermarried freely with the Chinese and, by the time the Rescue Society visited, few of the Jews of Kaifeng even looked Jewish. The society abandoned hope of "rescuing" the community but brought several of the Jews back to Shanghai, gave them jobs—one became a clerk for the Abrahams—and made them members of the synagogue.[10]

The insular Shanghai Jews were shocked by what they saw as the demise of the Kaifeng Jews. They considered intermarriage shameful; even a marriage between Yemenite and Baghdadi Sephardic families was frowned upon. To preserve their bloodlines, the Shanghai Sephardis often sanctioned marriages between close relatives, including first cousins.[11] By the 1920s, the Sephardis were a community of barely more than 1,000 people whose leaders controlled much of Shanghai's real estate and most of its fortunes. It remained a close-knit, conservative, and self-contained community. The Sephardis had minimal contact with other foreigners, but were closest to the British in manners, business practices, and political sympathies. Many of the rich Sephardis sent their sons to England for their education. They had even less contact with the Chinese, other than the compradores who worked for them and their amahs, houseboys, and cooks, some of whom spoke Arabic and could prepare Sephardic kosher food.[12] The notable exception was Silas A. Hardoon, a partner in E.D. Sassoon & Co. who built the Beth Aharon synagogue on Museum Road, near Soochow Creek, in his father's memory. Hardoon was a civic leader who at one time served simultaneously on the French Concession and International Settlement municipal councils.[13] But he angered his fellow Sephardis when he married a Eurasian woman named Luo Jialing and they adopted a large family of Chinese and Jewish children.[14]

The Sassoons continued to dominate the Sephardic community, although the family business remained based in India. In the 1920s, they donated funds to build a synagogue, Ohel Rachel, in honor of David's wife. It was a monument to the Sassoons' extravagance. The marble-columned edifice, with a high vaulted roof, sat 1,500 people, although the synagogue barely had 600 members. Next to the synagogue was a huge mikvah, almost one-hundred feet long, for the occasional conversion and the Jewish women's monthly cleansing ritual. It was located in the French Concession, far from the Hongkew homes of most Sephardi families. But when Chinese and Japanese forces battled for control of Hongkew in the early 1930s, many Sephardis moved to neighborhoods nearby the new synagogue.[15]

The Sassoons also expanded their holdings in Shanghai real estate. In 1929, they built Sassoon House on the Bund, an eleven-story hotel and office tower modeled after the finest Manhattan buildings. The top six stories were the Cathay Hotel, the most luxurious hotel in the Far East, with marble baths and a sprung floor ballroom. Noel Coward was among the first guests and, greeted with a bout of Shanghai flu, spent four days in bed in the hotel writing a draft of *Private Lives*.[16]

In 1931, Sir Victor Sassoon, the inheritor of his family's interests in Asia, moved his business from India to Shanghai—apparently to avoid British taxes on his vast fortune—and Sassoon House became his headquarters. Sir Victor was nearly a lifelong bachelor, an English-style gentleman who was educated at Harrow and Trinity. He wore a monocle and walked with a cane—he had a severe limp from a 1915 plane crash during a training run with the Royal Naval Air Service.[17]

Sir Victor continued to invest his family's wealth in real estate and built much of Shanghai's skyline along the Bund. The city's grandest hotels and office buildings—the Metropole Hotel, Grosvenor House, the Embankment Building, Hamilton House, and Cathay Mansions—were built with Sassoon money. The value of the Sassoon's Shanghai properties had almost tripled in value by 1935, despite the increasing threats from the Japanese.[18]

Sir Victor's lavish parties and costume balls at his villa on the outskirts of the city were the highlight of the Shanghai social season.[19] He also spent thousands of pounds buying and training racehorses, hoping to fulfill his lifelong ambition of winning England's legendary event at Epsom Downs. "There's only one race greater than the Jews," Sir Victor liked to say, in his dry English fashion, "and that's the Derby."[20]

He also continued his family's tradition of philanthropy for the poorer local Sephardis. That generosity didn't extend to the growing Russian Jewish community, which was founded in the early 1900s but grew rapidly to more than 4,000 people after the Bolshevik revolution and then the Japanese occupation of Manchuria. The Sephardis were suspicious of the Russian Jews, who spoke Yiddish and Russian instead of English and practiced different traditions. They were alarmed that the Russians blurred the line between foreigners and the Chinese, taking jobs as manual laborers; they were scandalized by the Russian Jewish women who worked as bar girls and prostitutes and lived with or married non-Jews. For the most part, the Sephardis had little to do with the Russian Jews and expected the wealthy Russian businessmen to take care of their own.[21]

The children of Russian and Sephardi families did mix in sports activities, scout troops, and at the Shanghai Jewish School next to the new synagogue. But in the early 1930s, the Sephardis threatened to expel the Ashkenazi children when their community couldn't pay its share of school expenses. That problem, if not the conflict, disappeared in February 1937, when the Kadoorie family established the Shanghai Jewish Youth Association (SJYA). The Kadoories, who lived in a mansion known as the Marble Hall, responded with typical noblesse oblige to the poverty and malnutrition they saw among Russian Jewish schoolchildren. They also saw an opportunity to impart some culture. "The realisation that it is by them that the Jewish community would be judged and the opinion of other races towards the Jews in general would be formed, made it clearly our duty to give our Jewish youth a fair start in life and to try to teach them the responsibilities attached to being a Jew," Sir Horace Kadoorie wrote in 1940.[22]

The SJYA was not entirely a charity, however. It charged nominal fees for most of its activities, including business classes, an employment bureau, a summer camp, and sports leagues. It also supported local scout troops and sent gifts and a letter to any refugee children who were ill.[23]

The rich Sephardis didn't hesitate to assist the next wave of refugees, the Jews from Germany and Austria. Their reasons for helping the European refugees and virtually ignoring the Russians aren't entirely clear. The new refugees were mostly Ashkenazis, like the Russians, and many of them spoke Yiddish. But the Europeans shared the Sephardis' commitment to culture and education. The Sephardis' ties to Great Britain also meant that they shared with the refugees a hatred of Adolf Hitler and the Nazis. There was a limit, however, to how far they would go to assist the refugees from Europe.

With contributions from the Sassoons, Kadoories, and others, the Komor Committee registered the refugees when they arrived, helped them find housing and jobs, and provided many with loans to start their own businesses. Initially, Komor also offered refugees rent and food allowances and provided meals, but those functions were taken over by the Committee for the Assistance of European Jewish Refugees in February 1939. The Komor Committee also established a milk fund to offer free milk to infants and sick children.[24]

Hundreds of people lined up daily at Komor's office at 190 Kiuking Road seeking assistance. Komor discouraged the refugees from taking manual jobs, hoping to avoid the further disgrace of Jews doing menial work. He also was concerned that the European refugees would create resentment in the community if they displaced other foreigners. Yet only a few hundred refugees could find work because there were few opportunities for people who spoke almost no English and were trained as lawyers, engineers, and academics.[25]

The remainder of the refugees lived on what little money they had been able to bring from Europe or support from abroad. Some German Jews received checks from the Hebrew Immigrant Aid Society when they arrived. Others sold their jewelry, silver, household goods, and clothing at second-hand markets to pay for food and rent. The Komor Committee opened a thrift shop to help refugees sell their belongings.

Refugees with some resources rented apartments in the French Concession or bought inexpensive buildings in Hongkew where they could live and collect rent from other tenants. The poorer refugees rented in Hongkew, where apartments were much cheaper. And those with almost nothing lived in the dreary, increasingly crowded camps.

The relief committee at first rented the former British Old Women's Home on Washing Road and used it as a home for sixty to seventy refugees. But with the increasing numbers of refugees, and the high cost of treating their illnesses at the municipal hospital, the committee converted the home into a hospital, headed by Sam Didner.[26] Sassoon then donated the first floor of his Embankment Building as a dormitory. In the following months, the committee opened refugee camps on Ward Road, Wayside Road, and Kinchow Road.[27]

By the summer of 1939, nearly 3,000 of the refugees were living in the camps and more than 5,000 were receiving meals there. Another 1,500 were receiving monthly rental allowances from the relief committee. The total relief effort was costing about $15,000 a month, with thousands more refugees on their way from Europe. Only about 350 refugees had found jobs.[28]

The Shanghai newspapers were writing regularly about the despair and poverty in the refugee camps, particularly among the older refugees, some of whom had been prominent academics or professionals in Europe. The Shanghai Municipal Police reported that three of the professional men had committed suicide early in 1939. The police also expressed concern about two reports of refugees attempting "to secure money by fraudulent means."[29]

Some press accounts showed clear hostility to the refugees. A White Russian newspaper reported early in 1939:

> According to our information, only about 30 percent of them [the refugees] are really in need. Among the others there are not a few who have managed to take with them their entire fortunes in money and valuables. . .Our own investigation shows that

these "needy" people reside in the best apartments of the Cathay, Palace, Plaza, Park and Royal hotels, dine in the restaurants of the Cathay and Palace hotels, drink champagne at Delmonte Cafe and buy provisions from the best wine and delicacy stores. Our investigations show that the "refugees" have brought with them diamonds worth millions of dollars.[30]

There was some resentment in the English-language papers as well. An April 1939 account in the *Shanghai Evening Post and Mercury* by John Ahlers reported that the economic competition created by the Jewish emigration:

constitutes a serious menace to part of the established western communities as well as to certain classes of the Chinese in Shanghai. While there is no anti-Jewish discrimination in Shanghai, there ought not to develop anything like a pro-Jewish discrimination. It would be an appalling injustice if established Shanghailanders were forced out of business and employment merely to make place for the new emigrants from Germany.[31]

Ahlers' article cited unsubstantiated reports that Russians and Chinese were losing their jobs to the new immigrants and that some were working without pay in an attempt to gain employment. The article concluded with what appeared to be something of a threat: "It is in the interest of the Jewish emigrants themselves that such practices should be discontinued immediately," Ahlers wrote, "in order not to create anti-Jewish feeling in Shanghai."[32]

With conditions deteriorating and the influx continuing, the Shanghai philanthropists apparently had neared the end of their charity. They took steps to put an end to the immigration.

On May 25, 1939, Sir Victor Sassoon and Ellis Hayim, a leader of the Committee for the Assistance of European Jewish Refugees in Shanghai, met with Japanese officials and reportedly urged them to halt the flow of immigration. Sassoon and Hayim assured the Japanese that world Jewry would not oppose the restrictions.[33]

In June, the relief committee sent its public relations chairman, Michel Speelman, an elderly Dutch Jew, to meet with Jewish relief officials in New York, London, and Paris to appeal for more aid. "Under no circumstances can Shanghai absorb all these people," Speelman wrote in his report to the JDC in Paris.[34]

The Japanese, who controlled Hongkew and most of the city but continued to show respect for foreign control of the International Settlement, spoke on August 9. In a press conference, the Japanese naval authorities announced that no additional refugees would be permitted to live in Hongkew after August 21. The Japanese cited a shortage of housing but also noted that "the Jewish committee" was concerned that more arrivals would threaten the livelihood of those already in Shanghai "and did not want a further influx of refugees." All refugees living in Hongkew at the time would have to register with the Japanese authorities and fill out questionnaires to receive a permit to remain there.[35]

The Shanghai Municipal Council, still the ruling authority in the International Settlement, made the crucial annoucement on August 14, prohibiting additional refugees from entering the settlement. "We've already done more than our share here in Shanghai," one official told the *North China Daily News*. "But the point has been reached where Shanghai cannot absorb any more refugees."[36] The next day, a council official said it was not clear whether refugees already on their way, aboard the *Guilio Cesare* and the *Conte Biancamano*, would be permitted to land.[37]

The only remaining refuge for European Jewry was closing its doors.

II
COMMUNITY
(1939–1941)

5

Didner

Sam Didner pedaled his Brennerabor bicycle along the tree-lined streets of the International Settlement, past St. Peter's Church, the police station, and the high stone walls that concealed all but the red-tile roofs of the Tudor-style mansions on Avenue Road. This warm, dry day in late August 1939 was the best Shanghai had to offer, a lull between the stifling humidity of summer and the heavy rains that would flood the streets in October. But it wasn't enough to calm Didner's building anger. He was on his way to settle a score.

It had been eight months since Didner had greeted his first shipload of refugees. More ships were arriving each week, adding patients to the already overcrowded Emigrants' Hospital. Didner, the hospital's medical director, worked long hours and had a familiar routine. He still slept at night on a cot in the hospital dispensary. In some ways, his practice had changed only slightly since he left Austria. Nearly all of his patients were Germans and Austrians—each foreign community relied almost exclusively on its own doctors. His contact with the Chinese was limited mostly to pharmacists and an occasional medical emergency.

Didner allowed himself little time for relaxing and socializing. He occasionally went to small dinner parties hosted by wealthy European doctors who were established in Shanghai before he arrived. Didner also attended a few parties and balls put on by prominent Sephardic and Russian Jews. His professional standing and his Austrian charm made him a welcome guest.

His most difficult adjustment was facing the unusual medical conditions in Shanghai. Dozens of Chinese froze to death on the streets during the cold winter months. In warmer weather, virulent diseases spread rapidly in the poor sanitary conditions. The Europeans were particularly vulnerable to lethal strains of dysentery—unheard of in Europe—which killed hundreds of them. Didner had few resources with which to work.

But he had learned to adapt to what was available. The Washing Road hospital was primitive, but initially was able to handle most cases. In the first few months that winter and spring, he treated one patient with typhoid fever, two with malaria, and one with pneumonia. Most of the admissions were for influenza or respiratory problems. In the meantime, he had helped train fifteen nurses and now had a French colleague, Dr. Gabriel Altmann, who was both competent and personable. The warm weather months brought a dramatic increase of severe illnesses[1] and the sixty beds were always full. The patients, Didner often said, were packed in like herring.

The scarlet fever epidemic in May, apparently carried by an arriving refugee, had been a serious threat. Didner and the other refugee doctors had to act quickly. On the first day of the outbreak, thirty-two cases were reported. Another seventy-four cases showed up in the next three days. The doctors decided to isolate all of them. They found room in a new dormitory on Chauofoong Road, which had just been renovated but hadn't yet been occupied. The quarantine worked. The outbreak peaked early—one week into the epidemic there were only nine new cases reported. By late that month, 128 patients were being treated. In a small, crowded community, an epidemic like this one could have claimed thousands. But only one person isolated at the Chauofoong Road camp died.[2]

Didner and his colleagues were not so fortunate in dealing with the dysentery cases that summer. The first appeared in June, with five patients coming to the Emigrants' Hospital with symptoms of amoebic or bacillary dysentery. The disease is usually contracted from drinking contaminated water, and Shanghai's filthy Whangpoo River was an ideal breeding ground for bacteria and parasites. Although most of the refugees had been careful not to drink the water or to eat unwashed or uncooked fruits and vegetables, hundreds were still becoming ill. Clever Chinese vendors were part of the problem. Many of the fruit sellers routinely injected oranges with river water to make them seem fresh; more unscrupulous sellers even injected water into watermelons to add to their weight. Their schemes to make a few extra cents had fatal consequences for some of their customers.

Didner had treated many patients in Austria with the same disease, but the Shanghai strain was far more powerful and often deadly. Patients were doubled over with severe abdominal pain and their diarrhea lasted for weeks. There was no treatment other than bed rest and injection of a salt solution to overcome dehydration. In July, Didner had thirty-three more cases of dysentery, along with twenty-two cases of diarrhea and enteritis. Two of the dysentery patients died in July, the first deaths from infection at the Emigrants' Hospital.[3]

At the time, epidemics like scarlet fever and parasitic infections like dysentery defied medical treatment. The best doctors were primarily good diagnosticians; medical practice involved more observation than treatment. Before the manufacture of penicillin and other antibiotics, there was little physicians could do for many ailments, particularly bacterial infections. Some severe infections were almost always fatal.

Earlier that year, Didner had seen one of those severe cases at the hospital. A seventeen-year-old named Albert Budak was brought in by his father with a very high fever. Another doctor already had seen Albert, but his father wasn't satisfied and decided to bring him to the hospital for a second opinion. The high fever was unusual, but Didner recognized the other symptoms—weakness, fatigue, and aching joints. His diagnosis was that Albert had infective endocarditis, a bacterial inflammation of the heart's inner lining that often destroys the heart's valves or causes heart attacks and strokes.[4] Combined with the high fever, Didner knew it was almost certainly fatal. Didner gave Albert aspirin to reduce the fever, but it didn't help. His temperature remained at 104 or 105 degrees and he was near death. There was only one hope for his survival.

Before he left Europe, Didner had read about German research into sulfa drugs. They had proved extremely effective in fighting some bacterial infections. The earliest of these drugs, Prontosil, was being manufactured when Didner emigrated to Shanghai.[5] Was it possible that this drug could be found here in Shanghai, halfway around the world? Didner already had discovered that the Chinese pharmacists could acquire almost anything. After a few inquiries, he located a supply of Prontosil and began a six-week series of injections for Albert.

Didner was impressed and fascinated by the results. Albert's fever subsided quickly and, after a few weeks of treatment, his symptoms disappeared. He would be left with an enlarged heart but in good health. For Didner, this was an introduction to a new era. Sulfa drugs and, within a few years, penicillin and other antibiotics, were about to reshape modern medicine. Doctors could now become healers, not mere diagnosticians.

There was another twist to Albert's case that also would change Didner's life. It introduced him to Albert's sister, Grete, a thin, dark beauty from an exotic Jewish family. The Budaks were Turkish Jews who had been raised in Berlin, fled to Shanghai, and established a profitable carpet business. Didner was immediately attracted to Grete, but romance would have to wait. She admired the doctor who had saved her brother's life, but found him rather cold and arrogant. Her father liked him more than she did. A few months later, when Grete was hospitalized with influenza for a week, she softened a bit.

But it wasn't Grete that was on Didner's mind this sunny August day as he bicycled down Avenue Road. He was on his way to confront Dr. Tibor Kunfi. The more he thought about him, the angrier he got and the faster he pedaled.

Kunfi was one of his colleagues on the medical board of the Committee for the Assistance of European Jewish Refugees. He also was a fellow Austrian, although he originally came from Hungary. Kunfi was a dark, tall man and a bit eccentric—he liked to operate with his bare hands and seemed proud of it. He took other risks, too. He was rumored to be having an affair with the chief refugee physician's wife.

But Didner had a different score to settle. The previous day, the medical board had had its weekly meeting and Didner, who was working at the hospital, couldn't attend. After the meeting, one of his colleagues called on him. He told Didner that Kunfi had used the meeting as a opportunity to level charges against Didner. Kunfi claimed, among other things, that Didner had incorrectly diagnosed a woman with an ovarian cyst and sent her to Shanghai General Hospital.

Didner knew that Kunfi's charges were lies and that he could prove his medical competence. But he was furious that a colleague would attack him behind his back, when he had no chance to defend himself. This was not the same as Obersiebenbrunn, where old Dr. Urschitz had made charges to try to protect his practice and undermine his new competitor. Kunfi, Didner felt, was simply driven by ambition and wanted to discredit Didner so he could take over as head of the Emigrants' Hospital.

Didner pulled his bicycle up the stairs and then walked into Kunfi's office, right past his open-mouthed secretary. Kunfi was standing by his desk and forced a polite smile when Didner burst in. The smile faded quickly. Didner was clenching his fists in anger.

"What kind of ethical behavior is this when you make charges against me and I am not there to answer those accusations?" Didner yelled. He could feel the blood rushing to his head.

Kunfi kept his distance, at first trying to deny that he had made the charges. But Didner would have none of it.

"You are a liar!" he yelled. "A filthy, scheming, dishonest liar!"

Didner's insults cut deep, and Kunfi seemed taken aback. Then suddenly, he lowered his head and charged across the room at Didner, looking like an enraged animal. Kunfi apparently hadn't heard about Didner's brief boxing career.

Didner threw only one punch, an uppercut that caught Kunfi squarely on the jaw. The force of the blow surprised Didner almost as much as Kunfi. The skinny Hungarian straightened up as his head snapped back, then stumbled backward across the length of his office, crashing into a floor lamp and bookcase as they all toppled over. Didner left Kunfi sprawling on the floor and again walked past his alarmed secretary. He bicycled back to the hospital, pulled out his typewriter, and began to type a letter. He had decided to resign.

Didner wrote the medical board that he felt compelled to leave his position and gave them two weeks notice. Kunfi's attempt to discredit him was unethical, he wrote, but he, too, had been unethical by striking him in retaliation. He felt he had no choice but to quit as medical director at the hospital and enter private practice.

If Didner had made his decision on purely economic grounds, it would have been foolhardy to open his own practice. The refugee community included hundreds of doctors and dentists but only a handful of patients with the funds to pay for private medical care. Most relied on the free services offered by the relief committees.

The other foreign communities—the British, Japanese, Russians, et al.—had their own systems of medical care. Didner would have to depend on hard work and long hours to make a living.

Early in September, Didner rented a room on Chusan Road, in the middle of the refugee community and not far from the Ward Road jail, and hung up a small sign with his name on it.

His wasn't the only new business in Hongkew that fall. Entire blocks had been remodeled into thriving businesses. Refugees had rented storefronts from the Komor Committee and rebuilt them with loans from Sir Victor Sassoon. Most of Chusan Road was filled with stores, offices, and restaurants. Flatow's butcher shop, at Wayside and Chusan roads, had added an outdoor cafe. The tables and chairs crowded under five big umbrellas had become a popular gathering place for the refugees.[6] West of Chusan Road, where Wayside merged into Broadway, were Abraham's dry goods store, Feiner and Reich's Broadway Pharmacy, and a European-style bathhouse run by three refugees. The Wayside Theatre also had opened, showing the latest MGM and other American movies. (It seemed fitting in Shanghai that the Broadway Theatre was on Wayside and the Wayside Theatre was on Broadway.) New restaurants, such as the Imperial and the Florida, had opened recently as well as several authentic Viennese pastry shops, a temptation even the most impoverished Austrian couldn't resist.[7]

Farther west, toward the Garden Bridge, were Brecher and Schwarz's Cafe Colibri, a two-story restaurant and cafe frequented by Japanese businessmen, Taussig's Garden Bridge Restaurant, Weinberg's cigar store, and Silberman's stationery shop. Two refugees were now running a shuttle service, in a small Ford, from the Garden Bridge to Wayside Road.[8]

A few refugees had started their own small factories, manufacturing everything from margarine to coal and employing dozens of refugees. Others went to work for Russian furriers, Chinese laundries, and Japanese paper factories. Two families who had manufactured candles and perfume in Vienna, Engel and Weiss, established a similar business in Shanghai. They began by selling *yahrtzeit* memorial candles to the Chinese, leaving samples burning at Chinese shops. When the amazed shop owners found the candles would burn for twenty-four hours, they bought dozens of them. It soon became quite common to see Jewish memorial candles burning in Chinese homes.[9]

But most refugees who had found jobs were serving their own growing community. Second-hand shops paid cash for the silver and jewelry refugees could no longer afford to keep. Tailors who turned old suits and shirts inside out and *Flickschusters* (cobblers) who could salvage torn shoes and soles were in great demand. Other refugees worked in the camps, cooking or delivering food. One older man ran a wake-up service, awakening camp residents at a designated hour and telling them the weather conditions so they could dress properly.[10]

Didner's office was like many other businesses, a large first-floor room that served as his home at night and his office during the day. He bought a used examining table, with stirrups for gynecological examinations, and equipment for minor surgery, then opened for business.

In his work at the hospital, Didner usually had seen only the most serious cases. But in private practice, he saw a wide variety of health problems as the refugees tried to adapt to their new environment. Those who lived in the camps, and the large number of families without any income, began to show signs of poor nutrition that made them more vulnerable to disease. Some older refugees without families lost the will to take care of themselves and slowly wasted away. The rush toward war in Europe was destroying any hope that the refugees' stay in Shanghai would be a short one.

These difficulties forced some refugees to make impossible choices. A few, including the wives of former professional men and academics, began to work as prostitutes. Didner knew a dental technician who brought his wife to work at a brothel every evening. Other women worked in Shanghai's seedy nightclubs as bar girls.

The bar girls were attractive young women who sat at the tables and bars and talked with male customers who bought them drinks. It was an obvious ruse. The "cocktail" the bartenders served the bar girls was tea instead of liquor, and the customers' drink money would go to the girls at the end of the night. Some of the bars had live jazz bands, and the bar girls danced with the customers. But many of the customers wanted more. Bartenders often doubled as pimps for the bar girls.[11]

In Europe, the idea of a Jewish prostitute was unthinkable. Here in Shanghai, the old moral standards could not hold. Few people condemned those women who did what they had to and saved their families from starvation.

For Didner, the loose moral conditions in Shanghai meant an increasingly large caseload of venereal disease. For sexually active men who felt a burning sensation when they urinated, Didner's office became known as the place to go for treatment. The cure at the time could be quite painful. Gonorrhea, for example, was treated by injecting silver nitrate into the urethra.

But Didner's most difficult cases were the young women who wanted to abort their pregnancies. Some were prostitutes, but most were young married women who felt they could not afford to raise children in the deteriorating conditions in Shanghai. Didner had already handled some of these cases at the Emigrants' Hospital and, under the instructions of the Komor Committee, he had reluctantly performed several abortions. They were illegal in Shanghai at the time, but that law, like so many others, was regularly ignored.

These were not Didner's first abortions. He had done many of them in Obersiebenbrunn, mostly as a result of botched farmhouse abortions that threatened a woman's life. It seemed for a while, Didner recalled, that every time he returned home from a late night visit to Vienna, a farmer would be waiting for him at the train station to take him to operate on his wife. Their conditions were often critical. Didner remembered one particularly bloody dilation and curettage he had done to try to clean up a septic abortion. He operated in a farmhouse by the light of a kerosene lantern held by the woman's husband. In the middle of the operation, the light disappeared. Didner turned to find the farmer lying on the floor. He had passed out from the sight of blood.

Most of these botched country abortions were performed by a Czech woman in her stable. Not long before Didner left Obersiebenbrunn, the Czech woman attempted to give herself an abortion. Didner was called in to save her. She survived the surgery and then abandoned her abortion business.

In Shanghai, Didner performed an average of two abortions a week. But in every case, he tried to discourage the women from the operation. A few changed their minds and kept their babies. Most of the women pleaded with Didner—some even fell to their knees to beg him—to abort the fetuses. It saddened him to do it, but he understood that many of the women had no choice.

Didner's practice grew as conditions worsened. He developed a good reputation and was always available. Most of

Didner's practice consisted of house calls. Didner bicycled across town day and night to see patients with typhoid fever, dysentery, cholera, dengue fever, and dozens of other illnesses.

But his Brennerabor bicycle proved an attractive target for the local thieves, who ran a thriving market in stolen bicycles. It was stolen twice in his first few weeks of practice, but recovered both times by Detective Kramer of the Shanghai Municipal Police. After the second theft, Kramer advised Didner to keep the bicycle with him at all times. So Didner regularly dragged his heavy bicycle and large, black medical bag up two or three flights of narrow stairs when he went on house calls. It helped keep him fit. He was strong enough to once carry a sick 230-pound man down two flights to a waiting ambulance.

When he found time for recreation, Didner went to boxing matches at the Shanghai Auditorium. He soon became a regular at the fights, and the refugees made him their unofficial physician. He sat near their corner of the ring and treated their cuts and bruises.

The first refugee boxing matches were organized in July 1939 by Max Buchbaum, a refugee and a renowned German amateur boxer. The best refugee boxers—Sam Lefko, Kid Ruckenstein, and Laco Kohn—defeated the top American, French, and even Japanese boxers that summer. They made Didner's job easy because they were rarely hurt, except for an occasional broken rib. The Jewish refugee boxers developed a reputation throughout Shanghai, and hundreds of fans from all nationalities would come to the auditorium to root for Lefko and the others.[12]

The biggest sport in Shanghai was soccer. The refugees first joined the Russian Jews on the Jewish Recreation Club team but soon had enough good players to form their own teams in the Shanghai league. (They also formed their own league, with teams sponsored by camps, restaurants, and newspapers, and competed on a field at the Kinchow Road camp.) The sports pages of the English-language newspapers featured articles about the refugee stars, including Erich Zomma, Karl Marishel, Hy Wind, and Max Kopstein. But no one could rival Leo Meyer, the sports teacher who had starred in Dusseldorf.

Meyer, a quick, agile center, was always among the leading
scorers. A refugee team lost a close championship match to the
Italians in the summer of 1939, but Meyer led a seven-member
team to the minisoccer championship later that summer.
Thousands of soccer-mad Chinese fans cheered wildly at the
games and would mob the well-known players when they
walked through the city.[13] Didner also played some soccer. But
when he was called one day to substitute for a sick player, he
found he was nearly too exhausted to handle a difficult
delivery later that day.

Didner kept his office on Chusan Road for only a few
months. To save money, he decided to share an office and
home with a Viennese dentist, Dr. Desider Molner. Molner, his
wife, and two daughters had been living on Bubbling Well
Road in the International Settlement, but the rent was
becoming too expensive. They moved to a house on East
Seward Road, a few blocks west of Chusan Road, and invited
Didner to join them. A Chinese man ran a bar on the first floor.
Molner and Didner shared a waiting room and adjacent offices
on the second floor, next to a kitchen and a small bedroom
where Didner slept at night. The Molners lived on the top floor
and kept a small pen outside where Mrs. Molner raised
rabbits. She did all the cooking and Didner gave his earnings
to her for safekeeping. But there wasn't much money to keep.

Didner had found that most of the refugees in Hongkew
were at least as poor as he was. He refused to charge them for
his services; his only income was from fees at the Shanghai
General Hospital, where he was affiliated and sent some of his
patients, and the occasional refugee who insisted on paying.
The General Hospital helped introduce Didner to another
world, the wealthy British community in its dying days of
colonial glory.

The British doctors made their living on medical contracts, a
type of socialized medicine in which all members of the
community paid a doctor of their choice an annual fee, in
advance, which covered all medical services for the year. The
system seemed to work wonderfully—for the doctors. Most had
spacious, well-furnished offices, with potted palms and leather
couches in the waiting rooms. They worked short days with

long lunches and spent their evenings at the club or at lavish British parties. Their weekends were dedicated to riding through the swamps with the Paper Hunt Club or betting at the Shanghai Race Course.

The weekend races indirectly brought some business to Didner. James Canning, who owned a large piano factory, called Didner one Saturday, suffering with a bad abscess of his tonsils and severe pain. Canning had a contract with a British doctor, but despite Canning's distress, he had refused to see him that day. The doctor was on his way to the race course. "Sorry, old boy," the British doctor had told him when he called, "but I'm off to the races." Didner examined Canning, immediately admitted him to the General Hospital, and performed an emergency incision and drainage.

Canning, his wife, and son became regular patients, and Didner and Canning became good friends. Canning sometimes invited him to parties at his home in Hungjao, near the golf course, where the British and some of the wealthy Sephardic Jews, like the Ezras, drank, danced, and gambled through the night. The favored whiskey was Johnnie Walker, and Didner was amazed at how much these Shanghailanders could drink. With the war in Europe under way after Germany's invasion of Poland, some of the British talked about leaving the pleasures of Shanghai and joining the war effort. Didner, simmering with anger toward the Nazis for what they had done to him and his family, began thinking about emigrating again.

At the British consulate, Didner signed up to join the British forces training in Australia. The consul also enlisted him to secretly help the Allies by giving physicals to recruits for the Chinese underground who were on their way to fight in Burma.

Canning also introduced Didner to some officials of the Swedish consulate, including Consul Hellerude, who befriended him as well, and Didner treated one or two consular officials. (The Swedish consul later arranged for Didner to treat a group of Finnish sailors who were stranded in Shanghai when the war in the Pacific began.) A Japanese dentist and his daughter, who lived in Hongkew, also regularly came to Didner for physicals. The dentist occasionally brought

Didner other patients. The most prominent was a Japanese naval officer. During a routine dental examination, the dentist had discovered an ulcer in the officer's mouth and called Didner to his office for his opinion.

At the dentist's office, Didner did what was called a "kick" diagnosis. He took one look in the officer's mouth and pulled the dentist aside.

"Put that man in the hospital immediately," Didner said. "He has an acute leukemia. He will probably die in a few days."

Didner's instant diagnosis was a flourish of bravado, one that impressed the Japanese dentist and enhanced Didner's reputation. Didner had seen the same kind of diagnosis during his residency in Vienna, where the legendary Dr. Chwostek, a seedy-looking alcoholic, would sweep into an auditorium filled with students and other physicians and examine a patient on a stretcher. Chwostek would sniff the air, perhaps touch the patient's skin, and then, based only on the evidence of his senses, pronounce his diagnosis. He was always right, but it was no parlor trick. Chwostek may have looked unimpressive, but his diagnoses were based on long experience and careful observation.

In the case of the Japanese officer, Didner's diagnosis was accurate, too. The officer died within a few days. But without taking a blood test, the diagnosis was a foolish show, displaying the arrogance Grete had sensed in Didner when she first met him. He had wanted to prove to the Japanese doctor that he, the well-trained doctor from Vienna, had no doubts.

Hubris, perhaps, is an occupational disease in the medical profession. It overwhelms some doctors, who begin to see themselves as gods, with the power to pronounce death or to overcome it. For others, like Didner, it can be a warning, a lesson to be learned. The years in Shanghai would help teach him the limitations of his profession and his own limitations as well.

6

Levin

It was, Levin had to admit, a rare tribute. Few people, after all, get a chance to read their own obituaries. But there it was, in bold letters, on the obit page of *The Shanghai Jewish Chronicle*. He sat up in his hospital bed and put on his glasses.

The account was rather flattering. There was the usual family background and personal history and a review of Horst's eight months in Shanghai, from his start as a piano player to his work as a newspaper critic and advertising salesman. There was praise for his work in founding the refugee radio program as well as his fund-raising activities for the new community center. Levin, the article said, had become one of the most respected members of the Shanghai refugee community. It all seemed accurate to him, except for one thing: He wasn't dead, at least not yet.

Outside his hospital room, the October monsoons continued to pour on Shanghai. The streets were knee-deep in water and rickshaws had become the only reliable transportation. It was the worst flood in the city's history, the *North China Daily*

News reported, and Shanghai had become the "Venice of the Orient." [1]

———————

It had taken several more visits that spring with M. Marcus, the MGM advertising executive, before Levin had closed the deal. But after weeks of lunches, dinners, and visits to Marcus's home, Levin landed a contract for six months of MGM movie ads in *Shanghai Woche*. The paper had been struggling financially and Levin's new account helped it survive. Its editor, Wolfgang Fischer, nicknamed Levin *Der weisse Rabe* (the rare bird) for rescuing the weekly.

Levin also had become a writer for the paper, translating news articles from the English dailies into German and occasionally writing a concert review. (His first review, of a piano concert by Hans Baer, upset the German virtuoso, who later told Levin he had slighted him by calling his performance a "routine.") He also reciprocated MGM's patronage by regularly publishing their press releases and stories about their new movies.

Levin was visiting the MGM offices in April to pick up a publicity package when Marcus stopped him and invited him into his office. Marcus poured drinks for both of them and announced he was about to leave China to return to the United States for six months. He offered to take Levin out for dinner.

That night over dinner, the two men talked some more about sports and music. But Marcus seemed reflective and, now that he was about to leave, particularly concerned about Levin. He had become rather fond of him, he said, and worried about his future in Shanghai.

"It's always seemed to me that you're uncomfortable selling these newspaper ads," Marcus said. "Is this what you want, or do you see yourself doing something else?"

Levin sensed that Marcus' concern was more than idle. He thought for several moments before he answered.

A few weeks earlier, Levin and another refugee had been guests on a talk show on XCDN, a radio station owned by the *North China Daily News*. They both had talked about their concentration camp experiences and about the cruelty of the Nazis. At the time, Levin had been fascinated by the power of radio—it could reach so many people so quickly. He had visions of a refugee newspaper sponsoring its own radio show and could see himself as a radio personality, reading the news and sharing stories and commentary with his listeners. Now, talking with Marcus, Levin articulated his ambition for the first time: He would like to run a radio program for Jewish refugees.

"That's a great idea," Marcus said. "In fact, my good friend, Roy Healey, runs the American radio station. Let me talk to him. You should wait a few days and then give him a call." It was as if Marcus had waved a magic wand and granted Levin's wish.

Levin telephoned Healey later that week. Healey already had talked with Marcus and sounded eager to meet with Levin. He invited him to the studio, on Race Course Road just south of the Shanghai Race Course, the next day. Levin was uncharacteristically nervous.

But Healey seemed eager to please him when they met at Radio Station XMHA the next morning and took him on a tour of the station, including two small studios.

"It's probably a lot smaller than what you're used to in Europe," Healey said, "but we have a strong signal that reaches all over China and sometimes abroad."

Levin didn't bother to tell him it was the only studio he had ever seen, other than his brief appearance on the talk show. Healey also showed him XMHA's record library, an extensive collection that was considered to be the largest in Asia. (XMHA was an NBC affiliate and, because RCA owned NBC, it had a nearly complete set of RCA Victor recordings.) Levin was impressed.

As they walked down the halls, Levin told Healey about his German-language newspaper and about the growing community of artists, musicians, and journalists who could be guests on a radio program. Although he hadn't made arrangements with any of them—in fact, he hadn't discussed the program with anyone but Marcus—Levin tried to appear confident, as if everything already was lined up.

"It sounds terrific," Healey said. "We have a free hour in the afternoon where we could fit you in. Can you start in two weeks?"

Levin was startled, but tried not to show it. He hadn't expected anything to develop this quickly. He nodded his head.

"Two weeks. That should be fine."

Healey asked him to come back in a few days with an outline for the program. "We'll discuss the business end of it then, too," Healey said.

Levin felt as if he were floating as he strolled outside. He would be the envy of everyone, the voice of the Jewish refugees. They had begun building a community in this desolate diaspora and now Horst Levin, a twenty-two-year-old who had walked out of Sachsenhausen less than five months ago, had hustled his way to the top.

He first brought the good news to Fischer, his editor, who quickly called together the writers and editors of *Shanghai Woche*. They agreed to help sponsor the radio program and suggested programming ideas to Levin. Fischer wrote a front-page article about the new program for that week's paper.

Within a few days, Levin had lined up Walter Friedmann, the balding, stocky actor and comedian, to perform on the show as well as dozens of other actors and actresses, lawyers and doctors, rabbis and cantors, editors, and political commentators.

Later that week, Levin again met with Healey and told him more about his plans. Healey said the show that would run six days a week, from four to five each afternoon, and for a half hour on Sundays. But he had one big surprise for Levin—the position carried no salary. There would be some revenue from XMHA's major advertisers, but most of the money to run the program would come from paid commercials Levin and other refugees would have to solicit. Despite Marcus' intervention, Levin would have to be an ad salesman once again.

On the afternoon of May 2, 1939, Levin slid the bulky headset over his ears and settled in behind the microphone in one of the XMHA studios. His throat was dry, but Levin felt some comfort as he looked through the window in front of him and saw virtually the entire *Shanghai Woche* staff—Fischer, a photographer, several reporters and editors—crowded into the waiting room to watch him inaugurate the new German-language program.

The engineer sitting behind him put a recording of the opera *Faust* on the turntable and, as Levin had instructed him, introduced the show with the opening bars of the *Soldier Chorus*. It was to become Levin's signature. Then, as the music faded out, the engineer signaled Levin and he began. His first words were rather stiff. It would take him several weeks to learn the conversational style of radio.

Attention, attention! This is an entertainment program in the German language on station XMHA, at 600 kilocycles.

My dear ladies and gentlemen, with these words we will announce ourselves from now on, every weekday at exactly 4 o'clock, to offer to you an hour of diversion of all kinds. In this one hour, you should be entertained in various ways and informed about all things that interest you.

So we shall bring to you daily the latest news about everything from all over the world; additionally, we'll give you the names of the ships that are arriving in the course of the week, with the arrival times, if possible. Likewise, we will report to you the departure times for airmail letters.

Besides these daily recurring announcements, you will hear entertainment in versatile and daily different ways; nevertheless, educational information will not be given short shrift. Thus, you should have the opportunity to receive English instruction from Professor Carstens twice a week on Wednesday and Saturday. We plan to allow science and even housewives a chance to be heard . . .

We would hope that this daily hour might appeal to the general public, and we will strive to heed every wish as we, of course, seek to make use of suggestions from our listeners. Likewise, we hope to be able to give a series of artists the chance during this hour to inform you about their various arts. [2]

Levin then introduced Fischer, who made some introductory remarks. Friedmann and his wife, Hilde, read some passages from Thomas Mann and then Levin read the day's leading news events, which he had translated into German from the English-language papers: President Roosevelt had opened the New York World's Fair with a call for peace; Hitler had criticized the U.S. boycott of German goods in a series of May Day speeches; the Japanese forces in China were pushing west, accompanied by heavy bombing near the Han River.[3] Levin completed the program by playing some of his favorite sonatas from Bach, Beethoven, and Schubert.

The hour had gone by so quickly that Levin had forgotten his initial nervousness. After he signed off, Healey entered the studio and congratulated him.

"I didn't understand much of what you were saying," Healey said, "but it sounded OK. Keep it up. And good luck."

In the following weeks, the afternoon program became a feature of daily life in Hongkew. Some of the refugees had brought their radios from Europe and could listen to the show at home. Others crowded into the European-style cafes and restaurants to hear it. And Ernst Karliner, a German engineer from Halberstadt, exploited the new demand by building and selling hundreds of inexpensive radio sets to the Hongkew refugees from his shop on Chusan Road.

The success of the program attracted some of the more prosperous Hongkew businesses to advertise on the show. Rudolph Mosse, an elderly man who had worked in publishing in Berlin, became Levin's assistant and handled most of the advertising. He also wrote humorous commercials that became a highlight of the show.

There were some complaints, too, but Levin tried to respond to them. After some listeners noted that his newscasts were simply a rehash of what they had read in the local newspapers, XMHA provided Levin access to the Reuters, United Press, and Associated Press wires. Each afternoon, he ripped copy from the wire machines and translated the latest dispatches for the show.

The variety of talented and intelligent guests was the show's greatest asset. Raoul von Toms provided regular commentary on world events; local physicians appeared on the show to discuss health and hygiene; lawyers explained Chinese law and how to establish and run a business. Levin made sure the show was entertaining—he wrote out scripts with his guests in advance and often opened his interviews with a series of jokes and clever German puns. But the most popular guests were the artists who performed on the show every day.

The Shanghai community now included some of the finest actors, comedians, and musicians from Europe. Several had been major figures in the rich cultural worlds of Berlin and Vienna. But like the other refugees, they, too, had to find ways to survive in a difficult, new environment. Those artists who could adapt accomplished far more than making a living for themselves. The comedies, plays, concerts, and art they produced helped the refugees transcend their problems and bring the community together. The artists gave Hongkew life.

The musicians often performed in the camps. Those who could play dance music had little trouble finding work in Shanghai's bars and nightclubs. A refugee chamber orchestra performed under the direction of Dr. Erich Marcuse, and pianists like Baer, Ferdinand Adler, Miriam Magasi, and Robert Kohner drew audiences from the entire foreign community. Other refugees directed music for the local Russian opera.[4]

Ten refugees had joined the Shanghai Municipal Symphony Orchestra. Its conductor, Arrigo Foa, was an Italian Jew who had been with the orchestra since 1921. The first German refugee to join was violinist Otto Joachimsthal (also called Joachim), who arrived in 1934 and later organized the Jewish orchestra. His brother, Walter, was a cellist who came to Shanghai from Malaya in 1940 and eventually joined the orchestra and taught at the National Conservatory of Music in Shanghai. Wolfgang Fraenkel, a composer, came to Shanghai in 1939 after he was released from a concentration camp. He performed in the string section and also taught at the Conservatory, where he introduced his Chinese pupils to Schoenberg and other modern musical theories. The greatest musician among the refugees was Alfred Wittenberg, a well-known Berlin concert violinist who played in the Shanghai orchestra after he emigrated in 1939 and taught at the Conservatory and university.[5]

The refugees performed Yiddish music as well, with stars like Raya Zomina, Hersh Friedmann, and Gretl Kleiner. Lily Flohr sang popular music in a half-dozen languages at the best nightclubs in the city. Herbert Zernik, who started as a bar musician, became the most acerbic and popular comedian in Shanghai. He drank heavily, but always was sharp enough to silence hecklers with quick retorts. In the great tradition of Jewish comedy, Zernik drew his best material from the sorrow around him. His jokes about the filth and insects in the camps, even about the women who made their living as prostitutes, turned tragedy, at least for a few moments, into laughter.[6]

The actors performed their first comedies and operettas in the dining hall of the Ward Road camp. The productions starred Jenny Raussnitz, a Viennese actress who specialized in playing the roles of older women, and Gerhard Gottschalk, a lanky Berlin actor and comedian who could make an audience laugh hysterically with his mocking facial expressions and a wave of his long, bony fingers. (When the artists played the press in soccer, Gottschalk was the goalie, wearing gloves, a tophat, and a Jewish star on his shoulder. He hung drapes on his goal and pulled them closed when the other team tried to score.)[7]

As the community grew, performances were staged in theaters and the newly opened clubs run by refugees. (German actress Eva Schwarcz also produced German-language plays on XCDN.) The actors performed the classic plays and operettas, from *Oedipus* to *Die Fledermaus*. They also performed many original works by talented refugee playwrights, including Karl Bodan, Alfred Dreifuss, Fritz Melchior, and Mark Siegelberg. Some of the plays were pointedly political and brought the refugees into conflict with local authorities.

Siegelberg, a Russian-born Viennese journalist who had been imprisoned in several concentration camps, and Hans Schubert wrote *The Matrimony of Dr. Brach* in Shanghai. It tells the story of a Jewish journalist in Austria whose Aryan wife plans to divorce him until he is sent to a concentration camp. She then fights successfully for his release and emigrates with him to Shanghai. Siegelberg submitted the play, as required, to the Shanghai Municipal Police for their review. The police, concerned about its political content, refused to permit Siegelberg to stage the play at the Kinchow

Road camp. They eventually granted approval to stage it at the British Press Attache's office on the Bund after Siegelberg revised the play and changed the title to *Die Masken Fallen* (*The Masks Fall*). It featured Zernik, Flohr, Gottschalk, Raussnitz, and other stars of the community.[8]

Before the first performance, Michel Speelman, chairman of the Committee for the Assistance of European Jewish Refugees, wrote a letter to the *North China Daily News* discouraging refugees from attending. Siegelberg was forced to show it free of charge because of the controversy. When the German consulate officially protested and hinted at reprisals against Jews remaining in Germany, the play was canceled after two performances.[9]

Many of the artists, like Gottschalk, Boris Sapiro, Walter Friedmann, and Zernik, became regulars on Levin's show. Some musicians, like Rosl Albach-Gerstl, made their debuts on the program. Levin added a regular feature, "From Burned Books," with actors and actresses reading from the works of Thomas and Heinrich Mann, Franz Werfel, Jakob Wassermann, Lion Feuchtwanger, and other Jewish writers whose books had been burned by the Nazis.

Levin also occasionally read letters on the show from listeners who picked up shortwave broadcasts of XMHA in Australia, Europe, Mexico, and the United States. One letter came from the interior of China, from a group of German physicians who had emigrated there in the early 1930s and were working at a small hospital in central China. They wrote how amazed and pleased they were to hear the voices of German Jews on their radios.

On Saturdays, Levin played musical requests he received in letters and telephone calls to the studio. Some refugees even loaned him copies of popular songs to play on the show, including such classics as Sophie Tucker's "My Yiddishe Mama." One Saturday, after he played that song, he immediately received a telephone call from a woman with a thick Russian accent.

"Mr. Levin, we are sitting here crying over that beautiful song you just played," she said. "Could you please play it one more time today?"

Levin politely declined, pointing out that he had many other requests to play that day.

"Never mind that," the woman replied. "If you play it once more today, you can come to my house next Saturday evening for a nice roast duck dinner."

It was an offer Levin couldn't refuse.

As the radio show flourished, Levin became more involved in community activities. When several refugees approached him asking for funds to help refurbish a building in the Pingliang Road camp for a community center, Levin joined the fund-raising effort. He and several other prominent members of the community sponsored a full-dress ball at a local nightclub and raised thousands of dollars.

Levin also was in demand as a critic and essayist. He wrote not only for *Shanghai Woche* but also for Ossie Lewin's newspaper, *The Shanghai Jewish Chronicle.* Lewin attracted some of the best writers in Hongkew, including Siegelberg, Fritz Friedlander, and Ladislaus Frank, and his paper, founded six weeks after *Shanghai Woche,* became a daily. Lewin and other editors appeared weekly on Levin's show with political commentary.[10]

The editors and writers, many of them prominent journalists in Europe, produced a variety of newspapers, magazines, and journals. Like the artists and performers, the refugee press helped Hongkew become a community. A.J. Storfer, a psychologist and student of Freud's from Austria, published an intellectual monthly magazine, the *Gelbe Post,* which eventually became a daily newspaper and competed with Lewin's paper; Fischer's weekly published a midday bulletin with war news, which became an evening paper (*8-Uhr Abendblatt*); Ferdie Eisfelder (who later changed his name to Fred Fields) published *Sport,* a weekly sports paper connected with the *Chronicle.* There were even small, short-lived medical journals, literary magazines, and business papers.[11]

By the fall, Levin had become a major celebrity in the community. He was working long hours to prepare the show and to write his newspaper columns. He also had stepped up his attempts to bring his mother and sister to join him in Shanghai. Shortly after he started the radio show, he received a cable that his father, Fred, had died after another heart attack. His mother, Betty, was still suffering from depression, although her doctor reported that she was showing some improvement. His sister, Ruth, who had worked so hard to rescue him from Sachsenhausen, continued to run the Cafe Hansa in Berlin.

Even after the immigration restrictions were issued in August, it was still possible for refugees to bring family members to China with a permit issued by the foreign concessions. But Levin's efforts to rescue Betty and Ruth ended when he fell ill that fall.

Early in October, Levin was slowed by a severe cold. He got some medicine from a doctor who lived nearby and tried to ignore it. But the cold lasted for more than a week. He coughed constantly and lost his appetite and energy. He also had trouble sleeping. One night, Levin woke up in his bed covered with sweat. His chest felt tight, as if his lungs were collapsing from the pressure. He pulled on his pants and stumbled down the stairs to wake up the doctor down the street. He banged as hard as he could on the door, using all the energy he had left, then collapsed on the front stair.

Levin remained unconscious. The doctor sent him by ambulance to Shanghai General Hospital. The diagnosis was a severe case of pleurisy, an inflammation of the lining that surrounds the lungs. The surgeons at the hospital removed a rib, drained some of the fluid from the pleural cavity, and inserted a tube in his chest to continue the draining. But there was no real treatment for the underlying infection.

Levin spent weeks in the hospital, still in pain and needing morphine injections to sleep at night. His fever remained high. The doctors then tried a second operation to empty the remaining fluid. The fever and the pain finally began to subside.

At XMHA, Walter Friedmann and Gustav Wolff took over the radio program and issued daily bulletins about Levin's health. Ossie Lewin also called the hospital to check on Levin. One of the Chinese telephone operators at the hospital apparently misunderstood Lewin when he called one day. She told him that Levin had died the night before. The next day, the *The Shanghai Jewish Chronicle* published Levin's obituary.

Levin remained hospitalized for several more months but was eager to prove that reports of his death were premature. When he finally was released in April, his surgeon told him that, because of his missing rib, he would have trouble walking for the rest of his life. Levin walked with a cane for weeks but soon was able to stand up straight and walk without assistance. He served as a judge for the Miss Shanghai 1940 pageant and even played for the press team in their soccer match against Gottschalk and the other local artists.

Healey welcomed him back to XMHA, and Levin again took charge of the refugee radio program. He was proud to be the voice of the community again. But when he read the news from Europe as the Nazi armies moved west that spring, he was overcome with sadness. He had lost contact with his mother and sister in Berlin while he was in the hospital, and now he began to lose hope that he would hear from them.

Levin did have a chance to assist some other refugees who were desperately trying to contact their children in Europe. Shortly after he returned to XMHA, a group came to the studio and told Levin that they had sent their children to refugee camps in Holland and Belgium before they left for Shanghai and, until the German invasion that spring, had received letters from them regularly, reporting they were well. Now they had lost contact and were worried about their children's safety. They asked Levin to broadcast an appeal.

Levin was skeptical that he could be of much help, but he knew that XMHA's shortwave broadcast band could reach all over the world. For two weeks, he broadcast a message from the families on each show, urging anyone abroad who heard the broadcast to repeat it on the shortwave band. When a ham radio operator's message reached England, a British newspaper tracked down the children at a refugee camp near London. A few weeks later, the parents in Shanghai got the message that their children had been evacuated to England before the Nazis arrived.

But most of the news remained grim, as the Nazis conquered the Netherlands and Belgium. That spring, about sixty refugees volunteered to join the French forces in Asia.[12] France collapsed that summer, and Britain was suffering relentless bombing from the Luftwaffe. In August, British troops moved out of Shanghai, and the first contingent of British residents sailed to Australia to train for military service.[13]

On October 1, 1940, the eve of Rosh Hashanah, Levin read greetings from the foreign consulates, a tradition he had begun in his first year on the show. The British consulate's message was a fiery attack on the Nazis and a pledge to help restore freedom to the Jews and other oppressed people of the world.[14] But Levin also used the occasion to read his own commentary, a message of hope and survival:

> From all over the world, reports reach us that speak of the misery, death and destruction of Jewry. All of us who have found refuge here in the hospitable harbor of Shanghai, which grants us safety, should never forget that there are thousands and thousands of people who envy us and our first obligation should be to help them.
>
> And how many, if not all of us, have family and friends still out there, either in Germany or emigrated from Germany, but then further pursued and harassed by the cruel, brutal forces which are presuming today to seize the whole world?
>
> And in this hour, at the beginning of the New Year, a hope glimmers, a trust in the future that still lies dark in front of us. We have heard of the seven bitter years and of the seven happy years that the people of Israel had to endure. It was seven years ago that the evil regime came to power that has today set the world in flames, that regime which the freedom-loving democratic powers have met in a decisive, life-or-death struggle.
>
> It has been seven years since a power was legalized in Germany, which had taken for itself as its program the ruthless

destruction and extermination of all Jewry. Much has occurred in these fatal seven years. Still, this thought gives us courage, that the attempt to make Jewry disappear has not succeeded.

On the contrary, although they were able to torture us, rob us and expel us from the country that was our homeland for centuries, new centers of Jewry have arisen. Proudly, we look at the Jewish accomplishments in Palestine. New Jewish life has arisen in South America. And, not least, here in Shanghai, where now a deliberate, hardworking Jewry is rallying around the Jewish community in order to put down deep roots here as well.

In the past seven years, many fragile twigs and remains of the tree of life of Jewry have broken off, but new shoots have sprung up which have provided for continued propperity with fresh strength. And let us hope that we have arrived at the end of these seven bitter years and that seven happy years lie before us. In this sense, I wish all my dear listeners *L'Shanah Tovah*.[15]

7

Kantorowsky

Eva Kantorowsky had never seen anything quite like the Sassoon Building, Sir Victor Sassoon's eleven-story edifice at the corner of Nanking Road and the Bund. The lobby was lighted by giant crystal chandeliers and decorated with pink and gray marble and large oil paintings. The corridors were lined with mirrors, mahogany paneling, and golden brocade couches. Cigar-smoking foreign bankers and businessmen circulated in every hallway.

After she and her father reached Paul Komor's fourth-floor office, Eva looked out at the harbor below, where British and American gunboats were surrounded by sampans, ferry boats, and junks. The outskirts of Hongkew were barely visible on the other side of the river.

The war seemed so distant here. Only three months earlier, Eva had been huddled with her friends in an air raid shelter in Berlin, listening to the hum of airplanes overhead, the pop of antiaircraft guns, and the faraway thud of British bombs. But in the Komor Committee office, the only sounds were the clicking of typewriter keys and polite conversation.

Eva and her father, Rabbi Georg Kantorowsky, were here to see Komor, the head of Sassoon's committee to assist the Jewish refugees. With his tall, thin frame and fragile features, Komor looked like someone who should be receiving aid, rather than giving it. He was a kind, decent man and was doing his best to make Eva and her father feel at ease.

Eva had been looking for work since she had arrived with her parents in November 1940, yet there were few positions suitable for a nineteen-year-old rabbi's daughter. Her father's status gave her access to prominent citizens like Komor, but little else. Early in December, Horace Kadoorie, another one of the pillars of the Sephardic community, had given her a typing test in his office. When she failed it, he loaned her a typewriter to practice with. Her years of German education had taught her Latin, French, and English, literature and philosophy, science and mathematics, but little about typing. Now, late in January 1941, Komor had a job he thought would be suitable for her.

Komor was planning to open a new school for refugees on Seward Road to teach Basic English. It was a method developed in the late 1920s by Charles Kay Ogden, an American linguist who believed that English could be taught with a vocabulary of 850 words and a few simplified rules. Ogden also believed Basic English held promise as a universal language that would have more appeal than Esperanto. By the late 1930s, there were dozens of books published in Basic, from science textbooks to the New Testament, and it was being taught in Japan, China, Czechoslovakia, Denmark, and Greece.[1]

Eva surprised Komor by telling him she already knew something about Basic. Her brother, Hans, had studied it in Berlin and taught her some of the rules. Hans and his leftist friends were drawn to Basic because of its potential as a universal language; they saw it as a way to help bring the world together. Eva was more skeptical. She thought of her brother as a dreamer, full of good intentions yet hopelessly naive. But she was discreet enough not to share that thought with Komor.

Komor's plan was to help the Jewish refugees adapt as

quickly as possible to Shanghai, where English was the lingua franca. Professor Carstens, who often appeared on Horst Levin's radio show, had left the committee and opened his own private school to teach English. So Komor finally had succumbed to the persistent pleadings of a Viennese refugee named Ferdinand Kars and agreed to open a school for Basic English.

Komor told Eva he was impressed with her English and thrilled that she already knew something about Basic. He offered her a job teaching in the new school, starting in February. Eva quickly accepted.

Like all other employees of the Komor Committee, Eva would receive 125 Shanghai dollars a month (about 20 U.S. dollars) for her work. With the worsening inflation in Shanghai, it wasn't much, but Eva was excited to finally have a chance to contribute to her family's income and have some spending money for herself. The idea of teaching for the first time frightened her a little, but she was confident she could handle it.

A few days later, before classes began, she met with Kars, who explained Basic English to her. He was too intense for her to interrupt, and Eva was too polite to tell him she knew almost everything he was telling her. Kars also gave her a textbook, Ogden's *The ABC of Basic English*. He smoked constantly as they talked, and Eva couldn't help thinking how disheveled and odd he was, with his rapid speech and wide-eyed stare. But what surprised her most was his grammar and vocabulary. Kars, who was to be in charge of the school and teach classes as well, didn't seem to have much command of the English language.

School began on the morning of February 3. Like most teachers on the first day of school, Eva was nervous before she walked into the classroom. And, since she had been taught to respect her elders, it worried her that all of her students would be older than she.

The students in the Seward Road school were mostly Germans and Austrians. There were two groups of classes, a morning class for some of the newer refugees and an advanced evening class once a week for Komor Committee staff members. The morning class met for nearly two hours every day but Saturday.

The classroom was modern and bright, particularly when the morning sun occasionally shone through the big windows that covered most of one wall. Sassoon, the benefactor of the Komor Committee, had furnished it well, too, with new rattan desks and chairs for each student and a huge chalkboard that covered the front wall, all the way to the ceiling. Eighteen words were neatly printed in the corner of the blackboard. They were the verbs at beginning of a Basic English list known as "operations": come, get, give, go, keep, let, make, put, seem, take, be, do, have, say, see, send, may, and will.

Eva's biggest problem with teaching Basic English was the difficulty of using only the selected 850 words when she lectured to her students. She also dictated passages for them to write and had them translate simple German stories into Basic English. Her students studied hard, and she was surprised to discover that, in just a few weeks, they could communicate in English. But there was a problem with this teaching method. Although the students could make themselves understood, they had a lot of trouble understanding other English speakers who didn't limit themselves to Ogden's vocabulary list.

There was one other problem with the job, but it had nothing to do with Basic. At least once a week, an administrator from the Komor Committee came to the classroom to collect the token tuition payments from the refugees and go over the books with Eva in the office next door. When they were alone, he seemed more interested in Eva than the books and constantly tried to put his arm around her shoulder as they worked. The more she pushed him away, the more he seemed to pursue her.

Eva was an attractive young woman with bright, dark brown eyes, an easy smile, and long, wavy black hair. She also was a constant source of concern for her parents. When she wasn't working at the school, she was out dancing or going to movies and concerts. Eva liked her life in Shanghai, but sometimes she wished she were back in Berlin. She worried about her brother Hans, who remained in Germany, and longed to see Samy, the boyfriend she had left behind.

It had taken many years for her mother to convince her father to leave; now it was Eva who regretted leaving.

———————

Her father, Georg, was from Loslau, in Upper Silesia east of Breslau. His hometown had become part of Poland after the Treaty of Versailles, but Georg seemed more like a proud German patriot than most native Germans. He frequently quoted Goethe and Schiller and had a broad knowledge of both German and Jewish culture. Like many German Jews of his generation, he was a member of the Centralverein Deutscher Staatsbürger Jüdischen Glaubens (German Citizens of Jewish Faith). He was above all a German; his faith simply happened to be Jewish. Georg never quite believed the Germans could accept Hitler as their leader. When they did, he was certain the Nazis would not survive for long.

Georg, who was born in 1883, trained to be a rabbi at the theological seminary in Breslau. It was there that he met his future wife, Frieda Schönfeld. She was born in Breslau and was studying in the seminary there to become a teacher. But she was forced to leave school to take care of her mother, who had suffered a stroke, and never completed her training.

Georg and Frieda were engaged for eight years, finally marrying when Georg completed his studies and was ready to head his own congregation. His first position was in Bernburg, a small town on the Saale River about eighty miles southwest of Berlin. Their first child, Hans Erich, was born in Bernburg in 1913. During the war, Georg also worked in the mobile army hospitals and was awarded a medal for his service.

Frieda, accustomed to the more cosmopolitan life of Breslau, soon felt confined by the small-town clannishness of Bernburg and was eager to move. Four years after Hans was born, Georg was hired to head a Liberal Orthodox congregation, the Jüdische Brüdergemeinde in Neukölln, a working-class district in southeast Berlin where leftist ideas thrived.

Like all clergymen in Germany, Georg's salary was paid by the state from the religious tax collected from everyone except those who declared themselves atheists. In addition to running the synagogue, Georg taught classes at several public Gymnasiums and lyceums during the day and religious classes for Jewish children in the afternoons. The Kantorowskys lived on Kaiser Friedrich Strasse, across the street from one of the Gymnasiums where Georg taught.

The synagogue was on Isar Strasse. On Friday nights and Saturdays, Georg conducted services there. Much of the service was in German, and he organized an amateur choir, but men and women sat separately. Like many liberal rabbis, Rabbi Kantorowsky wanted to steer his congregants away from rote repetition of prayers, encouraging them to understand the ideas behind Judaism, not simply the ritual.

Eva was born on August 6, 1921. When she was nine, the Kantorowskys moved to a new building on Geyger Strasse and lived in a nice third-floor apartment above a drugstore. They were across the street from the parks and grand apartment buildings that lined Sonnen Allee and a few blocks from the synagogue.

But Eva didn't spend much time at the synagogue. Many of her friends were non-Jewish and her governess, Lotte, was the daughter of a church sexton. When Lotte went to help her parents at the church, Eva and Lotte's little brother played hide and seek among the pews.

Eva's mother, Frieda, rarely seemed to be home. She worked as a volunteer, doing social welfare work in the poorest sections of Berlin. Frieda also was active in women's organizations and supported abortion rights at a time when doctors faced severe penalties for performing abortions. But she shared little of this with Eva. Despite her mother's feminism, Eva remained a sheltered child. It was her older brother, Hans, and not her mother, who taught her about the facts of life.

Hans was an idealist and was deeply influenced by his communist teachers at the Karl Marx School. Like his father, Hans didn't simply parrot his beliefs, he lived them. Hans sometimes came home on winter evenings without his coat. When his parents asked about it, he said he had given it away to someone who needed it more than he did. Georg often cursed Herr Studienrat, the history teacher who had first interested Hans in communism. Hans planned to pursue his interest in Marxist economics in college. He graduated from Gymnasium in 1931 and, as a concession to his parents, he studied law as well economics at Berlin University. But Berlin had become a dangerous place for radical leftists and, in May 1933, Hans moved to Prague to study at the German university there.

Eva had enrolled in the Karl Marx School in 1930. Its leftist leanings were tempered as the Nazis came to power, and some of the more radical teachers left or were imprisoned. By 1934, the uniformed Hitler Youth had the run of the school. Eva often faced jeers from the young Nazis ("We'll put you Jews on a one-way street to Jerusalem"), but she didn't fear them. Her favorite teacher, Herr Hoffmann, always made sure to protect Eva.

The Kantorowskys first felt the direct effect of the Nazi regime in the fall of 1935. That September, the Nazis had proclaimed the Nuremberg Laws, the decrees that deprived Jews of many of their basic rights. The Kantorowskys were forced to dismiss their maid (Lotte had died of tuberculosis several years earlier) because Jews were now barred from employing Aryan women under age forty-five as servants. (That provision, first proposed in *Der Stürmer*, was designed to discourage mixing of the races, because German boys often had their first sexual experiences with the family maid.[2]) But the real impact on their lives came after the Karl Marx School fired Director Karsen, the liberal who had headed it for years.

Rabbi Kantorowsky had been teaching at Karl Marx and often walked with Eva to school. One day that fall, as they walked into the school courtyard, Georg and Eva were stunned by what they saw on the school bulletin board. There, where every entering student and teacher could see it, was a horrifying *Der Stürmer* cartoon, depicting two fiendish, long-nosed Jews cutting open the necks of blond children and draining their blood. It was so vile, in fact, that the Nazis had banned that issue of the newspaper. Georg turned Eva away and took her home. The next week, he enrolled her in Lessler, an exclusive private school in Grunewald, far from Neukölln on the western outskirts of the city.

Eva found Lessler unsettling, with hundreds of new Jewish students enrolled and new Jewish teachers from throughout Germany who had lost their jobs in the public schools. The school also didn't have a license to give the *abiturium* exam that qualified graduates for college. So Georg, who considered the *abiturium* mandatory, eventually transferred Eva to two other schools. At one of the schools, Eva received her first *blauer Brief*, a blue letter indicating poor marks in school. In the fall of 1937, her father enrolled her in the respected Goldschmidt School in Halensee, even farther from home, but licensed to administer the coveted *abiturium*.

At first, Eva was unhappy at her new schools, because she had to ride the subway and street car for more than an hour each way. She lost touch with most of her non-Jewish friends in Neukölln; the few new friends she was able to make as she switched schools all lived on the other side of the city. She rarely got to see them after school and at dance lessons on weekends. Now that she was becoming interested in boys, dating was difficult. One night, when she went to a dance lesson in the evening and to a social at a friend's home after that, she returned to Neukölln after midnight. One of her dancing partners escorted her all the way home. But when they arrived at the Karl Marx Strasse subway stop, Eva's father was there waiting for her. He yelled at her about being out past her curfew, then slapped her in the face. "And where do you live?" Georg bellowed at the frightened young man. He lived in Charlottenburg and somehow would have to travel all the way back to the other end of Berlin. Eva and her father left the boy at the station. She didn't see much of him after that.

As Eva wrestled with her teenage crises, Frieda struggled to convince her husband that it was time to leave. Some of Berlin's rabbis, using their connections abroad, already had emigrated, and Frieda urged Georg to go to New York and look for a position with the help of her cousin, Eric Cohen. Cohen, president of Goodman's Matzoh and a prominent member of the Jewish community, had offered his help. But Georg was hesitant, afraid of the unknown and unsure that he could adapt to a new country and new language and again become a respected rabbi.

But by early 1938, as a series of tough new laws took effect, their lives became more difficult. The Jewish community had to pay exorbitant new taxes, reducing the salary it could pay to rabbis and teachers. That spring, the Kantorowskys had to register their assets with the government.

On November 10, Eva commuted across town to the Goldschmidt school as usual, early in the morning. After the elevated train passed the Zoological Garden stop, she could see smoke rising from Fasanenstrasse below, the site of a large synagogue. Eva knew something had happened, but still was innocent of the terror of *Kristallnacht*. When she reached her school, the teachers were outside at the entrance, hustling the students out the back door and telling them to go home. An hour later, when she returned home, her mother told her that her father would be away for a few days. Eva learned later that his synagogue had been vandalized early that morning, but her father had left home the night before.

Like hundreds of Berlin Jews who knew a pogrom and mass arrests were being planned, Rabbi Kantorowsky and a neighbor had been riding the subway for hours, switching cars whenever they saw Gestapo approaching or when other passengers looked at them suspiciously. They rode all night. On the afternoon of November 10, Georg went to his widowed sister's apartment in Schöneberg, expecting that the Nazis would not look for him there. But after a day at his sister's, he was uncomfortable, unable to fall asleep in a strange place for his daily afternoon nap. He returned home and, within an hour, the Gestapo arrived to arrest him.

Georg was gone for six weeks. Friends and neighbors occasionally visited with news that he had been taken to Sachsenhausen and was all right. With her father imprisoned, Eva couldn't concentrate in school and failed her Cambridge examinations that winter. Frieda worked desperately to find a way to get Georg out of the country. With the help of the Jewish community organization, she booked three tickets to Shanghai.

Georg returned home on December 21, 1938, trudging laboriously up the stairs. When he entered the apartment, Eva was horrified. He looked like a bum from the street, with his rumpled clothes reeking of disinfectant. His head was shaven and he was terribly thin. But he said nothing about what had happened to him. Eva wrote in her diary: "Father returns. He looks dreadful and totally changed. The fifth night of Hanukkah."

He rested in bed for a few days before Frieda told him about the tickets to Shanghai. But Georg, despite the obvious suffering he had endured, was not ready to leave and remained afraid of starting a new life. "What should I do in Shanghai?" he asked Frieda. The next day, over his wife's objections, he returned the tickets to the community office.

In the months that followed, however, Georg finally agreed to make an effort to emigrate. The Kantorowskys had been forced to give up their apartment in Neukölln early in 1939 and register all their assets. They stored their household goods and moved into small, furnished rooms, first in Schöneberg and then Charlottenburg. Georg's salary had been reduced, but the Nazis provided them with coupons with which they could purchase food each afternoon from four to five. Because of shortages during wartime, there was little food left by that time of day, usually only vegetables like beets or cabbage. They were not allowed to purchase any shoes or clothing.

That spring, they were required to turn in all their silver and gold. Eva gave two of her favorite rings to a non-Jewish girlfriend. In their back yard in Schöneberg, her father buried a gold pocket watch his father had given him. He turned in everything else, but applied to the Gestapo to reclaim items he needed for rabbinical functions: a *kiddush* cup his congregation had given him in 1937 on his twenty-fifth anniversary as a rabbi, two silver candlesticks that were family heirlooms, and a spice box. Georg was encouraged when, a short time later, he was allowed to retrieve those items, although they were badly dented and scratched.

That spring, with the help of Frieda's cousin Eric, Georg was offered a job with a congregation in New York. But when the contract finally arrived, the U.S. consulate in Berlin— apparently convinced the job didn't exist but was simply a ruse to avoid the U.S. immigration quota and get the Kantorowskys out of Germany—refused to recognize it and issue a visa. Meanwhile, Eva passed the *abiturium* at the end of the school year and was assigned to do household work in the Goldschmidt boarding school annex. She also was put to work writing letters in English to secure affidavits of support from her father's relatives in the Midwest.

While Georg and Frieda worked on other plans for emigration, Georg's older brother, Hugo, prepared to leave for Shanghai. Hugo's small business in Görlitz had been liquidated a year earlier and he had moved to Berlin with his wife to join their daughter and son-in-law there. With their assets gone and no source of livelihood, they had no reason to stay in Germany. Hugo and his family booked passage to Shanghai on the *Conte Biancamano*, which left from Genoa on May 31, the same voyage that took the Heimanns there. The Kantorowskys saw their relatives off at the train station, saddened that they were headed for such an awful place.

After Hugo left, and following Germany's takeover of Czechoslovakia, the Kantorowskys made arrangements to rescue Hans from Prague. He had remained active in leftist groups and was in danger there. Frieda had another cousin who lived in France, not far from the Czech border, who agreed to help Hans get out. His luggage was shipped, but Hans didn't make it. Instead, he surprised his family by showing up in Schöneberg in July. Hans reported his return, as required, to the Gestapo. After a few weeks, they sent him to Bielefeld, an agricultural training commune run by the Jewish community that would prepare Jews for emigration to South America.

In the fall of 1939, the Kantorowskys began to receive letters from Uncle Hugo in Shanghai. He wrote that he was doing well—he was a partner with another refugee in a coal company—and wanted them to join him. There were complications, however. The Shanghai authorities had agreed to stop immigration beginning in August, but now planned to allow limited immigration beginning in October. Hugo, an affable man who could charm almost anyone, wrote that he was hard at work trying to acquire immigration permits for the Kantorowskys.

Between August 22, when immigration was to end, and October 1939, more than 1,100 refugees arrived in Shanghai. Most already had been on their way—519 arrived on the *Guilio Cesare* on August 28 and 321 on the *Conte Biancamano* on September 18[3]—and the Shanghai authorities, after considerable debate, allowed them to land. But the influx slowed to a trickle by late September. After repeated appeals from the refugee community and from Jewish organizations outside Shanghai, local officials in October agreed to issue new regulations that would drastically limit, but not outlaw, immigration into the city. The century-old status of Shanghai as an open port had come to an end, but this small opening would allow another 2,500 Jewish refugees to land in the following two years.

The new system was designed to exclude any refugees who would need financial assistance. There were two ways for refugees to enter Shanghai. The first was to deposit four-hundred dollars (or one-hundred for a child) in one of several designated Shanghai banks. The shipping lines were required to receive a notice from the local Committee for the Assistance of European Jewish Refugees verifying that the funds were on deposit before issuing a ticket. The second way to enter was with a permit issued by the Shanghai Municipal Council. Such permits were to be issued to immediate family members (parents, spouses, or children) of refugees already in Shanghai who could establish "certified financial competency"; to anyone who could produce an employment contract with a Shanghai firm; or anyone who could show they intended to marry a Shanghai resident.[4]

There were few objections to the new rules among the refugees. Those with relatives remaining in Europe would still have a chance to sponsor their emigration to Shanghai. Beyond that, there was no support in the refugee community for any further influx, which would have forced even more refugees into poverty. Even the most prescient in the community had not imagined that turning away immigrants was tantamount to sentencing them to death.

Applications for permits were to be made to the refugee

committee and then submitted the Shanghai Municipal Police for investigation before the council would issue a permit. The permits were valid for four months. New residents would be permitted to live only in the International Settlement; Hongkew remained closed to newcomers.

The new system led to widespread abuses. Relief organizations in Europe, including the Hebrew Immigration Aid Society and Jewish Colonization Society (HICEM) office in Brussels, posted four-hundred dollars for some refugees in a Shanghai bank, then asked those refugees to return three-hundred dollars of it when they arrived in Shanghai so it could be used to allow another refugee to emigrate. The local refugee committee considered this a circumvention of the new rules and declined to intervene when some of the arriving refugees refused to return the money.[5] A few employers accepted bribes of up to three-hundred dollars to issue fake employment contracts.[6] A refugee lawyer, who claimed to have influence, charged refugees thirty dollars to help them acquire a permit, but his unsavory reputation probably reduced their chances for success.[7] Some employers issued employment contracts to help relatives escape, but had no plans to provide them with jobs when they arrived. The Municipal Police rejected more than 1,000 applications based on questionable employment contracts. The police expressed sympathy for those trying to rescue their relatives from Nazi-occupied territories but reported: "The issue of a permit has, it is realized, the effect of releasing men and women from concentration camps, but the point at issue [violating the requirements] must not be overlooked even on humanitarian grounds."[8]

In the first six months of the new system, only 460 refugees arrived, 193 of them with permits and the rest by posting funds. The council had issued permits for more than 1,200 people, but only a small percentage of them were able to book passage and reach Shanghai within the four-month time limit.[9] Despite Japanese objections, many of those who arrived settled in Hongkew, the only place most could afford to live. The Japanese controlled most of Shanghai but had not yet taken over the International Settlement.

It was an odd truce. The Japanese government had

frequently promised it would not interfere with foreign rights in China, but local military officials often made seemingly contradictory statements, warning they would enter the settlement to put a stop to anti-Japanese activities.[10] Japanese forces had seized some territories once claimed by the Municipal Council and also controlled the Chinese organizations that eventually took over the utilities, post office, and major banks in the settlement. Anti-Japanese journalists frequently faced assassination attempts.[11]

Until April 1940, the Japanese continued to try to limit settlement in Hongkew, which was fully under their control, by issuing only a handful of permits. But the rules changed that spring when the Japanese campaigned for control of the Shanghai Municipal Council.

The council had nine seats. The British held five of them and the Americans and Japanese two each. Five Chinese sat on the council in an advisory role. Although the Japanese had virtually complete military control over the city and had thoroughly intimidated the settlement authorities, they now hoped to win political control of the settlement as well. The Japanese put up five candidates and developed a scheme to win the election. They would seek the votes of the Jewish refugees and issue immigration permits to those who supported them.

The odd election rules in the settlement seemed to give the Japanese an advantage. Any property owner—from a refugee who bought a half-demolished home in Hongkew for $100 to the owner of the $30 million telephone company—had one vote.[12] More than five hundred refugees were eligible to vote.[13] The Japanese sidestepped the established Jewish relief committees and established an Electioneering Association.[14] It was headed by a refugee named Robert Peritz, a tall, aristocratic-looking man with a mysterious past.

Peritz had been born in Berlin in 1895 and had emigrated to Italy in 1932. He ran a lodging house in Milan for six years but left for Hong Kong when Mussolini announced a series of anti-Jewish laws in the summer of 1938. He was detained by the Hong Kong harbor police for carrying a forged German passport, and then he headed for Shanghai, arriving in

January 1939 on the *Empress of Russia*. He opened a lodging house on Yulin Road and the Palm Garden Restaurant on Thorburn Road. But both businesses failed. By the end of 1939, Peritz was working as a translator for Japanese businessmen and had developed close links with high-ranking Japanese officials. The Japanese selected him to help run their campaign for the Municipal Council.[15]

Peritz and a Japanese advisor to the foreign ministry, Mitsugu Shibata, set up an office on Muirhead Road and hired a number of Jewish refugees, including Peritz's cousin, Gustav Heimann, to work for them soliciting votes and issuing permits. Some Japanese officials accepted bribes to secure permits[16] and Peritz was widely suspected of using his position for personal profit.

But the Jewish relief committees refused a Japanese request to endorse their candidates for the Municipal Council. Instead, recognizing the links between the election and the issuance of new permits, committee leaders expressed fears about a new influx of impoverished refugees. The committees threatened not to provide assistance to immigrants with permits they had not approved.[17] Relief officials also worried that the election campaign might foment a wave of anti-Semitism in Shanghai. One pre-election advertisement on a British radio station asked: "Do you wish this International Settlement to be ruled by the Japanese and German Jews or by the British and Americans?"[18]

Shortly after the April 10–11 election, the Japanese officials kept their promise and issued more than 1,000 permits to refugees who had worked for and endorsed their candidates.(The Heimanns, who owned three buildings at the time, collected twenty-seven permits and used seventeen of them to bring many of their relatives from Germany to Shanghai.) Ironically, the Japanese campaign failed to win them any new seats on the council. Two of their candidates placed eighth and ninth in the voting, retaining the two Japanese seats on the nine-member council.[19] (A year later, after a violent campaign during which a member of the Japanese Ratepayers' Association shot a member of the Municipal Council, the Japanese finally won a third council seat.[20])

The Japanese permits set off a new wave of emigration. Getting out of Europe, however, was becoming increasingly difficult. When the Nazis conquered France and Italy entered the war in June 1940, all the sea routes from Europe were closed off. There was only one remaining escape to China: across the Soviet Union on the Trans-Siberian railway.

The Japanese permits from Hugo came in the mail late that summer. Hugo never explained how he got them. He simply wrote that they should come to Shanghai as quickly as possible. But Hugo had made a tragic mistake—he had sent only three permits. He had assumed that Hans would be going to Chile after his agricultural training and would not need to come to Shanghai. Hugo didn't know, however, that Hans's visa for Chile was invalid. Without a Shanghai permit, Hans would be forced to remain behind in Europe.

But even without Hans, Georg was now ready to leave for Shanghai. The British had begun bombing Berlin at the end of August, and the long nights in the air raid shelters were hard to bear. Eva spent the nights in the tunnels with her new Jewish friends, listening to the loyal Germans at the other end of the shelter loudly singing patriotic songs to drown out the noise of the bombers overhead. And she had a new boyfriend now, a Russian Jewish boy named Samy Schönhaus who had met her brother at the Bielefeld labor camp and shared Hans's leftist politics. Samy had returned from the farm and now lived with his parents near Neukölln. Although his family seemed poor and Eva felt they came from different social classes, she found Samy handsome and romantic. He visited often as her parents prepared to leave for Shanghai.

Georg and Frieda were eager to get out. But there was one more requirement before they could leave the country. They would need Russian and Manchurian transit visas before they could buy tickets for the railroad trip across the Soviet Union. Frieda's American cousin, Eric, agreed to post the money they would need for the Manchurian visas. Georg got a new passport—his original one had been taken away several years earlier—and he went to the Soviet consulate to get his visa.

But the consulate refused to issue it. Although the new passport listed Georg as a teacher, the Soviets considered him to be a clergyman and would not give visas to religious officials. Georg left the consulate dejected, convinced that none of his family would get out of Germany. But on the subway ride home, he ran into an old friend from his hometown in Upper Silesia. After Georg told his friend what had happened to him, his friend assured him that he could help because of connections he had at the Russian consulate. They returned there immediately and, in no time, Georg got his transit visa.

When her father came back and told her they would be leaving in nine days, Eva thought about how much she would miss Samy. "I am beyond myself," she wrote in her diary that night. On October 24, 1940, the Kantorowskys left home for the last time to take the night train from Charlottenburg station. It was scheduled to depart shortly after ten, about the time when the British bombers had been flying over every night. Eva was frightened that the planes would attack while they were waiting. But Samy had come to join them, and she forgot her fears when he handed her a gold bracelet. As they boarded the train, Eva had begun to cry. Samy ran to catch the local elevated train that ran parallel to theirs and at each stop in Berlin on the trip east he was waiting there, waving goodbye. Her tears fell onto her hands as she clutched the bracelet to her breast.

After they passed through German customs and Russian passport control, it took two days and several train transfers to reach Moscow. There they had a tour of the city from an Intourist guide and stayed in the Hotel Savoy. The stores in Moscow were crowded, but seemed to have even fewer goods than the stores in Berlin.

They boarded the Trans-Siberian railway the next day. The Kantorowskys traveled second class, four in a compartment, so they all could be together. A Russian officer was the fourth passenger, and Eva could speak Russian well enough to carry on conversations. He sometimes took Eva with him to join a group of officers in the dining car for meals. Many of the passengers contracted dysentery on the trip. Eva caught the disease, too; she followed the soldier's advice and drank vodka to settle her stomach.

It took a week to reach Otpor, on the Manchurian border, where they parted with the soldier (Eva discovered too late that he had stolen her watch) and passed through customs again. Then they boarded a slow, ancient train to Manchouli where they stayed in the Hotel Astoria, which doubled as a bordello. There were bugs everywhere; the Kantorowskys slept in their clothes.

The next day they took a Japanese train to Harbin, where members of the Jewish committee greeted them and put them up with the Stern family. They stayed for four days, and a former student of Rabbi Kantorowsky's took Eva out for dinner on two of the evenings there. While they were in Harbin, Frieda went to the bank to withdraw the money her cousin had deposited to pay for the Manchurian transit visa and Georg visited the U.S. consulate, ever hopeful he would be able to emigrate to the United States.

The train for Dairen left on November 9, and they stayed in the Oriental Hotel there for a night before boarding a freighter, the *Tsingtao Maru*, for China. There were two other couples on the trip. The ship left shortly after midnight and took two days to reach Shanghai, with a brief stopover to load and unload cargo in Tsingtao. The passengers were not allowed to disembark at Tsingtao, which remained under German control, but from the freighter Eva could see the red-tile roofs of the German villas that made the port look strangely like a Bavarian town. Eva spent her days lounging on a deck chair in the sun and enjoying the lavish eight-course lunches. She discovered a love for curry.

Eva and her parents stood on the deck as they approached Shanghai on November 12. Hugo was waiting for them at the wharf, as jovial and talkative as ever. But Frieda was still deeply angry at his failure to send a permit for Hans. Hugo took them to a lane house he had rented for them on Broadway in Hongkew that had no plumbing and was so close to the harbor that they could hear the fog horns all night. At first, Eva thought she was hearing the air raid sirens in Berlin again.

In a few days, they had found a better apartment in a newer building at 305 Kungping Road. It had a bathroom and running water. After they settled in, Eva began to look for work. She also visited with some of Samy's relatives who had come to Shanghai and met some people she had known in Berlin.

After months of living in fear and near-poverty in Berlin, Shanghai was beginning to seem exciting. There were new movies almost every week, like *Anna Bella Makes a Tour* and the kitschy *Isle of Destiny*; Mozart evenings at the Alcock Road camp; and German dramas, like *XYZ*, almost as good as those performed by the Jewish Kultur Bund in Berlin. Many nights, Eva would go dancing at the Tabarin or to one of the many Hongkew coffee houses. She dated Horst Levin a few times and a well-to-do doctor her parents liked. Her mother thought Eva was heartless and uncaring for going out all the time.

On some evenings, Eva visited with her Uncle Hugo or her parents' friends. Hugo had founded an organization for refugees from Upper Silesia, and Eva and her parents joined him every week for meetings at a coffee house. Eva thought the meetings were long and boring, but she had another motive for going. Heinz Angress, a handsome young man from Breslau, also was there with his parents. He was just as bored as Eva. They sat in the back of the room and talked quietly. Like everyone else, Eva called him Bob, the name he first called himself when he was little and couldn't properly pronounce *Bubi* (German for little boy). After a few meetings, Bob asked Eva to go out with him and they often stayed out late at night in a coffee house, talking and surreptitiously holding hands. But there wasn't much privacy in Hongkew. Some nights, if the streets were quiet, Eva and Bob would steal a kiss on a dark streetcorner as they walked home.

8

The Administrator

From the beginning of the relief effort late in 1938, it had been obvious that there was a great deal wrong with the administration of the aid program in Shanghai. The American Jewish Joint Distribution Committee, which was providing nearly all of the funds by 1941, had been receiving letters from refugees and rival relief organizations for nearly two years that detailed charges of inefficiency, corruption, and countless injustices. The JDC had met with Shanghai officials in New York and sent staff members to Shanghai, yet the problems—and the complaints—did not subside.

But the JDC, founded in 1914 by mostly liberal, assimilated, German-American Jews,[1] had a strict policy of not intervening in local relief programs. Its goal was to encourage local Jewish communities to operate on their own and draw as much financial and administrative support as possible from their own brethren. Shanghai, with its established, fabulously wealthy Sephardic community, had seemed like an ideal location for this hands-off philosophy. Yet it became clear to the JDC that local leadership was failing and that the JDC would have to take a more active role.

The opening came early in 1941. With the virtual cutoff of further Jewish immigration from Europe, U.S. State Department officials now had room in their small quota for some of the refugees stranded in Shanghai. But the consulate there had neither the staff nor the expertise to handle the emigration bottleneck. So the State Department officials asked the JDC for help.

That spring, the JDC sent Laura M. Margolis, its only woman overseas staff member, to Shanghai. Margolis was a social worker who had spent nearly two years in Cuba helping Jewish refugees from Europe get to the United States. She was born in Constantinople and spoke German, Spanish, and several Middle Eastern languages. Her instructions were to help the U.S. consulate in Shanghai communicate with potential emigrants and speed up the process of getting eligible refugees out of China. The JDC also had another, less pressing, assignment for Margolis in Shanghai. She was encouraged, if she had the time, to look into the continuing problems of the relief effort.[2]

Margolis arrived in May and was accommodated in an elegant suite at the Cathay Hotel with a marble bath and brass fixtures. She was quickly introduced to the colonial society. Her initial meetings with U.S. consular officials and Sephardi community leaders took place at parties and balls in Shanghai's finest mansions, including the opulent ballroom of the Kadoorie's Marble Hall. Margolis was unprepared for this lifestyle—she had flown on the Pan American Clipper with only a few suitcases of work clothes—and she had to buy evening dresses for the parties and dinners held nearly every night of the week.[3] "I went out to do a job and found myself dancing," Margolis said later.[4]

She was even more unprepared for the other side of life in Shanghai. When she first toured the refugee camps, Margolis was dismayed by the crowded, filthy housing conditions. One of the dormitories, she reported, had two old toilets for more than 400 people. The refugees were receiving only one small meal per day, usually two ladles of thin vegetable stew with a little meat and some bread. Most of the refugees on relief were over forty, Margolis reported, many of them former lawyers and engineers, who were suffering from malnutrition and broken spirits.[5] As for the Chinese, she said, many foreigners believed "they were just something you stepped on."[6]

The JDC had become nearly the sole source of support for the Jewish refugees. In a little more than two years, it had contributed half a million dollars for food, medical care, and housing.[7] Nearly 2,000 refugees were living in the Alcock, Ward, Wayside, Chaoufoong, and Pingliang camps; another 6,300 who lived outside the camps received free meals daily, most of them at the Ward Road camp. More than 500 refugees had jobs with the relief organizations.[8]

The situation was far worse than any Margolis had seen in her years as a Jewish social worker in Cleveland and Buffalo during the Depression. And it was quite different from what she had faced in Cuba in 1939–1940. (Margolis was in Havana when the Cubans stopped further immigration and refused to allow a boatload of refugees on the *St. Louis* to land there.) But her first priority was emigration. She discovered that the U.S. officials were eager to cooperate if she could talk with the refugees and identify the priority cases.[9] Margolis began the slow process of interviewing and checking files for hundreds of potential emigrants.

The task of feeding and housing the refugees remained in the hands of the Committee for the Assistance of European Jewish Refugees in Shanghai (CFA), chaired by Michel Speelman. It was controlled by local Sephardic Jews, some of whom contributed funds to the committee. Paul Komor, after a series of disputes with the committee, had resigned (his International Committee had merged with the CFA) to run his own operation with Victor Sassoon's funds. Komor was among those accusing the CFA of ignoring widespread graft; Sassoon hired an accountant to document profiteering by medical and food suppliers.[10]

Despite her efforts to focus on emigration, Margolis also began to hear complaints about the relief committees, mostly from refugees who claimed they had been treated unfairly by the CFA. The aggrieved refugees lined up daily at her hotel room, where she had set up her office.[11] Yet as Margolis tried to concentrate on getting the refugees out of Shanghai, she found that CFA officials had stood in the way of solving the emigration problem as well. She documented several cases in which the local officials had arbitrarily blocked refugees from receiving visas.

One involved a German couple, Martin and Charlotte Wolfskehl, who had been cleared for emigration. The Wolfskehl's relatives in the United States had agreed to sponsor them and were sending money for a visa and transportation, but the U.S. consulate required them to post an eighteen-dollar visa fee within two days. The Wolfskehls asked Ellis Hayim, a wealthy Sephardi who was Shanghai's top stockbroker and a CFA board member, to loan them the eighteen dollars from HICEM funds he controlled. But Hayim refused, Margolis reported, even after the Wolfskehls offered to give him their bed linens as security. They then went to see Komor, who readily gave them the money. By the time they returned to the consulate, however, Hayim had called to question their credibility. The consulate reversed its decision and refused to grant them a visa. Mrs. Wolfskehl suffered a nervous breakdown.[12] Margolis, who had met one of the Wolfskehls' relatives before she left the United States, intervened and helped them get out of Shanghai.[13]

Margolis became convinced that the CFA and its leaders were treating the refugees unfairly and administering the relief operation poorly. After Komor and Sassoon made their accusations, the CFA had hired a former dock superintendent for the Hamburg-Amerika Line, Captain A. Herzberg, to supervise the camps and the feeding of the refugees. Margolis wrote to the JDC that Herzberg, a German Jew born in Shanghai, handled the finances honestly. But he treated the refugees the same way he treated Chinese coolies on the docks, demanding obedience and acting without compassion. She also was certain, she wrote, that many of the 6,000 refugees on relief who lived outside the camps could afford to pay for their own food.[14]

As she continued her work in Shanghai, Margolis became increasingly hostile toward the leaders of the CFA. Herzberg and Hayim acted like dictators, she wrote in a July 2nd confidential letter to the JDC:

> The result is that any refugee dependent on the Committee who has the starch to talk back gets his relief suspended or some other kinds of stupid punishment.There is no distinction made between "troublemaker" and a man with a bona fide complaint. Therefore thousands of people, afraid of having their relief suspended, sit back and hope for the day when they can be independent. Now I understand the look of absolute hopelessness on the faces of people in the camps.[15]

In an August 11th letter,[16] Margolis offered a more thorough rundown on the CFA and its leaders.

*Michel Speelman, chairman:
[He] is, I am sorry to say (and this is confirmed by many of his friends here) getting senile. He's really very nice and a good-hearted person. He has been in this thing practically from the beginning and it's worn him down. Herzberg was his life saver; and now he's satisfied with anything as long as the refugees don't bother him.

*Eduard Kann, chairman of the CFA Immigration Department:
Mr. Kann's greatest fear is that there would be too many refugees in Shanghai. . . . In the past year it has become increasingly difficult to get a Settlement permit, even when one has the necessary relatives here in Shanghai to give the guarantee. But agents, some Russians, some refugees, have been able to get permits for varying sums. In the meantime, the Committee insisted that people apply for permits through the Immigration Dept. of the CFA. . . . Then they wait months. . . . While people applying through the CFA rarely get a permit, others working through agents get theirs.

*D.E.J. Abraham:
He and Mrs. Abraham (latter is sister of Ellis Hayim; all Baghdad Jews and very religious) are really the two kindest people I've ever met. They are very wealthy and very charitable, but absolutely blind on the subject of their orthodoxy. . . . They are the only people who at least look at the refugees as human beings instead of as derelicts.

*Horace Kadoorie, chairman of the Schools:
The Kadoorie family endow schools all over the Near and Far

East. Education is their hobby; they do an excellent job of it. But investigation shows that the money for the schools comes from a multitude of sources, private contributions, etc. and that all the money does not come from the Kadoorie family. They are fabulously wealthy; and therefore I took the stand that the local people with Kadoorie's help could at least finance the education of the refugee children. And it worked.

*Dr. Reiss, chairman of the Medical Board:

The hospitals are pretty sad looking and the doctors in charge a pretty heartless lot. The attitude right down the line is that they [the refugees] should be glad they have any kind of place at all.

*Hayim, vice chairman of the CFA:

He is really the one and only voice in the whole outfit. . . . Mr. Hayim holds reception hours for refugees in his office between 12 noon and 1. Then he sees dozens of them at a time, giving each just a few seconds. Refugees discontent with their relief allowances go to him. He decides yes or no, on an entirely personal basis. Sorry if I must interject my psychiatric training here, but the man is actually a sadist who has done unheard of cruel things to refugees; then, on the other hand, in a streak of generosity (probably guilt) he will grant an unheard of request to someone who doesn't need the help. Decisions are entirely a matter of mood; no one contradicts him.

Margolis asked the JDC to inform the local committee that "the present administration of the monies has not been found satisfactory" and to request a reorganization. She also asked for an assistant to help her implement the changes and suggested that the Komor Committee or other local people could help take over from the CFA leadership.[17] The JDC, increasingly concerned about reports of imminent war in the Pacific, had cabled Margolis to sail to the Philippines.[18] She replied:

I am going to Manila in order to await further instructions about the work in Shanghai from your office. I have absolutely no fear of personal safety or discomfort, although the prospects are anything but pleasant. But I simply cannot take the pressure brought on me by the refugees to help them while my hands are tied. It's like being a soldier in a front line trench without a gun. In order not to create any unnecessary panic here, I've told everyone that I'm going down on temporary assignment for the office in N.Y. and hope to be back here by middle or end of September. There is so much hysteria here already, without giving the impression that I'm evacuating for personal safety.[19]

There was one more reason for concern as Margolis prepared for her voluntary exile from Shanghai. Japanese officials had notified the CFA that they planned to evacuate 1,000 Jewish refugees, most of them originally from Poland, from Kobe, Japan to Shanghai that fall. More than 400 of the new arrivals would be rabbis and yeshiva students, including the entire Mir Yeshiva. The Shanghai community, already overwhelmed by 18,000 Jewish refugees, was totally unprepared for a new influx.

The Polish refugees were among 14,000 Jews who had found refuge in Vilna when war broke out in Europe. The Soviets, in their pact with Hitler, had taken over eastern Poland in September 1939. But they had left Vilna, which had been part of Poland since World War I, as part of the independent state of Lithuania. Jews from throughout Poland, including about 2,500 rabbis and students, fled to Vilna. In June 1940, the Soviets occupied Lithuania and annexed it to the Soviet Union.[20]

The Vilna refugees were trapped, but the Soviets would let anyone emigrate who had proper transit visas and end visas. The Dutch consul in nearby Kaunas, after appeals from the stranded refugees, agreed to stamp hundreds of refugee documents with the phrase "No visa to Curacao is required," apparently permitting their entry into the Dutch island of Curacao. (The stamp was not, in fact, an end visa because the governor of Curacao had sole authority to grant a landing permit.) The Japanese consul in Kaunus, Senpo Sugihara, then issued transit visas to Japan to those who had the Curacao stamp. Sugihara apparently recognized that the end visa was worthless, but he acted to assist the refugees, defying instructions from his own government. Hundreds of other refugees made counterfeit copies of the Japanese visa.[21]

Beginning in July 1940, 2,166 Jewish refugees from Lithuania, carrying documents with the Dutch and Japanese stamps and financed by American organizations, received Soviet exit visas, purchased Intourist tickets and crossed the Soviet Union into Japan. Among them were hundreds of yeshiva students and rabbis.[22] Most took the same Trans-Siberian route as the Kantorowskys and 2,500 other German Jews who were on their way to Shanghai.

Japan cut off further immigration in the spring of 1941. After that, Jewish leaders in Japan, Shanghai, and the United States launched a desperate effort to acquire Shanghai permits and transit visas for the thousands of rabbis and students who remained in Vilna. Only about a hundred of them made it to Shanghai, traveling via Vladivostok, before that route was closed when Germany invaded the Soviet Union in June 1941.[23]

Most of the 2,000 Polish refugees who reached Japan were settled in Kobe. There was a small Jewish community established there, and the JDC provided support for those who needed it. About half of the Polish refugees eventually emigrated to Australia or the West; as Japan prepared for war in the fall of 1941, it sent the remaining Jewish refugees to Shanghai.[24]

The Japanese authorities in Shanghai set only one restriction on the new immigrants arriving from Japan—they were prohibited from settling in Hongkew, the Japanese-controlled area already overcrowded with Chinese and Jewish refugees.[25] Before Margolis first arrived, in the spring of 1941, Russian and Polish Jews in Shanghai established a committee for the Eastern European Jews—known as Eastjewcom, or EJC—to work with the established CFA and to aid the incoming Polish refugees.[26]

The alliance between the EJC and CFA was a disaster from the start. As the Polish refugees began to trickle in, the CFA insisted that the new refugees move into the camps, like all the previous immigrants, despite the Japanese prohibitions. The EJC refused to defy the authorities and demanded private housing outside Hongkew where the rabbis and students could continue their studies. The new refugees also required strictly kosher food and therefore requested more money for food than the other refugees. After lengthy negotiations, the JDC granted each Polish refugee a food allowance that was nearly double the amount then being received by the German and Austrian refugees in Shanghai.[27]

By the end of August, with Margolis still in Manila, the CFA tried to abandon the problem of the new immigrants altogether and leave them in the hands of the local Russian and Polish Jews. The Abrahams offered temporary housing for the Polish refugees in Beth Aharon, the large, nearly abandoned synagogue Silas Hardoon had built on Museum Road, across Soochow Creek from Hongkew. The yeshiva students studied there, and all the Polish refugees slept on the floor on old, dirty mattresses. But the CFA refused to look for additional housing or provide for food, handing the money from the JDC to Rabbi Meir Ashkenazi, the head of the Russian Jewish community. Ashkenazi eventually found housing for some of the Poles at the old Jewish Club on Moulmein Road. He also turned to his own community for assistance.[28]

Unlike the Sephardis, most of the Russian Jews were relative newcomers to Shanghai. A few had arrived in the late 1800s, and in 1902 about twenty-five families established a synagogue. In the wake of the Russian Revolution, hundreds of new Russian Jewish families settled in Shanghai. By 1926, there were more than 1,000 Russian Jews in Shanghai— already larger than the Sephardic community—and they hired Rabbi Ashkenazi, a Lubavitcher originally from Vladivostok, to head the congregation. The rabbi led a successful fund-raising effort in his first year, and the community built a new Orthodox synagogue on Ward Road in the center of Hongkew.[29]

The major Russian Jewish community in China remained in Harbin. But when the Japanese took over Manchuria in the 1930s, the Russians began to flee south. By 1939, just as the major influx of European Jews was to reach Shanghai, more than 4,000 Russian Jews were settled there. None was as wealthy as the Sassoons and Kadoories, but some had established themselves as furriers and in the import–export business and lived in large mansions in the French Concession. Most owned small shops, bars, or restaurants; some took low-paying menial jobs previously shunned by the Sephardis, working even as rickshaw drivers and prostitutes.[30]

Although a few Russians attended the Sephardi synagogue and most sent their children to the Shanghai Jewish School, the two communities remained isolated from each other. The Russians established their own Zionist groups, including a Betar chapter, the Jewish Club, with its own sports leagues and social and cultural activities, and a Yiddish and Russian newspaper. Just before Passover in the spring of 1941, the Russians opened a huge new synagogue on Rue de la Tour in the French Concession.[31]

There also were few links between the Russian Jews and the Central European Jews who followed them to Shanghai. The Russians provided some assistance to the newer refugees— they sent a group of the poorer German and Austrian children to a summer camp on the coast in 1939[32]—but left most of the relief work in the reluctant hands of the Sephardi community. A few European refugees found it ironic that the Russians and Poles in Shanghai now shunned them, because a generation earlier it had been the Berlin and Viennese Jews who had looked down on the Polish and Russian Jews when they emigrated west during World War I.[33]

Some of the refugees worked for Russian businesses, but social connections between the two communities were unusual. One of the few exceptions was the marriage of Karl Marishel, a young Viennese who arrived in December 1938, and Sylvia Gohstand, a Russian Jew whose family originally came from Odessa. Karl spoke no English when he arrived and made a living doing odd jobs. His success as a soccer player eventually helped him establish a clothing store. Sylvia, whose family had migrated to Shanghai early in 1938, lived with her family near her uncle's pharmacy in the French Concession and attended the Shanghai Jewish School. In 1939, her family moved to Hongkew, where her father opened the Wayside Pharmacy next to the Broadway Theatre in the middle of the newly thriving refugee community. After she and Karl met, Sylvia tutored him in English and they started dating a year later. Following a long engagement, they were married by Rabbi Ashkenazi during the war.[34]

But more typical of the rivalry between Russian and German Jews was a September 1941 editorial in the Russian-Jewish newspaper, explaining the need for a separate relief committee for Eastern European Jews. "We do not want the Eastern European refugees to be lowered to the sad level of the Jewish refugees from Germany," the editorial stated.[35] That same month, the publication *Asiana* offered the opposite prejudice, suggesting that the Russians and Poles were jealous of the Germans and Austrians: "The development of Hongkew from its former state of shambles into a busy area and the wealthy affluence of a fair number of the German emigres has also aroused the fear that they may usurp the position of the Russian emigres."[36]

Margolis returned to Shanghai early in October 1941. JDC officials had telephoned her to say that the U.S. State Department was convinced there would be no war in the Far East. The JDC also had granted her request and written Shanghai relief officials authorizing her to take over a reorganization. Captain Herzberg met her at the dock on her return from Manila, carrying a sheaf of correspondence between the CFA and the Russian and Polish Jews. He complained that the Eastern European Jews were uncooperative and unreliable and left all the relief work to the CFA.[37]

But Margolis no longer had to worry about bruising egos. She criticized Speelman and Hayim for refusing to even meet with Rabbi Ashkenazi and blamed them for dumping the problem of feeding and housing the Polish refugees in Ashkenazi's hands. Because she now had direct control over the JDC funds, she advised the CFA that no more money would be released until they had straightened out the relief problems.[38]

She also began a series of meetings with Ashkenazi and the EJC. "The situation of this new group is entirely different from the 20,000 already here," Margolis wrote in an October 26th letter. There were about 1,000 Polish refugees, she wrote, about half of them yeshiva students and rabbis. Of that group, 238 were from the Mir Yeshiva.[39]

At first, Margolis had to meet with the members of the Mir Yeshiva separately because they would not accept Ashkenazi's leadership. She wrote:

> They consider themselves a separate and distinct entity. They fled en masse from Poland, are still intact and intend to remain so. I needn't tell you they have no conception of realities, limitations or of anything else except their own immediate problem.[40]

The other yeshivas also had to be kept together with a place to study and pray. "Anything else is simply inconceivable to them," Margolis wrote, "and, strangely enough, everyone accepts this locally." The remaining Polish Jews, ranging from the nonreligious Yiddish Bundists to internationally renowned Zionist leaders, had to be housed in relatively expensive apartments in the International Settlement to comply with the Japanese restrictions. Margolis concluded, however, that the EJC was much more efficient than the CFA in eliminating assistance for those who did not need it.[41] And the EJC had done a great deal to raise money locally, collecting $75,000 from a benefit ball.[42] But in a subsequent letter, Margolis said "my own conscience hurts" because "the housing and feeding standard of the Polish refugees, and more so the religious group, is far superior to that of the Germans and Austrians."[43]

She also found that, although she was having some success in getting visas for refugees, the majority of cases receiving clearance were now coming from the small minority of yeshiva students and rabbis. "They must have good representation in Washington," Margolis wrote. "Who is it?"[44]

She had identified part of a dilemma the JDC had been facing since the beginning of its rescue efforts in Europe. Groups like Va'ad Hahatzalah (Emergency Committee for War-Torn Yeshivas), dedicated to saving the yeshivas trapped in Lithuania, had concentrated vast resources to raise funds and lobby officials on behalf of the rabbis and their students. Whenever the JDC showed unwillingness to give the yeshivas top priority—such as the reluctance to provide more food aid to the yeshivas than to the other refugees—it was inundated with telegrams and letters from leading rabbis and other Jewish officials.

JDC's position was that all refugees should be treated equally; there should be no special treatment for groups with powerful representation in the United States. But Va'ad Hahatzalah and other groups had argued that rescuing the rabbis and students, the scholars who would preserve the future of Judaism, was far more important than rescuing others. Their lives had more value, they claimed, than other refugees.* JDC compromised, in effect, by maintaining its control over general fund raising but permitting Va'ad Hahatzalah and others to make special appeals for the yeshivas throughout the war.[45]

As Margolis took control in Shanghai that fall, the JDC dispatched Manny Siegel, who had worked with Margolis in Cuba, to join her. He arrived in Shanghai early in November. By then, the U.S. Marines had departed, and new rumors of war were spreading throughout the Pacific. The rumors set off rampant inflation, cutting the value of relief funds in half. Margolis and Siegel worried that if war started, outside assistance would be cut off and local bank accounts frozen. She asked for JDC authorization to borrow funds from wealthy Shanghai residents in an emergency.[46]

Siegel and Margolis then met with the CFA and, at long last, reached an agreement to begin reorganizing the committee. But the reorganization never occurred. They had been scheduled to start a week later—on December 8, 1941.[47]

---

* Members of the Mir and other yeshivas have since argued that not only were the German and Austrian Jews less worthy of rescue, but also that their assimilation caused the Holocaust by bringing forth the wrath of God. See Yecheskel Leitner, *Operation: Torah Rescue*, Feldheim Publishers, New York, 1987, pp. 138–39.

III
WAR
(1941–1942)

9

Kantorowsky

As the hundreds of Polish refugees arrived in Shanghai in the fall of 1941, Eva Kantorowsky became their main link with the outside world. She was now secretary to Meyer Birman, manager of the Far Eastern Jewish Information Bureau.* Part of her job was to write letters in English to the refugees' relatives and to organizations in the United States asking for financial support and assistance in emigrating. It was a familiar role for her, similar to the work she had done for her father when they were trying to get out of Germany.

The information bureau had been based in Harbin until the fall of 1939, with a small Shanghai office run by a local Russian businessman. But when most of the Jews from Manchuria moved south, Birman transferred the main office to Shanghai. Before the Polish refugees began to arrive, the bureau's basic function was to distribute HICEM checks to

---

*The bureau was known as HIAS (Hebrew Immigrant Aid Society) in the United States and HICEM (an acronym for HIAS and the Jewish Colonization Society) in Europe and other countries.

arriving refugees. The checks, from $50 to $150 per person, were provided mostly to German refugees, including those released from concentration camps, who had registered before they emigrated.[1]

Many refugees, like the Heimanns, used the HICEM money to buy houses in Hongkew. Later, after immigration to Shanghai was restricted, HICEM posted the guarantee money that permitted refugees to land. Until the Polish refugees began to arrive, the bureau had no role in relief activities or emigration. But once the Poles began arriving from Japan, the Committee for the Assistance of European Jewish Refugees refused to take responsibility and left the new refugees' plight in the hands of Birman's bureau and other Eastern European Jews.

Eva was impressed with the resourcefulness of the Polish Jews, long accustomed to pressuring and outwitting hostile governments and bureaucracies. Their representatives in the United States, like Va'ad Hahatzalah and other religious groups, zealously lobbied government agencies, embassies, and relief agencies, particularly on behalf of the rabbis and yeshiva students. Even as emigration from Shanghai came to a halt for the Germans and Austrians who had arrived earlier, dozens of visas continued to appear at the U.S. consulate for the Polish Jews. There also was regular communication and a constant supply of funds from abroad, even after the United States had broken off contact with Shanghai.[2]

Although she felt she was doing some good, Eva hated her job. She saw Birman as a grouchy, uneducated old man who spoke broken English and sometimes dictated letters in Yiddish, which she couldn't understand. He also was agonizingly frugal. He required his secretaries to type letters on extremely thin rice paper to save postage and only issued new pieces of carbon paper from his locked cabinet after confirming that the old carbon was worn out.

Eva would have loved to be back working for Paul Komor and teaching Basic English. But she had been fired from that job just after the High Holidays. She had her father to blame for that.

When Rabbi Georg Kantorowsky arrived in Shanghai with his wife and daughter in the fall of 1940, there already was an established Jewish refugee community with two congregations. Most of the Germans and Austrians who came to Shanghai in 1938 and 1939 were far less religious than the Orthodox Sephardis from Baghdad and Ashkenazis from Russia. Many, particularly the Austrians, had virtually abandoned any practice of their religion. A few had converted to Protestantism or Catholicism in an attempt to hide or deny their Judaism; others had married non-Jews and several had brought their non-Jewish spouses with them to Shanghai.

But most of the acculturated Central European Jews, who had retained some links with their Jewish communal associations when they had lived in Europe, found a need for a similar community in Shanghai. Like the European *gemeinden*, the Shanghai community eventually served political, social, and cultural, as well as religious, needs. Even the most assimilated European Jews, crowded together with other Jews in the confines of Hongkew, joined in the life of the Jewish community.[3]

The European refugees in Shanghai at first formed *minyans* in the camps but held their first community-wide religious services during Shavuot in the spring of 1939. The Sephardi community leaders permitted them to use the virtually abandoned Beth Aharon Synagogue on that occasion, and more than 1,000 people attended. (Most of the Sephardic community had moved to the western end of the International Settlement during the fighting in 1937 and now worshipped at Ohel Rachel.) But the Orthodox Sephardis were uncomfortable with the use of more secular, German ritual in their synagogue. The refugees decided to form their own congregation.[4]

The refugee congregation initially was sponsored by the local relief organizations. But it became a separate Jüdische Gemeinde (Jewish community) at the end of 1939 and opened offices on East Seward Road. Because most refugees had arrived with almost no money or possessions, they had little to contribute to the Gemeinde. But the lack of funds seemed only to intensify the debate over leadership and ritual. Many of the refugees complained that the services were still too Orthodox and attendance at services declined. Lutz Wachsner, a refugee from Breslau, was appointed to develop observances that would satisfy the congregation.[5]

In the spring of 1940, a separate Jewish Liberal congregation split off and offered services that were more familiar to many of the German Jews. At their first services during Passover at the Eastern Theatre, Cantor Heinz Wartenberger introduced a mixed choir and organ. The liberal group began to hold regular Friday evening and Saturday morning services at the Helvetia Restaurant and then the Rosenthal Restaurant, later opening a prayer hall on the first floor of the Broadway Theatre.[6]

The competition spurred the original congregation to introduce its own organist and choir in the summer of 1940 during sabbath services at the Tabarin Restaurant. The changes helped the congregation grow again. It also added some of the traditional functions performed by Jewish communities in Europe. It formed a burial society and opened a new cemetery on Columbia Road after deaths from disease and old age had filled the available plots in the old Jewish cemetery on Baikal Road. A women's group ran *seders* and mended clothes for the poorer refugees.

A young German, Willy Teichner, was hired as the congregation's first rabbi, later joined by Rabbi Walter Silberstein, Gerhard Heimann's great-uncle. (Silberstein eventually was named chief rabbi for the Jewish liberal congregation.[7]) Rabbi Kantorowksy was hired by the congregation's rabbinical council when he arrived in Shanghai late in 1940. He became a familiar figure in the community. Although the younger Teichner was more popular and dynamic, Kantorowsky's broad knowledge and training brought him admiration among the German and Austrian Jews. He had found the esteem he valued so much and feared he would lose forever when he left Germany. (The growing population of Polish yeshiva students was not so deferential, however, murmuring their disapproval when they saw Rabbi

Kantorowsky carrying his umbrella on the sabbath, which they considered a sacrilege.)

The Gemeinde held its first elections in June 1941, selecting a board that represented much of the diverse refugee population. The board named Fritz Lesser as president and Felix Kardegg as vice-president.[8] Although the Jewish community organization had only limited powers, Japanese officials sought their assistance in apprehending minor criminals.[9]

But religious services remained the main function of the Gemeinde through the end of 1941. In September 1941, Rabbi Kantorowsky was given the honor of presenting his first Rosh Hashanah sermon in Shanghai. The service was being held in the Wayside Cinema (the new synagogue on East Yuhang Road wasn't scheduled to open until November[10]) and, as usual, it was filled to capacity for the High Holidays. There were more than a thousand people there, twice as many as the congregation in Neukölln.

Eva and her mother watched Rabbi Kantorowsky from their seats in the balcony—women and men remained separate even in the more liberal services. Eva felt proud on occasions like this; being a rabbi's daughter gave her a special status in the refugee community. But there was another side to it, too. Eva felt she was expected to follow a higher standard than other young women. She knew she was being watched when she went out on dates with Bob and other young men. The community was full of gossips. Wherever the rabbi's daughter went and whatever she did was sure to be reported back to her parents.

Eva was only half listening as her father delivered his Rosh Hashanah sermon. She respected his ideas, but thought his sermons were long winded and monotonous. Like most rabbis, he was exploiting his large, captive audience for the High Holidays to berate them for their moral failings during the previous year.

The Jewish people, Rabbi Kantorowsky was saying, had always stood on the side of the working class. The labor movement had won many important freedoms in Germany and was active here in China as well. And Chinese workers deserved the same rights, the same opportunities to earn a living wage, as European workers, he said.

Her father's sermon was now focusing on the ongoing strike of Chinese workers against the local hotels and restaurants. But what upset Rabbi Kantorowsky was that the hotels had hired strike breakers to replace the striking workers. That, the rabbi was saying, was immoral. It was wrong for anyone to take the job of a striking worker.

Rabbi Kantorowsky's sermon was clearly making some people uncomfortable. Some of the men turned to each other with raised eyebrows; others whispered loud comments among the members of the congregation. Perhaps the rabbi didn't know that dozens of his own congregants were among those hired as strike breakers or that most of the hotels were owned by the refugee community's most prominent benefactor, Sir Victor Sassoon.

For refugees without the skills and financial resources to start their own businesses, a job as a strike breaker was one of the few opportunities to earn a decent wage in Shanghai in 1940–1941. Most of the available jobs required difficult manual labor and paid little. The European Jewish refugees remained near the bottom rung of the foreign population—they were among the lowest-paid workers in Shanghai. In some cases, they were paid even less than the Chinese workers.[11]

Most of the jobs were in businesses founded by refugees in Hongkew, working as delivery boys in small factories or in bakeries and laundries. The work usually involved hard manual labor for ten to twelve hours a day, earning from 40 to 50 cents (U.S.) a day. One of the best jobs available was with an egg dealer, whose ten employees worked for twelve hours a day and had Sundays off, earning less than $3 a week. A Jewish taxi company hired refugees to work as chauffeurs for $10 a month plus tips. A refugee-owned chemical factory hired more than twenty immigrants to work for about $11 a month, at least $8 less a month than the minimum earned by Chinese who worked at foreign or Chinese chemical factories. Jewish night watchmen earned 25 to 30 cents a night, about a quarter of what Sikh watchmen earned for the same work.[12]

There were even fewer opportunities for women. Some women found jobs in workshops or did piecework at home. The home work rarely paid more than $6 a month. Nurses, cooks, and dressmakers could make as much as $8 a month.[13]

Few refugees could survive on such low wages. They generally paid more for food and rent than the Chinese and, as inflation soared under the Japanese occupation, even those with jobs had to rely on relief agencies for meals and housing. The large majority of refugees depended on assistance and on what they could raise by selling or pawning their belongings.

But the frequent strikes by Chinese workers offered a rare chance for foreigners to earn a decent income, at least by wartime Shanghai standards. In the summer of 1940, the Shanghai Gas Company hired Jewish and Russian immigrants to replace striking Chinese, paying them 65 cents a day, even more than the Chinese workers had made. In 1941, there were dozens of strikes by Chinese unions, protesting the shrinking value of their wages.[14] In June 1941, an English firm hired refugees to replace striking welders at nearly $1 a day. And later that year, the strike by Chinese hotel and restaurant unions provided dozens of good-paying jobs for Jewish refugees, who had formed an association to train and find positions for their own restaurant and hotel employees.[15] In most cases, the refugees were fired as soon as they strikes ended.[16]

As Rabbi Kantorowsky continued his fervent attack on the immorality of strike breaking, Eva and her mother listened uncomfortably from the balcony. They always had been apprehensive when the rabbi's sermons ventured into topical issues. Sometimes, they felt, he took positions without having all the facts; perhaps he should have been more cautious in criticizing the strike breakers. But Eva and her mother never openly questioned the rabbi's judgment.

A few days after Rosh Hashanah, Eva received a letter from the Komor Committee. It informed her that, due to "economic reasons," her services as a Basic English teacher would not be needed after the end of that week. Eva was sure her firing had more to do with her father's sermon than any shortage of funds. Komor, after all, worked for Sassoon and could not ignore the rabbi's criticism. Her father's status as a rabbi had helped her get the position in the first place; now his outspokenness had gotten her fired.

But Eva, with her marketable skills in English, had no trouble getting another position quickly. Birman sorely needed someone who could read and type letters in English, and Komor had little influence with the information bureau. Eva couldn't stand Birman, but she didn't have any choice if she wanted to work. Her new job, however, would only last three months. This time war, not politics, would force her out of work.

10

Levin

It was unusually warm for the middle of December and Horst Levin, host of the refugee radio program, had been sleeping outside on a covered terrace. Horst usually slept in a room on the second floor he rented from the Rosskamms, but the terrace seemed a good place to escape the heat. Yet even outdoors, it was too hot to sleep well and Levin was restless all night. As the sun rose, Levin thought he was still dreaming when he felt someone tugging on his arm. He looked up to see three Japanese soldiers standing on the terrace by his cot, armed with rifles and fixed bayonets.

As he turned toward them, the soldier who had been shaking his arm thrust a letter in his face. Levin reached for his glasses, but they weren't much help; the letter was in Japanese, on official-looking stationery. Yet it didn't take much imagination for Levin to figure out that they had come to arrest him. He got dressed quickly and the soldiers led him outside and into a military truck, which drove them up Broadway toward the Garden Bridge.

The truck stopped outside Broadway Mansions, the looming

office building and hotel just before the bridge. The soldiers took Levin into a large first-floor conference room, where dozens of people sat waiting. Levin recognized many of them; it was like a convention of foreign journalists in Shanghai. Nearly every British and American editor, reporter, and broadcaster was there, from the *North China Daily News*, *Shanghai Times* and *Shanghai Evening Post and Mercury* and from radio stations XCDN, XMHC, and XMHA, including Levin's boss, Roy Healey. But although Levin had often shared drinks and conversation with many of them, none of them acknowledged him or spoke. They were all worried that they were being watched and fearful of what was going to happen to them next. Every few minutes, a young Japanese woman entered the room, called out someone's name, and took him with her to another room. None of the journalists ever returned to the conference room.

It seemed like most of the day had passed before Levin's name was called. The woman led him to a large office, empty except for a huge desk and some chairs. A short Japanese naval officer, his uniform covered with medals and his sword on a table next to him, nodded to Levin, indicating he should be seated. The officer was fingering a thick folder on the desk in front of him. He studied it for a few moments and then looked up again, snapping out questions in perfect English: Name, address, nationality, occupation. After Levin had answered, the officer began to speak.

"Yes, yes, of course we know who you are," the officer said. "And we have monitored every broadcast you have made on XMHA." He fingered the folder again. "We know of your slanderous attacks against our German allies. Now that we are in full control of the Greater East Asia Co-Prosperity Sphere, we are dealing with you and other lying propagandists. Everyone I have seen today has been sent to the Bridge House."

Levin swallowed hard. Since Pearl Harbor and the Japanese takeover of all of Shanghai ten days ago, dozens of prisoners had been sent to the Bridge House. The cells there were rumored to be filled with typhus-infested lice; no one had yet returned alive. Had he survived Sachsenhausen only to die in a jail in Shanghai?

The officer interrupted Levin's morbid thoughts with another question.

"Do you know who I am?" he asked.

"No, sir, I don't know you." Levin stammered as he spoke, confused and afraid.

"I am Captain Inuzuka, head of the Japanese Naval Landing Party." Levin thought the name sounded familiar.

The refugee radio program had continued to be popular, right until the eve of Pearl Harbor. But in the past year, Levin had found it harder to earn a living from it. Advertising revenues had shrunk as the Japanese occupation led to shortages and fueled inflation. Several British and American firms, including some of Levin's best advertising clients, had left the city; those that remained didn't see much value in trying to sell their products and services to the increasingly impoverished Jewish refugees. To pay for food and rent, Levin had to draw on some of the money he had saved in his first year in Shanghai. Occasionally, he ate his meals at the relief kitchen.

Levin supplemented his income by writing reviews and columns for several of the refugee newspapers. There were real dangers, however, in working as a foreign journalist in Shanghai. The Japanese considered most journalists to be spies and arranged for assassinations of those who openly criticized them. Carroll Alcott, an American who worked for the Associated Press and whose biting commentaries on XMHA frequently targeted the Japanese, was shot at several times and always wore a bullet-proof vest.

But Levin's radio show continued without interference, airing readings from burned books, news events, music, comedy, and advice from guest lawyers and doctors. In the cafes and restaurants of Hongkew, where many unemployed refugees spent their days, Levin's program drew the community together.

Each fall at Rosh Hashanah, the British, American, and

other foreign consulates still sent their New Year's messages to the refugees over Levin's show. The Japanese had never expressed interest in issuing such a greeting. But in the fall of 1941, just weeks before Pearl Harbor, Levin received a letter from a Captain Inuzuka, offering the Japanese emperor's good wishes to the Jewish community.

Levin brought the letter to Healey, the station manager, and asked for his advice. Would it be wrong to broadcast this message over an American-owned station?

"I'm surprised at you, Horst," Healey said. "You've been running this program for years without my advice. What do you think you should do?"

"I think we Jews owe the Japanese a great deal," Levin said. "For one thing, they let us land here, in a war zone, when they could easily have sent us away."

"You're free to do whatever you want, Horst," Healey replied. "I won't interfere."

Levin's dilemma about the Japanese was shared by most of the European refugees in Shanghai at the time. Although the Japanese were now allied with the same Nazis who had imprisoned Levin and other Jews and driven them from Europe, they had not disturbed their sanctuary in Shanghai. They were ruthless in their conquest of China, yet, up to this point, had shown an almost benign neglect toward the Jews and other foreigners.

The refugees' uncertainty reflected an apparent confusion among the Japanese themselves. Japan's brief history with the Jews was a mysterious tangle of conflicting sentiments. There were strains of both anti-Semitism and friendship, of respect for Jewish wealth and power combined with the worst stereotypes of world Jewish conspiracies. Yet it all came from the same source, a Japanese pragmatism that made it possible to arrange alliances with both Nazis and Jews.

The Japanese first developed admiration for the Jews during the Russo-Japanese War of 1904–1905. Few nations had recognized Japan as a potential world power at the time, and financiers had offered little support for their military buildup. But Jacob H. Schiff, a German-born Jewish banker from New York, saw the conflict as a chance to punish Russia for its persecution of the Jews. His loans helped finance the expansion of the Japanese navy that was a key to Japan's victory.[1] The Japanese reciprocated by being among the early supporters of the Balfour Declaration and endorsing a Jewish home in Palestine during debates at the League of Nations.[2] There was only a tiny Jewish presence in Japan itself until the European refugees passed through on their way to China. The Sassoons had opened offices in Yokohama and Nagasaki after 1854, and the Jewish community in Nagasaki grew to more than one-hundred families by 1904. The Yokohama Jews resettled in Kobe after a 1923 earthquake, and the twenty-five families there later hosted the Polish refugees who were fleeing from Vilna.[3]

But the Japanese remained mostly uninformed about Jews and Judaism. Japanese military officers first learned about anti-Semitism when they joined military campaigns in Siberia in 1918 and 1922 to assist White Russians fighting the Bolsheviks. They were introduced to the *Protocols of the Elders of Zion* and other anti-Semitic propaganda and later translated some of these writings into Japanese. The officers spread the myth that cunning, unscrupulous Jews controlled governments, the media, and the gold supply and were plotting to disrupt national economies and set up a worldwide Zionist empire.[4]

After the Japanese conquest of Manchuria in 1931–1932, the Japanese condoned the violent anti-Semitism of the White Russian population against the Russian Jewish communities in Harbin and other cities. The Japanese refused to intervene when White Russians kidnapped and murdered wealthy Jews. These Jewish communities soon lost much of their wealth and status, and many Jews began to migrate south.[5]

Yet as early as 1933, the Japanese were considering a plan, first proposed by a Shanghai Sephardic Jew, to provide sanctuary for up to 50,000 German Jews in Manchuria. N.E.B. Ezra, editor of *Israel's Messenger*, suggested the proposal in a letter to the Japanese foreign ministry in September 1933, although it was not given serious consideration until 1937, a year after Ezra's death.[6]

Japan's strongest support for the Jews came in 1937-39,

when it sponsored three annual conferences in Harbin for the Jewish communities in the Far East. The first was attended by more than 1,000 Jews from five different communities. The Jews hoped Japan would guarantee the safety of their communities in Manchuria and China, including the rapidly growing refugee population in Shanghai. The Japanese had a different goal. As their relations with the West deteriorated, they hoped the Jews would use their influence to attract American investment in Manchuria and encourage a Japanese-American rapprochement. By 1939, some Japanese officials were proposing a settlement of at least 30,000 Jewish refugees in Manchuria or other parts of China, including those turned away when immigration was restricted in Shanghai.[7]

Strangely, the anti-Semitic literature then widely available in Japan bolstered, rather than hindered, these initiatives to seek Jewish support. If the Jews, in fact, controlled the money supply, the press, and world leaders, some pragmatic Japanese argued, then it would be in Japan's interest to seek their assistance.[8] The *Protocols* and other anti-Semitic literature helped foster the Nazi hate that led to the annihilation of the European Jews; it convinced the Japanese to befriend them.

The Japanese were disappointed by the world's lack of interest in their plans for a Jewish settlement. And they were frustrated by the lack of cooperation from Shanghai's wealthy Sephardic Jews and Sir Victor Sassoon's public criticism of the Japanese forces.

Sassoon had toured the United States in February 1940 and made critical comments about the Japanese armed forces in China, suggesting they were weakened by corruption and lack of support for the war effort in Japan.[9] A Japanese spokesman in Shanghai called the speech a "serious slander," reminded the Jewish community that the Japanese had gone out of their way to help the Jewish people, and called it "regrettable" that this "had not been appreciated by at least one member of the Jewish race."[10] A few weeks later, local Jewish leaders responded by issuing a statement praising the Japanese for their continued assistance. But the Japanese were stung again when their candidates for the Municipal Council didn't win Jewish votes, despite issuing entry permits for their relatives from Europe.

Most of the Jewish refugees from Europe who fled to Shanghai traveled on *Lloyd Triestino* Liners from Italy. The *Conte Biancamano* (above) made seven voyages between December 1938 and February 1940, bringing more than 3,600 refugees to China. Below, refugees descend the gangplank of the *Conte Biancamano* into Shanghai in February 1939. They were to enter a city already overcrowded and weary from years of war between Chinese and Japanese forces.

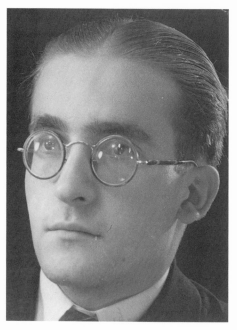

Among the refugees who arrived in Shanghai were (above left) Sam Didner from Graz, Austria, who arrived in December 1938; Horst Levin (above right) from East Prussia, who came in February 1939; and Gerhard Heimann (below left), who arrived with his family from Berlin in June 1939. After the war in Europe began, thousands of other refugees, including Eva Kantorowsky (below right) and her parents, traveled to Shanghai via the Trans-Siberian railway and Japanese ships. By the end of 1941, when further immigration was outlawed, there were nearly 20,000 refugees in Shanghai.

Most of the new refugees settled in Hongkew, which had been devastated by Chinese and Japanese shelling in 1937. Within months, the refugees rebuilt the area. Seward Road, where Didner shared an office with a dentist, is shown early in 1939 (above) and in 1940 (below), after the refugees had arrived.

The refugees opened dozens of cafes and restaurants, including the Roof Garden (above), on the roof of the Broadway Cinema on Wayside Road. There also was a variety of sports activities, including boxing and soccer. Leo Meyer (below, at left) starred in both the refugee and citywide soccer leagues. The community also provided English instruction for the refugees, including the Basic English school (below, at right) where Eva Kantorowsky taught. Eva, at far right, is shown with International Committee members who took evening classes.

Most of the refugee children attended the Shanghai Jewish Youth Association school, founded by a wealthy Sephardic Jew, Sir Horace Kadoorie. Mrs. Lucie Hartwich (above, at rear) was the headmistress and Gunther Gassenheimer (above, at left) was one of the most popular teachers. The first school was on Kinchow Road and included a modern kitchen, where girls learned cooking. Some children attended the Freysinger School, the Shanghai Jewish School, where most of the Russian and Sephardi children matriculated, and several religious schools.

BETH HATEFUTSOTH

The Japanese who controlled Shanghai required the refugees to move into a one-square mile ghetto area in Hongkew by May 18, 1943. By August 10, all refugees who wished to leave the ghetto for business or other reasons were required to carry a pass. The Japanese official in charge of issuing most of the passes was Kanoh Ghoya (at center, above), an unpredictable man who sometimes beat the refugees and made them wait in line for hours. The ghetto was patrolled by a self-policing force and signs, like the one shown above Ghoya's head (right) were posted on the borders. The refugees were required to remain in the restricted area until the end of the war in the Pacific in August 1945.

By the summer of 1940, the possibility of rapprochement with the West seemed remote as pro-Nazi factions gained control in Japan and the United States imposed an embargo on sales of scrap metal and aviation fuel to Japan, demanding Japanese withdrawal from China. The Japanese leaders in Shanghai made one last attempt at exercising the "Jewish card," again turning to the Sephardic officers of the Committee for the Assistance of European Jewish Refugees in Shanghai.

In August 1940, Captain Koreshige Inuzuka, the head of the Japanese Naval Landing Party in Shanghai, approached the Jewish officials with a request to wire a telegram to American Jewish organizations. (Inuzuka also was reportedly a leading writer and translator of anti-Semitic tracts.[11]) The telegram was to read:

> WE ARE GREATLY INDEBTED TO THE JAPANESE AUTHORITIES IN SHANGHAI WHICH ARE DESPITE THE DIFFICULT CIRCUMSTANCES ARISING OUT OF THE PRESENT HOSTILITIES GRANTING ADMISSION AND SYMPATHETIC TREATMENT TO A LARGE NUMBER OF JEWISH REFUGEES FROM EUROPE.
> LEST UNFRIENDLY INFLUENCE BE EXERTED UPON THE AUTHORITIES WHO ALLOWED THE MAXIMUM OF FREEDOM WHICH TENS OF THOUSANDS OF REFUGEES NOW ENJOY UNDER THE JAPANESE PROTECTION IN THE FAR EAST AS A RESULT OF THE POLICY BEING PURSUED BY THE STATE DEPARTMENT IN WASHINGTON VIS A VIS AMERICAN EXPORT TRADE TO JAPAN INCLUDING A FEW ITEMS OF GOODS ESSENTIAL TO JAPAN WE CALL UPON OUR BRETHREN IN AMERICA TO CONSIDER THE SERIOUSNESS OF THIS SITUATION AND TAKE WHATEVER STEPS WITHIN THEIR POWER FOR OUR COMMON CAUSE.
> ANXIOUSLY AWAITING YOUR REPLY.[12]

The CFA rejected the proposal. It replied to Inuzuka on August 15 that although it was "anxious to meet you in your request, we feel it outwith [sic] our province to do so as we are constituted purely as a philanthropic body."[13]

Inuzuka angrily responded to the committee on August 27:

The Committee rejected cooperation with the scheme broached
by Captain Inuzuka to Mr. Speelman on the ground that it was
a political scheme. Does not the Committee realize that no
country in the world admits aliens who do not render services
calculated to enhance the prosperity of the country which gives
them refuge, as well as their own prosperity? . . .

The Committee's attention is invited . . . to the fact that every
inch of Hongkew and Yangtzepoo areas in which the Jewish
refugees are now enjoying peaceful life was secured by the
blood shed by Japan's armed forces. And in view of the
sweeping anti-Semitic propaganda and anti-Semitism which it
is feared might spread to and be aggravated in the Far East, it
would appear to be to their own best interest for the Jewish
people living within Japanese-occupied territories to refrain
from any expressions of opinion likely to prove irksome to the
Japanese Authorities and people, and to endeavour at all times
to make the best possible impression upon them. Does the
Committee realize that this question is one having a direct
bearing on the happiness and welfare of the Jewish people in
Shanghai?

It is therefore suggested that the Committee should not let
slip this opportunity to cooperate with the Japanese Authorities
in the above-mentioned scheme, so that the Japanese
Authorities might be duly impressed with the sincere desire
which the Committee doubtless cherishes to assist Japan's
cause.[14]

Despite his threats, Inuzuka continued to paint a positive
picture of the Japanese attitude toward the Jews. Early in
1941, he told *The Shanghai Evening Post* that there was no
racial discrimination in Japan and no religious persecution.
"Asia is the best place for the persecuted Jewish people to live
in," he said.[15]

Even as late as the fall of 1941, Inuzuka pleaded his case,
sounding more like a disappointed father than a powerful
military leader who harbored anti-Semitic feelings. In a
memorandum to the CFA, he claimed to have intervened with
other Japanese authorities to find shelter for the Polish
refugees arriving from Japan, despite the decision to prohibit
further settlement in Hongkew. Yet the committee and the
refugees still refused to cooperate, he complained.

Refugees continued to settle in Hongkew without permits;

they had forced up the cost of living; some refugees had been involved in street fights with White Russians, Inuzuka wrote. But the committee had done nothing. It had ignored his proposal for a joint Japanese-Jewish real estate company; American Jews had failed to take advantage of the opportunity to assist Jewish resettlement plans in China or Manchuria. And Sassoon had continued to make anti-Japanese statements, Inuzuka wrote.

> From the very beginning, the Japanese Naval authorities, sympathizing with the distressed circumstances of the European Jewish refugees, permitted the refugees . . . to live in this area. . . . It is no more than natural for us to expect individuals who occupy a prominent position in the Jewish community to give us their full and active cooperation. However, not only have we been unable to obtain the desired cooperation, but there have actually been some who have openly engaged in anti-Japanese activities.[16]

Just before dawn on Monday, December 8—the morning of December 7 in Hawaii—the Japanese launched attacks in Guam, Wake Island, Hong Kong, the Philippines, and Malaya, coordinated with the crippling strike on Pearl Harbor.[17] In Shanghai, boarding parties from a Japanese gunboat pulled alongside the USS *Wake* and the HMS *Petrel*, two small gunboats anchored in the harbor, and demanded their surrender. No American officers were aboard the Wake—they were asleep in hotels in the city—and the Japanese took it without a fight. But the *Petrel*'s captain refused to surrender. The boarding party returned to their small boat and signaled the Japanese gunboat, which opened fire. The *Petrel* began to return fire when the massive HIJMS *Idzumo*, docked about a half-mile away at the Shanghai and Hongkew Wharf, fired a series of deafening blasts from its cannons.[18]

The *Idzumo* had been built in England; the Japanese had used some of Jacob Schiff's loan money to buy it toward the end of the Russo-Japanese war in 1905. The *Petrel*'s small guns were no match for it. The *Idzumo* pounded huge holes in the *Petrel*'s hull, and the boat exploded in flames. The British captain destroyed his secret codes, and his crew abandoned ship in a small launch. But the Japanese guns sank the launch, too. When the British sailors began to swim for shore, Japanese marines aboard the *Wake* and along the waterfront fired their rifles into the water. Yet only one British sailor was killed. Some of the wounded were rescued by Chinese sampans and then taken prisoner.[19]

Within hours of the attack, Japanese forces had gathered the officials of the British, U.S., Belgian, and Dutch embassies and consulates in the Cathay and Metropole hotels and put them under guard. Yet only about ten prominent foreigners were arrested, and other foreigners could still move freely throughout the city. The Japanese permitted the Shanghai Municipal Council to continue its functions, but removed Americans from jobs at the customs office, waterworks, and power company.[20] Other enemy nationals soon were required to register with the Japanese and wear red armbands designating their nationalities. The Jewish refugees, who had been declared stateless by the Nazis in November, were not considered to be enemy nationals.

Notices were attached to all Allied property that it was now under Japanese control. (Initially, there was open rivarly between the Japanese navy and army. The posted notices said the properties were being seized by both the army and navy, but naval officers scratched the word army off the notices and forced out soldiers who were occupying some businesses.) The navy took control of Allied banks and limited withdrawals, although the banks remained open, and confiscated shortwave radio sets to restrict access to foreign news.

The Japanese also took over the local newspapers and radio stations, including XMHA, and began publishing and broadcasting news of the attack on Pearl Harbor and issuing antiforeign proclamations. (After the German consul protested the antiforeign attacks, the Japanese shifted to criticizing only the British and Americans.[21]) Only one refugee newspaper, *The Shanghai Jewish Chronicle*, continued publication. The takeovers put an end to Levin's refugee radio program and his newspaper career.

Yet after some initial food shortages and gasoline rationing that kept all but military vehicles off the streets, it seemed to

Levin that life in Shanghai was returning to normal.
(Throughout the war, in fact, the Japanese and Nationalists did
little to stop—and in many ways encouraged—legal and illegal
trade between Japanese-occupied areas and the rest of the
country.²²) Levin's impression changed, however, when he was
rudely awakened ten days after Pearl Harbor and brought
before Captain Inuzuka, who had threatened him with a
sentence in the Bridge House.

"So you do remember me." Inuzuka was smiling now. "I was
the one who sent you the message from the emperor, and you
were wise enough to broadcast it on your show. You did me a
great favor. So now I must do you a favor."

Inuzuka lifted the folder from his desk and dropped it in a
wastebasket.

"You can go home now and wait until we call you again."

Levin walked slowly back to Hongkew, thinking about the
radio broadcast that had saved his life.

11

Heimann

Gerd had heard amazing stories about the Marble Hall. It was supposed to be the greatest mansion in Shanghai, built for the Kadoories in the early 1920s while they were out of the country. Their drunken, pompous American architect had designed a ballroom with a 65-foot ceiling, covered by intricate plaster designs and lit by eight giant chandeliers fitted with thousands of pink, blue, and red bulbs. There were black marble fireplaces at either end of the ballroom, topped by 20-foot mirrors framed by white plaster that came to a peak near the ceiling. Outside, the portico was decorated with four marble pillars and flanked by a covered, 225-foot veranda. On the walkway in front of the entrance, marble Greek statues of a young boy and young girl on pedestals greeted visitors. The Kadoories were dumbfounded when they returned to Shanghai to see their grandiose, half-finished edifice. After they learned their architect was in the hospital to recover from his alcoholism, they hired another one to complete it.[1]

Gerd thought he was looking at a fantasy as the van pulled in front of the Marble Hall on a cold January morning. When the van came to a stop, Mrs. Hartwich stood in the aisle and called for their attention. Gerd and his five classmates couldn't help staring out the windows at the giant, two-story brown and white building. Mrs. Hartwich said they would be going inside the Marble Hall in a few minutes to collect some things for Mr. Kadoorie while he was away. They could only stay for a short while and had to be very careful to keep together. They should go only where she took them. Gerd couldn't wait to get inside—he was hoping to see the famous ballroom.

For the children of European Jewish refugees in Shanghai, Sir Horace Kadoorie was like a kindly millionaire uncle. It was he who had built their first, lavish school and who sent them notes and baskets of fruit when they were sick. He came to their school plays and brought cakes and cookies for the *oneg shabbat* after Friday evening services. When the service was over, Mr. Kadoorie always would take that week's student rabbi home in his chauffered Rolls Royce.

The first Kadoorie School had opened in November 1939, four months after Gerd and his family had arrived in Shanghai. The school was on Kinchow Road, a few blocks from the camp where the Heimanns first lived and where Mr. Katz taught the children morning lessons in the dining hall. But the new school was nothing like the filthy, crowded camps. It didn't look exactly like a school either, at least not the schools that Gerd was used to. The Kinchow Road school, in the Kadoorie tradition, was something like a country club.

There were sitting rooms with upholstered chairs and a well-stocked library. The girls studied cooking in a modern kitchen and served meals to the boys, who were trained how to hold the girls' chairs for them while they were being seated. They all learned how to address each other and use their knives and forks properly. The Kadoories hoped to turn the rough little European refugees like Gerd into sophisticated colonialists.

Their education was modeled on the European system. Gerd's classes—and the quality of his teachers—were similar to what he would have encountered in a German Gymnasium. Mrs. Lucie Hartwich, a schoolteacher from Berlin who had come to Shanghai with her husband in 1939, was the headmistress and taught French and music. Most of the teachers were German, but there were other teachers from throughout Shanghai's foreign community—Russians, British, Norwegians, and Chinese. All classes were taught in English. But the teachers' accents were so diverse that many of the students spoke English with a conglomeration of foreign inflections.[2]

Gerd received a traditional liberal education of social sciences, mathematics, and languages. Each school day started with exercises in the schoolyard, led by sports teacher Leo Meyer, the legendary German soccer player. For the rest of the morning, the teachers instructed students in geography and history, reading and composition, algebra and trigonometry, Chinese and Japanese, Hebrew and Bible. Gunther Gassenheimer, a thin, bespectacled German, was Gerd's class teacher and nearly everyone's favorite.

Gerd was not a good student, but some of his classmates astounded their teachers. Hans Eberstark was the star pupil of the Kadoorie School. When Mr. Gassenheimer dictated math problems, Hansi could add the numbers in his head before anyone else finished writing them down. He was rumored to be memorizing the entire *Encyclopaedia Britannica*. But Hansi was also a klutz—he was too uncoordinated to eat lunch with a knife and fork.

The afternoons were set aside for games and for the students to prepare their homework. There were ballroom dancing classes and an after-school club run by Mr. and Mrs. Wilhelm Deman, where students learned trades, played chess and ping-pong, and took music lessons. Meyer taught calisthenics and running and supervised student track meets after school. He also was the school disciplinarian. Whenever students acted up, a few minutes in the schoolyard passing a medicine ball back and forth with Meyer was sufficient punishment. If the students made noise at Friday night services, one look from Meyer was usually enough to quiet them down.[3]

The school covered seven grades, each with an upper and lower division, except for the highest grade. It initially enrolled 380 pupils, but the school population neared 600 when an addition was built in 1940. Nearly all the refugee children were enrolled in school. A few continued to attend the more expensive Shanghai Jewish School in the western end of the settlement on Seymour Road—also partly funded by the Kadoories—along with the Sephardi and Russian Jewish children. In the spring of 1941, Ismar Freysinger, a refugee and former school principal who had taught in Germany for twenty years, opened a smaller elementary and middle school. He hired seven skilled teachers and offered a more religious curriculum. Freysinger competed with the Kadoorie School and eventually enrolled two-hundred pupils.[4]

The Komor Committee also sponsored a kindergarten for young children. Another refugee, Mrs. Alexander, ran her own kindergarten, first in the Wayside camp and later in a private home.

Because many of the refugee children, particularly the Austrians, had little religious training, a group of Orthodox Jews founded an afternoon Talmud Torah religious school. About 120 refugee children were enrolled by 1941. After the Polish refugees arrived, the Orthodox Jews even established a Beth Jacob school for girls and an all-day yeshiva with instructors from the Mir Yeshiva.[5]

The education of the Shanghai refugee children helped isolate them from the harsh conditions that haunted their parents. The teachers and parents created an environment to shield the children as much as possible from poverty, war, and the dangers of Shanghai. The long school day kept them away from the camps and the streets of the city. As the quality of life declined in Hongkew, teachers took extraordinary steps to care for the children. Later in the war, when lunch consisted of a drum of millet from the camp kitchens, Gerd saw an incredibly thin Mr. Gassenheimer serve lunch to all the children, then tip over the drum to scrape out a few spoonsful for himself.

But the Kadoorie School was forced to close in the summer of 1941. It was a major setback for the refugee community. The Shanghai Municipal Council had advised the Jewish community that it was reclaiming the Kinchow Road school building, which originally had been a Chinese school.[6] Kadoorie promised the refugees a new school, however, and began construction that summer on East Yuhang Road, west of the center of Hongkew and next to the site where the refugee community's new synagogue was being built. The school wasn't completed until early in 1942. In the meantime, Mrs. Hartwich tutored some of her pupils, including Gerd, at her home that fall and winter.

There were even fewer resources to protect the older children. The refugee schools ended their education at age fourteen. Children who had graduated, or who had finished school before they came to Shanghai, often languished in the camps, unable to find work or afford further education. At first, the only other option was a workshop for girls at the Kinchow camp, run by Mrs. Kann. About sixty girls made knitted goods, which they sold in a shop in Sassoon Arcades. They even sold some of their goods abroad until the war started. The workshop supported itself. Two new programs started in 1941. The director of the Pingliang Road community center, Mr. Blaut, set up apprentice workshops at the nearby camp. A German engineer taught older children trades and retrained unemployed adults. Eventually, three-hundred students took courses for furniture makers, locksmiths, electricians, and masons.[7] In the fall of 1941, Chaim Rozenbes, a Jewish refugee from Poland, opened a Shanghai branch of ORT. (ORT was founded in Russia and its name was an acronym for "Society for Promotion of Labor" in Russian.[8] Rozenbes had been an ORT board member in Poland.) The ORT's first classes were in electro-fitting, locksmithing, and carpentry and it originally enrolled as many as two-hundred students.

There were other professional schools for the Hongkew community as well. The Asia Seminar was founded in 1940 by a German refugee and amateur Sinologist, Willy Tonn.[9] It offered classes in sixteen Asian languages and a variety of other subjects.[10] In October 1941, the Demans—who had run the club and vocational program at the Kinchow Road school until it closed—opened a business school to teach young people typing, Gregg shorthand, bookkeeping, and other office skills. In the evenings, the school offered courses in Chinese and Japanese.

Although Gerd's life had changed little since he and his family first arrived in June 1939, life was increasingly difficult for his father, mother, brother Benno, and Uncle Sally. After living a week in the Kinchow camp, the dusty public housing with the bunk beds and bedbugs that had made his mother cry, they had moved in with the Wegerzyns, relatives of Uncle Sally. They stayed with the Wegerzyns for a few weeks while Gerd's father, Gustav, looked for houses he could buy with their HICEM checks.*

He found three nice houses on Chaoufoong Road, west of the center of Hongkew. They shared one house with Uncle Sally and rented out the other two, providing them with some income. The houses had the luxury of illegal toilets.

Gerd's mother, Julie, remained depressed about leaving Germany and rarely left the house. Uncle Sally did all the cooking. In the hot summer days, Sally walked around the house wearing only blue boxer shorts. Gustav looked for work as a clothes salesman, his occupation until his license was taken away by the Nazis, but, like most refugees, he couldn't find a job.

That summer, Sally decided to open his own business and invited Gustav to join him. He rented a shop at the end of Chaoufoong Road where it crossed Broadway, near the circle called the Diledgow where the trolley cars turned around and headed back to the city. Sally planned to manufacture and sell chairs and other furniture. In Berlin, he had invented an upholstered chair that folded out into a bed.

Sally's chair became a popular item for refugees living in the tiny lane houses in Hongkew who needed an extra place to sleep. Gustav's and Sally's confidence in the business grew when they signed a contract with the Silk Hat nightclub to manufacture all of their upholstered furniture.

Benno, Gerd's brother, worked with his father and uncle for

* Under the system of extraterritoriality in Shanghai, foreigners technically could not buy property. The title deeds for property they purchased were registered in the foreign consulates. See Feuerwerker in *The Cambridge History of China*, vol. 12, p. 131.

several months, but he couldn't get along with eccentric Uncle Sally. So Benno started his own business, offering to wash windows for other businesses in Hongkew on a monthly contract. It was a big success in the grimy, dusty city. Benno became well-known throughout the community, and his easy-going manner made him one of the most popular refugees.

Gerd's blond hair and cute smile made him popular, too. The Booths, a Christian family with a home in the Shanghai countryside, used to invite him to visit on weekends and play in their grassy back yard. The Booths reminded Gerd of his neighbors in Berlin who took him to the beach on weekends. But after Mrs. Booth asked the Heimanns if she could adopt their little boy, Gerd's parents refused to let him visit them again.

For Gerd, Hongkew seemed like one big, extended family. Since they first arrived, his father had helped most of his uncles, aunts, and cousins from Germany come to Shanghai with the permits he got when he worked at the electioneering office. Even his mother's uncle Walter—everyone called him Rabbi Dr. Silberstein—had arrived and was preparing Gerd for his bar mitzvah. The last to come were the Keibels, Uncle Adolf and his father's sister Thekla, who traveled on the Trans-Siberian railway in the fall of 1940. Yet Uncle Adolf always complained about Shanghai and refused to talk to Gerd's father, blaming him for forcing them to leave Berlin and come to this crowded, horrible city.

Gerd still thought of Shanghai as a kingdom of excitement. With school closed in the fall and winter of 1941, Gerd had even more time to wander around the city and play games with his European friends. He hadn't learned to speak Chinese (other than a few choice swear words) and didn't have much contact with the Chinese children who lived around him in Hongkew. Gerd tore around town on his whiproller, stopping by the docks to see the last of the U.S. marines leave the city. He explored the downtown shops and watched the *stoffneppers*—material sellers—walk into the exclusive offices and banks, flattering and bargaining with executives who bought their fake English lambswool for suits. The *stoffneppers* liked to celebrate their sales with sodas at a chocolate shop on

Nanking Road, and they usually would buy something for Gerd, too. Gerd hadn't thought much about a career, but he knew he wanted an easy job, just like the *stoffneppers*.

On the morning of December 8, as Gerd headed for his lessons at Mrs. Hartwich's house, the streets were strangely quiet. All the businesses in Hongkew were shuttered and there was hardly anyone outside. Many refugees had been awakened by the Japanese attack on the British gunboat in the Whangpoo and word was spreading about Pearl Harbor. Japanese soldiers were parading through the downtown streets; there were rumors that they had set up a machine gun nest on top of the Ward Road jail. But Gerd hadn't been worried until he saw the empty streets and stores in Hongkew. Then, just like the day after *Kristallnacht*, he became afraid and uncertain and returned home.

The Japanese takeover had little immediate impact on most of the refugees. Some lost their jobs when the Japanese closed some British and American factories. But others continued work in the factories the Japanese had taken over to produce goods for their war effort. Many small businesses in Hongkew survived, although some were forced to close by the inflation that followed the beginning of the Pacific war and the takeover of the foreign banks.

One of the businesses that suffered was Uncle Sally and Gustav's upholstery store. A few weeks after the Japanese takeover, they were no longer able to pay their Chinese workers and they closed the business. Sally then spent most of his time at home and Gustav joined Benno in the window-washing business. Not long after he started, Gustav landed his first big contract—he was hired to wash the hundreds of windows at the new East Yuhang Road School after it opened January 2. Gerd, however, was hardly pleased. It meant an end to his acting out at school—his father would be there watching him almost every day.

The windows were easier to wash now that the Shanghai air was finally clear. Some industries had closed, and the shortage of fuel had forced most buses, cars, and trucks off the streets.[11] But little else had changed. American movies were still being shown in the local theaters, preceded by Japanese propaganda films. Most shops reopened quickly the day after Pearl Harbor, and the Hongkew merchants quickly learned that almost anything—chocolate, caffeine, butter—could be had for a price. Chinese-owned warehouses around the city were well stocked with even the most exotic foreign goods, available in the black market throughout the war. Hoarding became one of the major new industries in Shanghai. Flints and tins of kerosene were among the most valued commodities. Even Gerd's Zionist Betar group continued to meet, although the Japanese had declared it illegal. Betar established elaborate communication networks, relaying messages and calling secret meetings, despite the risks. Gerd enjoyed the adventure—it was almost like being in the underground. At home, he helped his parents keep track of the new war. The Heimann house now had a map of the Pacific on the wall, and pins marked the progress of Japanese and American forces.

Although the Japanese showed little interest in the refugees, they began interrogating and arresting journalists and foreign nationals soon after the war began. Captain Inuzuka had a particular score to settle with the leaders of the Sephardic community, most of them British subjects. He had not forgotten their refusal to send messages to the United States in support of the Japanese and their lack of cooperation in controlling the refugee community.

Early in January, the Japanese began to question some of the wealthier Sephardis, including Horace Kadoorie and Ellis Hayim. A short time after the new East Yuhang Road School opened in January, they arrested Kadoorie.

When Mrs. Hartwich learned of his arrest, she decided to act on behalf of her school's friend and benefactor before the Japanese could occupy the Marble Hall. She gathered a small group of students after school, including Gerd, and brought them to the settlement in a van she had somehow commandeered. When they got to the Marble Hall, she and the students scurried through the mansion, pulling knickknacks and silver from the shelves and mantels and collecting them in the suitcases she had brought. It all happened so fast, Gerd forgot to look for the giant ballroom. Then they reboarded the van and headed back to their new school. Mrs. Hartwich brought the suitcases to one of the groundskeepers. He waited until after sunset to bury the valuables in the yard behind the school.

12

The Rosh Hashanah Plot

In April 1941, Colonel Josef Meisinger was named German police attache in Tokyo, the chief representative of the Gestapo in the Far East. Meisinger first had worked for the Gestapo in Berlin, investigating and arresting homosexuals. After the Nazi conquest of Poland, he established the Warsaw ghetto and became known as the "Butcher of Warsaw" for reportedly ordering the execution of 16,000 Jews.[1]

In the Far East, Meisinger controlled a network of spies and double agents. He was a corpulent, bald man, described by one journalist as "a grinning, swashbuckling, donkey-faced scoundrel."[2] For Germans living in Japan and China, he was the most feared man in Asia.

The colonel visited Shanghai frequently and established undercover agents throughout the city, ranging from the legendary Richard Sorge to the bizarre Trebitsch Lincoln. Sorge was a German double agent who was later executed by the Japanese on charges of spying for the Soviets.[3] Lincoln was a Hungarian-born Jew who once had served as a member of the British Parliament, later joined a Buddhist monastery in

China, and became a Nazi spy during the war. In May 1941, Lincoln nearly convinced Meisinger to grant him an audience with Hitler where, he vowed, he would make three wise men from Tibet step out of the wall and appear before the Führer.[4] Meisinger's faith in Trebitsch Lincoln damaged his already limited credibility with the Nazis in Berlin. It did little to diminish his dreaded reputation in the Far East.

After Pearl Harbor, Meisinger and the Gestapo stepped up pressure on the Japanese to take action against disloyal Germans and the Jewish refugees in Shanghai. But the Japanese were suspicious of the Gestapo and had lost all trust in Meisinger after the Sorge affair. (Legally, the Gestapo had no real authority over the former German Jews because their government had stripped Jews of their German nationality in November 1941.) Some Jewish refugees, however, saw Meisinger's influence everywhere, including in the Japanese decision in June 1942 to replace Captain Inuzuka with officials less sympathetic to the Jews and in the anti-Semitic articles that appeared in the local Chinese press. (Much of the anti-Semitic propaganda actually was fomented by White Russians.[5]) In the Shanghai Jewish community, where Meisinger had planted a number of spies and collaborators, *bonkes* (rumors) spread that the Gestapo was planning strict new measures against the Jews.

With some Jewish leaders in jail early in 1942, the Japanese approved a new committee to administer relief for the Jewish refugees. It included Speelman and Hayim, from the former Sephardic committee; two representatives from the Russian Jewish community, Boris Topaz and G. Shifrin; Felix Kardegg, the new president of the Jüdische Gemeinde; Fritz Kauffmann, a German-Jewish businessman who had been working in Shanghai since 1931; and Robert Peritz, who had worked for the Japanese on the Electioneering Association and now headed the International (formerly Komor) Committee. (Peritz had replaced Paul Komor after Komor was arrested in February.[6])

The new committee met regularly at the Shanghai Jewish Club on Bubbling Well Road. But late in July, the committee members were suddenly called to an emergency meeting in

Hayim's office. Mitsugu Shibata, who had worked at the Japanese foreign ministry and under Inuzuka, was there to meet with them.[7] Kauffmann discussed the meeting in a speech years later:

> We knew him [Shibata] well and were aware of his sympathies for our problems. . . . He was pro-American and against the war. He told us an unbelievable and frightening story. The day before, [the Japanese], under pressure from the Gestapo, had resolved to "liquidate" *all* Jews in Shanghai, not only the new arrivals. They had not yet decided in what manner this was to be accomplished. Some had suggested that all of the approximately 40,000 Jews should be loaded into old ships which then should be sunk in the open sea; others felt it would be preferable to transport us to the uninhabited island of Tsungming, in the Yangtze estuary, and starve us to death there.[8]

The action was scheduled for Rosh Hashanah, less than two months away.

> As far as he [Shibata] was concerned, there was only one way to prevent the execution of their plans. We had to get access to higher authorities, to the general who had the high command of central China, to the admirals of the marines in Shanghai and to the right people in the foreign ministry in Tokyo.[9]

Kauffmann and the other committee members were astounded by Shibata's warning and frightened for their own safety. The Sephardic and Russian Jews' earlier reluctance to assist the refugees had vanished. The committee members immediately went to work, secretly contacting people they knew who had influence with high-ranking Japanese officials.[10]

————————

In the months since Pearl Harbor, the living conditions for the Jewish refugees, particularly those living in the camps, had deteriorated badly. For the week following December 8, the two JDC officials in Shanghai, Laura Margolis and Manny Siegel, were confined to their rooms at the Cathay Hotel. With only limited JDC funds left and further assistance cut off during wartime, the refugees' bread ration was cut to six ounces and they were served only one free meal a day—a small bowl of soup—for the rest of December. The five-hundred refugee employees of the relief committee were notified that they would probably lose their jobs after January 1, adding another five-hundred to the relief rolls.[11]

In mid-December, Margolis and Siegel met with Captain Inuzuka, who had taken over Sir Victor Sassoon's penthouse at their hotel.

He helped them release funds then frozen in a local bank, providing enough money to feed the refugees for another six days. Inuzuka also authorized them to use the JDC's promissory note, which they had received early in December, to borrow $180,000 from local Jews.[12]

As the JDC representatives searched for wealthy residents who could underwrite the note, the Jewish Community published a notice in *The Shanghai Jewish Chronicle*:

PROCLAMATION TO ALL JEWISH MEN AND WOMEN IN SHANGHAI.

In this serious hour the Jüdische Gemeinde issues an appeal for help to you. A terrible calamity has reached a great number of the Immigrants. The public has already been notified that the help from the Joint in America has at present ceased. Hunger and disease threaten many of our brothers and sisters. Everything must be done to come to their aid as quickly as possible. We therefore request all Jews to declare their solidarity with the sufferers. To bring immediate aid the Jüdische Gemeinde requests:

1. Every family which does its own cooking shall daily give one main meal to at least one needy person.

2. Families which do not do their own cooking shall pay a sum of $30 (thirty) monthly instead.

3. Restaurant, coffee house and bar owners shall charge a 10% surtax on all bills, which shall go to the assistance funds of the Jüdische Gemeinde.

4. Provision stores shall also collect a 5% surtax on their goods.

5. It is the duty of every wealthy Jew to come to the

immediate assistance of his fellow Jews by contributing a generous sum.

All those to whom this proclamation applies are requested to get in touch personally, by letter or by phone, with the Jüdische Gemeinde (805 East Seward Road, Tel. 50192) without any loss of time.

COMMITTEE OF REPRESENTATIVES OF THE JÜDISCHE GEMEINDE.

Shanghai, January 11, 1942.[13]

The appeal produced only enough funds to continue feeding the refugees for another six days. In mid-January, the number of people receiving free meals was cut in half, from 8,000 to 4,000, leaving only children, the elderly, the sick, and the poorest refugees on assistance. The relief money was virtually exhausted. Appeals to the wealthy leaders of the Sephardic community—some of whom had been detained by the Japanese—had produced almost nothing. Wealthy Russian Jews refused to contribute unless the Polish Jews continued to receive more assistance than the Germans and Austrians. Margolis and Siegel reluctantly agreed to set aside one-sixth of their funds for the 1,000 Polish refugees, leaving the remaining five-sixths for the 18,000 others.[14]

By January 15, the situation looked desperate. Margolis granted an interview to a reporter for the *Shanghai Times*, now under Japanese control, to describe the refugees' plight. The next day, the paper published a detailed account of the malnutrition, starvation, and terrible housing and medical conditions. The publicity enraged Japanese officials, who at one point threatened Margolis and Siegel with arrest. But the article produced results. Local radio stations broadcast appeals for funds, and small donations began to pour in.[15]

By the end of April, Margolis and Siegel had raised nearly $180,000, covering most of the JDC note. The Jüdische Gemeinde's sponsorships (*patenschaften*) had provided support for dozens of other refugees. A small group of Russian Jews had broken with their community and set up a committee to feed five-hundred German and Austrian refugee children.[16]

But there was more bad news in May. A cable via South

America relayed word that the JDC was cutting off all contact, even indirectly, with Shanghai, to comply with U.S. Treasury Department rulings under the amended Trading with the Enemy Act.[17] Although HICEM and Va'ad Hahatzalah continued to send money to the Polish Jews in Shanghai through Switzerland and other neutral countries, the JDC would not circumvent U.S. policy.[18] Therefore, no more JDC funds, promissory notes, or even telegrams would be sent to Shanghai. The remaining money would run out in September.

In June, Margolis and Siegel decided to close the two refugee hospitals to save money. They fired the doctors and nurses and transferred patients to the Shanghai General Hospital. They also sent cables seeking aid from Sweden, Turkey, Portugal, and Switzerland.[19] That summer brought the worst conditions since the refugees had arrived in Shanghai. Weakened by malnutrition, hundreds of refugees were infected by a typhoid epidemic; a heat wave killed sixteen people on just one day in August.[20] The death rate was double that of the previous year.[21]

In July, Margolis and Siegel resigned from the relief committee, continuing as advisors but leaving the administrative duties to Lutz Wachsner and other refugees they had trained. They expected that they, along with other foreign nationals, would either be repatriated on neutral ships leaving Shanghai or interned in camps within the next few months. Shortly after their resignations, Peritz came to Margolis and Siegel with the remarkable story Shibata had told at the emergency meeting of the Jewish leaders. Peritz asked them to cable the United States for help.[22]

The two JDC representatives didn't trust Peritz or Shibata. They knew Peritz had an unsavory reputation and that he and Shibata had worked together in a racket in 1939–1940 selling Japanese landing permits to refugees. (Shibata also was in trouble with Japanese army officials for helping Topaz split with the White Russian Jews and set up a Jewish Chamber of

Commerce.[23]) At any rate, it would have been impossible, under the wartime restrictions, for them to contact the United States. They chose to wait.[24]

But Kauffmann and the other committee members had taken action. The Russian Jews contacted a Japanese general they had known from Harbin and officials at the Foreign Ministry in Tokyo. Peritz was assigned to talk with Japanese officers he had worked with in the Electioneering Association.[25]

No one on the committee knew anyone among the powerful Japanese military police (*kempetai*). But Kauffmann had worked with a Mr. C. Brahn, another German-Jewish businessman. Brahn knew a Japanese woman, Mrs. Nogami, who worked as an interpreter for the *kempetai* and had intervened when the police threatened to arrest Margolis and Siegel in January because of the publicity in the *Shanghai Times*.[26]

Kauffmann warned Brahn not to reveal that Shibata had told them of the secret Japanese plans because Shibata could be arrested and tried for treason. He suggested Brahn tell the *kempetai* that Jewish leaders were concerned about the recent anti-Semitic propaganda in the press and feared it could lead to actions against the Jews.[27]

But Brahn folded quickly when questioned by the *kempetai*. Two days later, with August temperatures well over one-hundred degrees, Kauffmann was arrested at his home by two *kempetai* officers and taken to the Bridge House. Kauffmann was interrogated for more than two hours, but stuck with the story he and Brahn had agreed upon; he did not mention Shibata or the emergency committee meeting.[28]

Kauffmann was held in a cell with four other prisoners. The next day, he discovered that all six members of the committee, as well as Shibata, were being held at the Bridge House. They were interrogated separately over the next few days. Speelman was the first to be freed, apparently through the help of a Vichy police commander from the French Concession. Two weeks later, Hayim was released as part of an exchange on the Swedish ship *Gripsholm*.[29]

When he was interrogated again after eighteen days, Kauffmann told the Japanese the real story; he explained the committee had been trying to protect the Jews against the planned actions. The *kempetai* officers strongly denied that the Japanese had plans to harm the Jews. They finally freed Kauffmann two weeks later when he admitted "spreading false rumors" and signed a statement that he would not discuss his treatment or interrogation with anyone.[30]

All of the other Jewish leaders, except for the two Russians, already had been released. Shibata was accused of being a traitor and deported to Japan. The Russians were freed a few days after Kauffmann but, a week later, Topaz, the head of the Russian Jewish Community who had worked with Shibata to establish the Jewish Chamber of Commerce, was imprisoned again. He was accused of being an American, British, and Soviet spy.[31]

Topaz was held in the Bridge House and tortured for more than eight and a half months. He later claimed that Peritz—along with a White Russian named Eugene Pick (alias Hovans), a notorious spy, murderer, forger, and extortionist whom the Japanese had released from prison after Pearl Harbor—had demanded ownership of a pawn shop Topaz owned in Hongkew. When he refused, Topaz said, they had him arrested.[32]

While Peritz was in prison that summer, several refugees formed a new relief organization they called the Kitchen Fund. Its first goal was to purchase used steam boilers and build a new, cost-efficient kitchen for feeding the refugees. They planned to raise the money through a *patenschaft* (sponsorship) campaign. Margolis and Siegel also opened secret negotiations to borrow up to $210,000 from local Russian businessmen—despite the fact that they could not guarantee the JDC would repay it—and turn it over to the Kitchen Fund to feed and house the refugees.[33]

The new kitchen was opened in December 1942, at a ceremony attended by Japanese officials. A month later, the Japanese arrested Siegel and interned him on Putong with other foreign nationals. Margolis was interned in a camp in Chapei a few weeks later.[34]

In January 1943, the *Gripsholm*, carrying freed prisoners from Shanghai, arrived in New York. One of the repatriated passengers—the name was deleted from the report—was interviewed by the U.S. Office of Naval Intelligence. The passenger talked knowledgeably about the condition of the Jewish refugees in Shanghai, but made no mention of the Rosh Hashanah plot. He stated that:

> a vice-consul of the Japanese consulate, named Shibata, [had] approached several wealthy Jewish residents of Shanghai and induced them to give him large sums of money, ostensibly for the relief of Jewish refugees. It was later discovered that his action was unauthorized by the Japanese authorities and that he had pocketed the money.[35]

The Rosh Hashanah plot, it appears, was part of a scheme by Peritz and Shibata that had spun out of their control. But like all *bonkes*, it started with a kernel of truth. The Japanese military had discussed measures for dealing with the Jews at a July meeting. The only proposal they seem to have discussed seriously, however, was to isolate the Jews in Hongkew, not to kill them.

They prepared to act on that proposal early in 1943. The Jews of Shanghai, like their brethren in Poland, were about to be herded into a ghetto.

IV
GHETTO
(1943–1944)

13

Kantorowsky

They were eating stew and millet again for lunch, but Eva thought the millet tasted musty. Bob's mother had worked hard to cook the meal over their stove—it was actually more like an upside-down flowerpot—heated by the weak embers of small, round briquettes made mostly of mud and straw. She had fashioned the stew from a cow's spleen and covered it with lots of onion gravy to overcome the taste. But there wasn't much she could do with the millet her husband had bought on sale at the Chusan Road market. It apparently had been stored in a damp warehouse and was discolored from mildew. Neither Eva nor her in-laws could afford to let food go to waste, however, so they ate without complaining. Whatever bargains Bob's father brought home—moldy millet, cracked wheat, half-frozen sweet potatoes, even the nearly inedible free food from the Kitchen Fund—they would eat, as the Germans would say, until it grew from their throats.

Most of the Jewish refugees in Hongkew had similar diets in the summer of 1943 and, as usual, they found humor in their misfortune. They liked to say that the Jews have a blessing

171

before eating food that grows from the ground and another blessing before eating food that grows from a tree. But what, they would ask, is the blessing for food that grows from the throat?[1]

(The dark humor sometimes got refugees in trouble. Comedian Herbert Zernik was nearly arrested after a performance at the Chaoufoong camp that spring for parroting the way Japanese soldiers searched pedestrians and for announcing that Adolf Hitler Square in Berlin had been renamed Stalin Square.[2])

Eva and her new husband walked to his parents' house every afternoon for tiffin, their big meal of the day. As bad as the food was, it was better than anything they had at home. For breakfast, they usually ate gruel, a mixture of water, flour, and sugar stirred in their small electric cooker. They washed it down with green tea; coffee was too expensive on Bob's small salary. If they ate in the evening, it would be a piece of bread, often dry and moldy, spread with lard Bob's mother had cooked or some of the strange-tasting margarine manufactured in Hongkew. A piece of cheese, or a slice of one of the shriveled salamis hanging over the door, was an occasional treat.

Bob and Eva lived in his aunt's lane house on Kinchow Road, similar to the houses in which most of the refugees now lived in the alleys of Hongkew. Most of the lane houses had thin wooden doors on the outside, leading to an alcove. A second door led to the living quarters, a cramped series of small rooms joined by narrow staircases. The housing conditions in Hongkew were so crowded that many refugees—including Bob and Eva—lived in the tiny concrete rooms that housed the electric meters.

The lanes veered off nearly every street in Hongkew—Chusan, Ward, Tongshan, Alcock, Dalny, and others—and many of them connected to other lanes. They were like little communities of their own, where there were few secrets and almost no privacy. Some lanes were occupied entirely by Chinese, others by the refugees. The Chinese and refugees lived in a few of the lanes together (some of the refugee children became fluent in Shanghai-dialect curses), but the

Chinese and foreigners mostly maintained the tradition of polite separation.

In the oppressive summer heat and humidity, it seemed impossible to breathe inside the houses, where mold and mildew grew on food, clothes, linens, and shoes and inside closets and chests. Few people could use fans because electricity was strictly rationed. The ubiquitous insects and mosquitoes added to the discomfort. In the evenings, nearly everyone moved outside into the lanes, where they played cards, gossiped, cooked, ate, and even slept. Men walked around in boxer shorts with sweat towels around their necks; most women wore only bras and panties, a few of them arousing sexual fantasies among some of the boys. The children seemed oblivious to the heat, running wildly through the lanes.

Bob and Eva's tiny concrete meter room was halfway up the stairs from the first floor. It normally was used as a bathroom or kitchen and had two small windows. There was barely enough space for their small brass bed, a portable wardrobe closet, a washbasin attached to the wall, a tiny table, and two stools. For privacy, they usually closed the window to Bob's aunt's room when they made love. They washed and bathed from the cold water tap over the basin and used a bucket in the room downstairs as a toilet. Every day, Eva carried their thermos to the water shop down the lane, where she used bamboo tokens to purchase hot water for drinking. (The water sellers used bamboo sticks as currency since small coins had disappeared because of inflation.)

The conditions were depressing, particularly for Germans used to cleanliness and hearty foods. Eva suffered from intestinal problems caused by the recurring dysentery she first contracted on the train ride across Russia; it was aggravated by parasites and her poor diet. Twice, upset when she feared she might be pregnant, she went to see a doctor she had known from Berlin who put her on a regimen of vodka and quinine to abort the pregnancy. It made her terribly weak and sick, but Eva and Bob knew they couldn't raise a child under these conditions.

They had only to walk down Ward or Alcock or Seward

roads to see others, living in the camps, who were worse off. Refugees who had once been distinguished lawyers and academics now held out tin cups to beg for money or food. They had sold all their possessions and burned their lice-infested clothes. Some wore outfits made from jute flour bags. Women who had worked as bar girls now openly solicited customers as prostitutes. Some twenty mothers even sold their newborn babies to raise money for food.[3] Several babies froze to death that winter in the refugee hospital's maternity ward.

The year after Pearl Harbor had been difficult, but conditions this year were much worse. Since the Japanese proclamation in February 1943 that required all the refugees to live in a designated area in Hongkew, nearly everyone suffered under poor living conditions and malnutrition. But Bob and Eva, young and in love, were rarely depressed. They lived to enjoy each new day with each other.

After the war in the Pacific had started, Eva had been laid off by Meyer Birman and the Far Eastern Jewish Information Bureau. She hadn't been happy there and enjoyed her free time. But by the spring of 1942, she had found a job with Robert Peritz, now head of the International Committee. Peritz was active in founding the Kitchen Fund, a refugee group that raised money for the new kitchen on East Seward Road and took over many of the relief activities at the end of that summer. Eva answered his telephone, wrote letters for him, and even went on temporary assignment with his friend Shibata at the Manchurian consulate. She sensed that Peritz had influence and was involved in a variety of schemes. But she didn't ask many questions, even when Peritz was sent to the Bridge House and Shibata was deported in August 1942 over their role in the Rosh Hashanah plot.

Eva maintained Peritz's confidence until the beginning of 1943. But Peritz was having an affair and he mistakenly suspected that Eva was reporting to his wife. Peritz fired her in January 1943.

By then, she had convinced her parents to let her marry

Bob Angress. He was the young man from Breslau she had met two years earlier when her parents took her to Uncle Hugo's gatherings of refugees from Upper Silesia. They had dated off and on for those two years, going to coffee houses and movies. Her parents were worried about Bob's disability—he walked with a limp and his left arm was slightly shorter than his right, impairing the movement of his left hand. The disability apparently was caused at birth, although Eva's parents feared it was genetic and even sent her to a doctor who tried to discourage her from marrying him. Yet her mother eventually gave in and won over her father. A dressmaker fashioned Eva's wedding gown from the dining room curtains her mother had brought from Berlin. Her father and three other rabbis from the Jüdische Gemeinde officiated at the ceremony. It was held in the new Kadoorie School on a miserably cold last day of January. The stove wasn't working and the guests shivered through the wedding dinner. But the newlyweds were happy.

Eva and Bob found a nice, small room in a lane house on Dent Road, in a fairly new complex of buildings where Eva's parents also lived. Two weeks after they moved in, they heard an announcement over their radio. They were stunned to hear the Japanese army and navy commanders proclaiming restrictions for the "stateless refugees":

> Due to military necessity, places of residence and business of the stateless refugees in the Shanghai area shall hereafter be restricted to the undermentioned area in the International Settlement. East of the line connecting Chaoufoong Road, Muirhead Road and Dent Road; west of Yangtzepoo Creek; north of the line connecting East Seward Road and Wayside Road; and south of the boundary of the International Settlement.
>
> The stateless refugees at present residing and/or carrying on business in the district other than the above area shall remove their places of residence and/or business into the area designated above by May 18, 1943. . . .
>
> Persons who will have violated this proclamation or obstructed its reenforcement shall be liable to severe punishment.[4]

Their new apartment was on the border of the designated area, but on the wrong side of Dent Road. With almost no money, the newlyweds would have to find another place to live.

An article in the *Shanghai Herald* defined the terms of the proclamation. "Stateless refugee" meant people who had arrived in Shanghai "since 1937 from Germany (including former Austria, Czecho-Slovakia), Hungary, former Poland, Latvia, Lithuania and Estonia, etc. who have no nationality at present." That definition covered almost all of the 20,000 refugees, the last of whom had arrived from Japan just before Pearl Harbor. It excluded most of the Russian and Polish Ashkenazi Jews who had preceded them to Shanghai.[5]

Refugees with jobs outside the designated area could be granted temporary permission to leave during working hours. Chinese who lived inside the area were encouraged to move outside to make room for the refugees.[6]

The Japanese claimed the proclamation was "motivated by military necessity" and was not intended as a form of oppression. "It is even contemplated to safeguard, so far as possible, their place of residence as well as their livelihood in the designated area," the military leaders announced. They were careful not to use either the word Jew or ghetto in their statement.[7]

The Japanese security concerns may have been affected by reports of black marketeering and other suspicious activities. Their main source of information was the Shanghai Municipal Police special branch, a unit dominated by anti-Semitic White Russians after all the British detectives had been interned. The police records report on a riot at a public meeting of refugees to discuss relief programs and on nuisances created by Jewish beggars. In addition, Japanese naval intelligence relied on reports from Pick Hovans, the White Russian ex-convict who had tried to extort money from Topaz and others, for information on the refugees. Hovans strongly advocated more controls over the Jews in Shanghai. Local newspapers also fed Japanese fears. Just two days before the proclamation, the *Shanghai Times* published a major story headlined: "Shanghai,

Hunting Ground of Thriving Jewish Racketeers: Prominent but Shady Part Played by Unscrupulous Jews in City's Economic Life and Development."[8]

Most refugees were shocked by the proclamation and not comforted by Japanese assurances. It meant an end to the relative freedom they had enjoyed and raised horrifying memories of centuries of oppression against the Jews and of enforced segregation, from Venice in 1515 to Lodz and Warsaw in 1940. There was added terror for the thousands of refugees who had been imprisoned in Dachau, Sachsenhausen, and Buchenwald and those whose families had been resettled in Poland. Was the proclamation to be only the first step?[9] Many refugees saw the influence of Meisinger and the Gestapo in the proclamation, although there is little evidence of this.

Beyond the psychological impact, the proclamation meant that about half of about 16,000 refugees who had registered with the Japanese would have to move within three months from their houses and apartments in the French Concession, International Settlement, Western District, and parts of Hongkew outside the designated area.[10] The biggest adjustment came for the 3,000 refugees who lived in the French Concession and International Settlement, most of whom lived in nice apartments and some of whom had tried to hide the fact that they were refugees.[11]

The exchange of apartments proved costly. Agents charged excessive rents for apartments and demanded large sums of key money, an illegal payment to a landlord for transferring a lease.[12] Few refugees could afford such sums. The proclamation also divided some families. Several non-Jewish German women who had come to Shanghai with their Jewish husbands registered at the German consulate so that they were exempt from the segregation order and eligible for German relief assistance, which they shared with their husbands.[13]

Yet for most refugees already living in the designated area, the proclamation had little immediate impact on their lives. Hongkew had been a de facto segregated area for years. In some ways, it strengthened their sense of community.[14] But the one-square mile area was badly overcrowded—100,000 Chinese as well as 8,000 refugees already lived there[15]—and had some of the poorest housing in the city. Shoddy lane houses built for three or four people now were crowded with ten or twelve.

Following the proclamation, the Japanese also began to supervise relief programs for the refugees. It proved to be a highly lucrative area for some officials, who extorted money from Russian Jews who were not affected by the segregation. On February 23, five days after the proclamation was announced, T. Kubota, the Japanese official in charge of organizing the relocation of the refugees, met at the Jewish Club with members of the Russian Jewish community. He appealed for their help in housing and feeding the refugees. The Russians were the only available source of Jewish philanthropy now that most of the wealthy Sephardic Jews were being held in Japanese internment camps.

The Japanese officials, who had dealt angrily with the pro-British Sephardic Jews, were curiously solicitous to the Russians. At the time, the Japanese government was exercising extreme care not to alienate the Soviet Union, which had remained neutral in the Pacific war. A number of Russian Jews, including some professed anticommunists, had recognized this and registered with the Soviet consulate in order to help protect them from the Japanese. (The Russians' affliation with the Soviets later made it virtually impossible for most of them to emigrate to the United States after the end of the war.)

But the Japanese held the threat of segregation over the Russian Jews and convinced them to form an aid organization, staffed by refugees, that was known as SACRA, the Shanghai Ashkenazi Collaborating Relief Association.[16] SACRA drove even deeper divisions between the Russian and refugee community. The refugees viewed the Russians as traitors, and many believed the ghetto proclamation was part of a conspiracy between the Japanese and Russians. The Russians saw their work for SACRA as a thankless task. Many continued to have little to do with the refugees and remained reluctant to provide relief. But the Russians agreed to finance some of the refugee resettlement costs, paid bribes to buy houses from Japanese inside the ghetto, and provided loans and "contributions" to a number of Japanese officials. In effect, the Russians were paying for the privilege of remaining outside the ghetto, although they still did very little to assist the refugees.[17]

Without money for a down payment, Bob and Eva couldn't afford a new apartment and were forced to move in with his aunt. After the proclamation, his aunt had exchanged her house outside the designated area for three small lane houses on Kinchow Road. Eva's parents also had to move and were given housing in a building taken over by SACRA.

Bob kept his job with a Russian firm in the International Settlement, a textile company that had been a subsidiary of a British firm before the war. Later that summer, he was able to get passes to leave the ghetto for work. Eva read, listened to the radio, and visited with their Viennese neighbors. She also looked after Bob's aunt, who had been virtually starving to death until they convinced her to come with them to tiffin at Bob's parents'.

Eva tried to remain cheerful. But just after they moved to Kinchow Road in the spring of 1943, she received a brief letter from her brother Hans via the Red Cross. It was the first time she had heard from him in months and the last letter she would receive. He had been back in Berlin, he wrote, and now was probably on his way to their father's old *heimat* (neighborhood). Eva understood the message—Hans was being deported to Poland. But he was going even farther east than his father's native town of Loslau, to the Polish village of Oswiecim. The Germans called it Auschwitz.

Other refugees in Shanghai were receiving similar messages. By the summer, nearly all of them had lost contact with their relatives in Eastern Europe. In July 1943, the Far Eastern Jewish Information Bureau in Shanghai sent an appeal to a Jewish refugee agency in Portugal:

Dear Sirs,
    During the last time we have begun receiving for our numerous applicants here replies of the International Red Cross Committee from various parts of occupied Poland—mostly from

the regions of Lublin, Radom, Kielce, Warsaw, also from the Baltic countries and occupied Soviet Poland. The replies are all the same, vis. that the relatives (respectively, parents, children, brothers, sisters, wives, etc.) are no longer under the given addresses and [have] left for unknown destinations. As to Litzmannstadt, formerly Lodz, replies are received that there is no mail connection with the ghetto, i.e. enquiries are sent back to us.

Such replies naturally cause acute mental anguish to the enquirers, and they constantly appeal to us asking to take further steps in order to trace their near of kin. Unfortunately, being so far away from European centres and for that reason not [aware] of the true state of affairs in East European ghettoes, we do not know what to undertake. Generally, we ask the applicants to give us several addresses of relatives in the same place and direct an enquiry to the I.R.O. Geneva for further investigation. But it is doubtful whether the relatives are still there and whether they would be able to give to the I.R.O. the information desired. Tracers are also directed by us to our affiliated organization in Stockholm, Zurich, Geneva, etc.

By the present we beg to apply to your esteemed organization with a request to inform us of the following—should you find it possible and convenient for you, naturally:

1. Whether Jewish residents were deported from the small cities of Lublin, Radom, Kielce and other regions of Poland, and if so where? We mean the constant residents of these places as well as those who in its time were deported there from Central Europe.

2. Do *"Jüdenrats"* exist (or similar Jewish organizations) in the occupied regions, and if so, is it possible to get in touch with them through neutral countries, i.e. whether tracers could be addressed to them.

3. Is there any possibility of sending any individual assistance there through neutral countries?

We are well aware that all the questions raised by us are extremely complicated at the present moment, and are not very hopeful, therefore. But the desire to know whether there is a possibility of helping our applicants at present, as well as the desire to know more about the situation in Europe, has prompted us to apply to you on the matter.[18]

14

Didner

It was still two hours before dawn and, as he walked out onto the dark street near the Bridge House, Sam Didner was having trouble finding his friend Herman Natowic. A few moments ago, Didner had signed a statement certifying that, as of today, July 26, 1943, Natowic was in good health. He hadn't seen Natowic yet, but it was the only way the Japanese would release him. The guards had told Didner he would find Natowic on North Szechuen Road, just across from the Bridge House, the eight-story white apartment building that was now Shanghai's most notorious prison. Yet as he squinted in the dark, Didner couldn't find him. The only person he saw nearby was an emaciated old man sitting in an alleyway. He walked up and down the block a few times but didn't see anyone else.

Didner returned to take a closer look at the old man. He was nearly six feet tall but extremely thin, well under one-hundred pounds, and had long, filthy hair and a red, scraggly beard. His clothes were torn into shreds, and lice were crawling over his skin and through his hair—he seemed like hundreds of other beggars Didner saw on the street every day. But as he leaned in closely, Didner thought he recognized something in the man's bloodshot eyes. He spoke to him in German.

"Herman? Is that you, Herman?"

The man nodded, ever so slightly. Herman Natowic, the burly soccer referee who had weighed nearly two-hundred pounds six months earlier, had been reduced to a half-dead skeleton. Didner tried to help him to his feet, but he could barely stand. So he lifted Natowic onto his shoulder—he seemed to weigh almost nothing—and carried him down North Szechuen Road and east on North Soochow Road, two long blocks to the Shanghai General Hospital.

Didner had Natowic admitted and helped the nurses wash him and put him in a cot. The hospital's nurses were French and Chinese nuns and most were kind and conscientious. But the doctors were White Russians and Didner considered them all incompetent. Two specialists came to see Natowic immediately after his admission and quickly concluded he couldn't survive. They recommended no further treatment. Didner decided to care for Natowic on his own.

He started him on an intravenous glucose and saline solution to build his fluids up, covered his skin sores with dressings, and began a series of blood tests. The results were worse than Didner had thought. Natowic was suffering not only from malnutrition, but also from several of the most virulent diseases known to Shanghai—typhoid, dysentery, beri beri, perhaps others. Maybe the White Russian doctors were right.

In the nearly two years since Pearl Harbor, Didner had seen his most disheartening cases. A severe shortage of drugs meant that even diseases for which there was a known cure could be fatal. One of his patients was a teenage girl with diabetes, whom he had treated for three years. Until the war in the Pacific had started, he had been able to find insulin for her. For a time afterward, Didner had searched for insulin in dozens of pharmacies and even on the black market. What he found often was well beyond its expiration date, but still effective. The supply ran out completely by the end of 1942, however, and Didner admitted her to the General Hospital, hoping that the nurses would have access to some insulin. But the hospital had exhausted its supply. Didner visited the girl every day as she sank into a diabetic coma and then died.

There was little he could do for many other patients, weakened by malnutrition from the meager food in the camps or what little they could afford to buy. Some could barely walk. Almost any disease—it was often pneumonia, but could be dysentery, typhoid, or a host of other diseases—would kill them. Dozens of refugees were dying every month. The only treatment Didner could offer was iron supplements for those suffering from anemia.

He was most upset by the death of Dr. Walter Cohn, another refugee doctor. Cohn was a German physician with an office near Didner's, a kindly young man with a beard who had been affectionately nicknamed Jesus of Stettin. Like Didner, he did house calls on a Brennerabor bicycle and treated patients free of charge. He never had enough to eat and suffered from malnutrition and possibly tuberculosis. Each time Didner saw him, he seemed to have lost more weight. One day early in the summer of 1943, Didner learned Dr. Cohn had died and he bicycled out to his funeral at the Columbia Road cemetery on a rainy morning. There was only one other refugee at the funeral. Didner was overcome with frustration and disgust as he watched the coffin lowered into the grave. Dr. Cohn had killed himself to save the lives of countless refugees, Didner thought, yet only one of them had enough gratitude to see him buried. It was a low point in Didner's years in Shanghai. He left the cemetery deeply depressed.

Didner was still living in the Molners' house, sharing his office with Dr. Molner and getting his meals from his wife. Mrs. Molner always cooked him enough to eat—Didner's favorite meal was a rabbit stew she would make from one of the rabbits she raised in the pen behind the house. He was able to pay her for food and rent with the help of his foreign patients. Didner's British patients had either sailed abroad before Pearl Harbor or, like his friend Canning, had been interned in one of the dozen camps and prisons for foreigners throughout the city. But he still received money from the Swedish consulate for treating Finnish sailors.

He treated his first sailor shortly after the Pacific war began. The sailor, who came to Didner with symptoms of venereal disease, told him that about forty of his fellow sailors had been stranded in Hongkew. The Japanese didn't bother them, but they had been unable to find passage from Shanghai. The sailors had little to do now but drink and sleep with prostitutes and bar girls. Most of them started coming to Didner for treatment, usually for liver and venereal diseases. He submitted bills to the Swedish consulate, which promptly paid him. But he felt sorry for the Finns, who badly wanted to leave yet could find no way out of Shanghai.

Didner had given up his own hope of joining the war with the British army in Australia. But he continued to work for the underground, examining Chinese volunteers before they were sent to Burma. Every few weeks, a young, streetwise Chinese boy would come for him and escort him to a basement room where he would conduct physicals on fifteen or sixteen Chinese recruits, most of them barely teenagers. Didner was discreet about his work, although he had slipped once and mentioned it to a Swede who worked for the consulate. It was a dangerous mistake. The Swede, he soon learned, lived with an Australian mistress who was a radio commentator and a spy for the Japanese. Didner feared she would have him arrested. But the Swede died of typhoid a short time later, before he told his mistress of Didner's work, and Didner was out of danger.

With his busy practice, Didner only occasionally had a chance to see Grete. He always hoped to take her dancing, but never found the time. His only recreation was attending sports events as the unofficial refugee physician. Most of the boxing matches ended after Pearl Harbor, but soccer continued to thrive, even in the ghetto. It was through soccer that Didner met Herman Natowic, a member of the Jewish Recreation Club's executive committee and the top soccer referee in Shanghai.

Natowic was born in Vienna in 1910. He was the second of three children, with an older brother, Joschi, and a younger sister, Mella. Herman always was overshadowed by Joschi. When they were boys, their grandfather would take Joschi to coffee houses and test him in front of the other customers with complex mathematical problems. Herman was quiet and shy and made his friends playing soccer and later as a soccer referee. Both sons worked in the family's soft drink and liquor business in the Twentieth District. But Joschi continued to be known as a genius—he invented a popular soft drink called Vienna Gold—and Herman remained in the background. Herman remained single; Joschi married a beautiful woman named Hella.[1]

It was one of Herman's soccer friends who warned the Natowices and their relatives early in 1939 that they should leave Austria. Joschi already had been beaten up by Nazi thugs, suffering a severe blow to his stomach from a rifle butt, and it wasn't difficult to convince the family to leave. They left for Shanghai from Trieste in February 1939, aboard the *Conte Rosso* with nearly four-hundred others. After they arrived on March 5, they lived in the Embankment Building camp for a short time and then rented a house at 169 Chusan Road. There they established one of the first refugee liquor shops, Elite Liqueur, on the first floor of their home, just across from the Ward Road jail.

It was difficult to find carbonated water, so Joschi couldn't manufacture Vienna Gold in Shanghai. Instead, he copied a popular Vienna apple cider drink called Obi and sold that. The shop also made money by selling distilled water. But it got most of its customers because of Hella. Dozens of men came into the store each day to buy a shot of schnapps at the counter and stare at her as she leaned over the counter to pour a drink, showing off her bosomy figure. The Natowices' father, Salo, who had been bald as long as anyone could remember, perpetually sat on a stool and watched.[2]

Herman may have been obscured in the liquor business, but he was an imposing presence on the soccer field. In his first game as a referee in Shanghai, he penalized Erich Zomma, one of the top Jewish stars, with two yellow cards, ejecting him from the game. But teammate Leo Meyer, the best player in Shanghai, who had played with Zomma in Germany, protested loudly, yelling at Natowic that he had no right to throw Zomma out. Natowic immediately threw Meyer out of the game, too, and was never challenged on the soccer field again.[3]

About a year after the Natowices arrived in Shanghai, Joschi died, apparently as a result of the injuries he sustained from the beating by the Nazis. Herman, Hella, and a salesman named Erich Seidl then ran the store. After Joschi's death, Herman developed a reputation as a tough businessman. He made some enemies, but none could have wished for the fate that befell him.

It began on February 24, 1943, six days after the Japanese had issued the ghetto proclamation. That morning, Herman received a telephone call from a man who said he was an employee of Joe Farren's nightclub on Great Western Road and asked him to bring some liquor samples to the club.[4] Farren was a Viennese dancer who had come to Shanghai after World War I and later opened one of the most popular clubs in the city. Russian dancing girls performed in Farren's ballroom, and he ran a gambling casino upstairs. But he had been in trouble with the Japanese authorities, who apparently wanted a share of his business.[5]

Natowic sent his salesman, Seidl, to see Farren with some samples. But when Seidl arrived at the club, Farren told him that neither he nor any of his employees had called Natowic. Seidl returned to the store and, a short time later, Natowic received another telephone call from the man who had called earlier. This time, he told Natowic to come to a restaurant called Jimmy's Kitchen and pick up an envelope that someone would later retrieve at his store. Natowic thought the request was strange, but he was always eager to please. He went to Jimmy's Kitchen and brought the unopened envelope back to his shop, where he put it under the counter.[6]

Three days later, a Japanese man came to the liquor store at about 3 P.M. to ask Natowic about his prices for cherry brandy. The man said his boss was opening a new store at Haining and North Szechuen roads. He left, then telephoned Natowic about fifteen minutes later and asked him to bring some samples to the new shop. Natowic said he would send someone else, but the man insisted Natowic come himself because he expected to make a large order. Natowic left his store with several bottles.[7]

But the Japanese had blocked the streets, as they often did to search for criminals and black marketeers, and Natowic was unable to get very far. When he returned to the shop, Hella told him the Japanese man had called again five minutes earlier, asking if Natowic had left. Natowic hired a rickshaw and set out again. When he finally reached North Szechuen Road, however, he couldn't find the shop. He called Hella on a pay telephone to tell her. As he was talking to her, the Japanese man who had come to his store earlier that afternoon tapped him on the shoulder. Natowic said goodbye, hung up the telephone, and walked with the man several blocks to a coffee shop.[8]

A group of Japanese soldiers surprised Natowic when he entered the coffee shop. Several of them threatened him and one yelled at him, accusing him of being a spy. Natowic, confused by what was happening, tried to object, but the soldiers beat him with their fists and sticks and forced him into a burlap sack. He was thrown on the back of a truck and driven to the Bridge House, a short ride down North Szechuen Road.[9]

When Natowic's relatives reported him missing, the Shanghai Municipal Police investigated. They learned Seidl also had been missing since earlier that afternoon. The police pieced together an account of the past three days, including Seidl's trip to Farren's and Natowic's visit to Jimmy's Kitchen. One of Natowic's relatives found the envelope that Natowic had left under the counter and turned it over to the police. The police opened it and found a sketch of a thirty-watt radio transmitter. They discovered it had been drawn by Karl Effert, a German engineer who worked for the Japanese *kempetai*. Effert admitted leaving the sketch in an envelope at Jimmy's Kitchen and telephoning Natowic to pick it up, but refused to tell the municipal police anything about Natowic's whereabouts.[10]

That evening, two Japanese *kempetai* officials came to the Wayside Municipal Police station and were asked about the case. Hella was at the station and recognized one of the men as the Japanese who had come to the store to ask about the cherry brandy. The two men acknowledged they were informers for the *kempetai*.[11]

The municipal police handed over the envelope and sketch to the Japanese and advised the Natowices they had no authority in the case. They were powerless to deal with the *kempetai*—several of their officers, in fact, had at one time been imprisoned by the *kempetai* in the Bridge House.[12] The next evening, Natowic called the liquor store from the Bridge House. He said he was safe and would be released the next day, yet asked someone to come with food and clothing. His sister, Mella, brought him the things he had requested.[13] Word spread throughout Hongkew of Natowic's imprisonment and refugees came to the liquor store every day to ask about him. But Natowic would not be set free until he had spent five horrifying months in the Bridge House.

The Bridge House was controlled by the *kempetai*, the feared Japanese military police, and located on North Szechuen Road, just one block past the bridge over Soochow Creek. The Japanese had taken it over in 1937 and constructed dozens of cells and torture chambers in what had once been apartments.[14] Hundreds of Chinese and foreigners accused of spying, operating shortwave transmitters, or other crimes were interrogated and tortured there during the war. Many died from torture and disease.[15]

Foreign newspaper and radio journalists, most of whom were suspected of being spies, were among the first held in the Bridge House, shortly after Pearl Harbor. Horst Levin's boss, Roy Healey, was confined there for about four months before being transferred to the Ward Road jail. Sailors from the USS *Wake*, several U.S. Marines, and eight of the captured Doolittle fliers also were confined in the Bridge House for short periods. The Jewish community leaders who had met to discuss the Rosh Hashanah plot were interrogated there in August 1942. And in the fall of 1942, foreign employees of the Shanghai Telephone Company and of several British firms were brought there on spying charges. Many prisoners were questioned about ludicrous accusations, including a sixty-six-year-old

American who was charged with inventing a pilotless airplane and an automated antiaircraft system. But it remains a mystery why Herman Natowic was brought there. Perhaps he had been set up, possibly as part of a scheme to get Joe Farren. Farren was arrested a short time after Natowic.

Natowic was held in one of the windowless ten-by-twenty-foot basement cells with wooden bars. At times, as many as thirty prisoners were crowded into one of these small cells. Men and women prisoners—including a pregnant woman—were held in the same cells. They all had to use one filthy bucket in the corner as a toilet. Each prisoner got one dirty blanket, which smelled of urine and feces, to sleep on. There sometimes wasn't enough room on the wooden cell floor for all the prisoners to lie down. In the morning, each cell was brought one bucket of water for drinking or washing. One of the Japanese guards sometimes took pleasure in washing his genitals and buttocks in the water before handing the bucket inside the cell.[16]

During the day, all the prisoners were required to sit cross-legged on the floor without shifting positions or talking. As punishment, guards would make some prisoners spend all day on their knees. Anyone who moved or whispered to another prisoner would be beaten. The prisoners' food consisted of a small bowl of *congee*, a kind of rice porridge, in the midmorning and four or five ounces of stale bread and some weak tea for the remainder of the day.[17]

The cells were filled with infected lice. Prisoners suffered from virtually every known disease, from leprosy to dysentery, and were refused medical treatment. From the floors above, throughout the day and night, they could hear the moans and cries of other prisoners being tortured.[18]

Natowic was called in for an interrogation about noon on his second day. One Korean and one Japanese guard brought him to a small room on the first floor. One of them pointed a gun at his head and ordered him to telephone the liquor store to tell his family he was fine and would be home soon. Then they stood him up and made him spread his feet and arms out against the wall. They accused Natowic of being a spy. Natowic tried to deny it, but they beat his hands against the wall with bamboo sticks every time he objected. The questioning and beating continued for four hours.

The next night, two other guards, both Japanese, took Natowic to a room on the third floor. They told him to take off all his clothes and kneel on the concrete floor in front of them. Then they asked him about his spy ring. Natowic replied he knew nothing about a spy ring. One of the guards screamed: "Never say 'I don't know'!" The two of them beat him with four-foot bamboo sticks on his back and legs until they drew blood. Next the guards took out an envelope and showed Natowic the plans for the shortwave radio that he had inadvertently brought to his shop. When he told them he had never seen the sketch before, they beat him furiously again.

On his fourth night in the Bridge House, Natowic was taken to a more elaborate torture room. There one guard placed him face up on a bench and handcuffed his wrists beneath it. Then he lashed Natowic's waist, knees, and ankles to the bench with a thin cord and finally wound a large towel in a circle around his nose and mouth. A guard named Suzuki straddled over Natowic and asked him about his spy operation. Each time Natowic failed to answer or denied any involvement, one guard held his head while Suzuki lifted a large bucket over him and began to pour filthy water into his nose and mouth. Natowic gagged and tried to swallow, but the water kept coming, held in a pool by the towel, until he nearly passed out. Suzuki jumped up and down on his stomach, forcing him to remain conscious, then repeated the questioning and water torture. Several times, they untied Natowic from the bench and hung him by his heels from a pulley on the ceiling so some of the water would drain out. The torture lasted for two hours.[19]

Different guards tortured him every night for ten days— beatings, water torture, even shocks from a strange electric machine that they attached to his thumbs. In their cells during the day, the prisoners sometimes surreptitiously exchanged stories of their torture. Some had the skin burned off their penises and testicles with cigars and cigarettes. Others were beaten with iron pipes, kicked in the shins with hobnailed boots, or had metal spikes forced under their fingernails. A few were ordered to write farewell letters to their families, taken out in the yard before a firing squad, lined up to be shot, then returned to their cells. Natowic was once told by two Japanese he would be killed the next day, but never heard from them again. He had thoughts of committing suicide, but was too weak to strangle himself.[20]

On his tenth night there, two guards beat Natowic with sticks and fists until dawn. A nurse came into the room about halfway through the night and gave them both injections. It drove them both into a wild frenzy, and they beat him even more furiously. When he returned to his cell in the morning, Natowic's body was covered with blood and pus. He didn't move for two days. When another guard brought him an official-looking document in Japanese to sign—apparently some sort of confession—he signed it without asking any questions.

The torture stopped after that. The next night, Natowic thought he heard Joe Farren screaming from a floor above. (Farren reportedly attempted suicide in the Bridge House and died at the General Hospital shortly after his release.[21]) He also discovered that his salesman, Seidl, was being held in the next cell, although he hadn't been tortured. Natowic sat cross-legged in his cell every day, watching dozens of new prisoners come and go, many of them near death. One day, the guards beat one Chinese prisoner in his cell until he was dead. Other prisoners moaned from their nightly torture and wasted away from lack of food and disease. But Natowic survived. His days as a referee had given him a strong sense of fairness—he was certain he had done nothing wrong and did not deserve to die.

Natowic could feel lice crawling all over him, but he didn't have enough energy to pick them off. He sometimes could fend off the rats who tried to stick their heads into his bowl of *congee*, but was too weak to stop a brown rat from carrying off an extra piece of bread a Chinese prisoner had brought him. He felt weaker and thinner each day. His severe diarrhea caused what little food he ate to pass right through him. Splotches were growing on his skin and his wounds were healing slowly, if at all.

After he had been there for several months, one of the guards handed Natowic a small mirror through the bars. He hadn't showered, shaved, or changed clothes in all his time there. Natowic lifted the mirror toward his face to look at himself, then turned suddenly to look behind him. He couldn't believe at first that the scraggly, bearded man in the reflection could be he. The guard slapped his knee and laughed hysterically.

There were a few kind guards in the Bridge House as well. To celebrate Emperor Hirohito's forty-second birthday on April 29, the guards had brought each of the prisoners an egg, but had refused to give one to Natowic. The other prisoners warned him to keep quiet, but Natowic complained to one of the guards. The guard was surprisingly sympathetic. Instead of beating him, the guard fed Natowic an egg through the bars and, when he was able to swallow it, fed him another. Another nice guard who spoke English occasionally talked to Natowic. He asked him about the war and about why he thought he had been in the Bridge House so long, when everyone else had been killed or let go. Natowic didn't know how to answer. That guard once gave Natowic a cigarette, but he was too weak to smoke it without burning his beard.

As the weeks wore on, the guards seemed to grow more worried about Natowic. His mouth had become swollen with sores, and he could no longer eat, drink, or even sit up. They decided to release him to die outside the Bridge House. On July 26, at about 1 A.M., a guard opened the cell door, walked in and stood over him. "Natowic," he said, "you are free." He asked for the Natowic family's telephone number so they could be called to have him picked up. Natowic could barely speak and couldn't remember it. From the next cell, Seidl yelled out the number.[22]

The guard who telephoned Hella told her to send a doctor for Natowic. She called Didner immediately. After Didner got Natowic to the hospital, he resolved to see him through, despite the hopeless diagnosis. For the next six weeks, he virtually abandoned his office practice and spent all of his days by Natowic's bedside, watching his fluids, changing his dressings, and talking to him when he showed signs of consciousness.

After a few weeks, the swelling in his mouth subsided and he was able to eat solid food. He wanted to talk about soccer, and asked Didner to fill him in on the Jewish Recreation Club. Natowic laughed at the rat who stood up near his bed, telling Didner it reminded him of the rats he had fought with over his rice bowl. His health slowly improved and he was released from the General Hospital on September 6. He spent several more weeks recovering at two refugee hospitals before he was well enough to go home.

News of Natowic's return spread quickly through Hongkew and was cause for celebration. Prominent members of the community came to visit him; actors and actresses like Walter Friedmann and Jenny Raussnitz showed up at his home to perform his favorite Viennese operettas.[23]

Natowic returned to work that winter and was refereeing soccer games again in the spring. His survival and recovery amazed everyone. He was back to his burly, broad physique and rounded, ruddy face. A few months after Natowic regained his health, he married Hella.

But he never escaped the fears and nightmares from the Bridge House—they would haunt him for the rest of his life. He woke up Hella on many nights with his screaming and would sometimes run in terror if he saw a Japanese soldier on the streets. He was not a hero, but a surviving victim. Perhaps, some in the community later suggested, Herman Natowic also was a victim of fate, chosen to suffer for the Jews of Hongkew as millions of Jews who remained in Europe suffered far greater horrors.

15

Heimann

Szuran's barbershop was particularly crowded that afternoon in the spring of 1944. It was the day before Passover, one of two times a year when yeshiva students traditionally had their hair cut. The yeshiva students had been coming in all day, and the regular customers were there, too, waiting on the six stools inside the shop and in the alley outside. The work was slow—all the cutting had to be done by hand because the Japanese were rationing electricity—and there were only two barber chairs in Friedrich Szuran's shop at 599 Tongshan Lane.

Szuran was concentrating on one of his customers, but he looked up when an intense-looking young man entered the shop. He recognized him as one of the yeshiva students from next door. Szuran didn't have much use for his neighbors. They didn't give him much business and they could barely communicate with him, as Szuran didn't speak Yiddish and few of them spoke German. In fact, Szuran didn't have much use for anything to do with Judaism; he had considered himself an assimilated Austrian, not a Jew, until the Nazis forced him to emigrate.

But the student was demanding his attention. In broken German, he was trying to tell Szuran that the head rabbi of the yeshiva was about to come for his haircut. Szuran would have to sterilize his clippers, the student said, and collect the *rebbe*'s hair in a paper bag to be disposed of in the river. The other customers would have to wait, he said, until the barber took care of the *rebbe*.

The waiting customers, mostly Austrians like Szuran, were not impressed. As soon as the student left, they began to mock him and criticize the "pushy" religious Jews who always had to have their way. Their head rabbi, or whoever he was, one of them said, could wait his turn like everyone else.

Five minutes later, the student returned with three other students, ushering the head rabbi into the shop. They were virtually carrying him in, as the rabbi modestly tried to discourage their attentiveness. When the crowd of students parted, Szuran and his waiting customers got their first look at the rabbi. He was an elderly man, perhaps in his eighties, with white hair and a flowing white beard. But it was his face that captivated them: his all-knowing countenance seemed to possess the wisdom of God. The customers suddenly fell silent. All of them, including the one sitting in the barber chair, got up and cleared the way for the rabbi.

"Quickly," Szuran ordered his apprentice, Gerhard Heimann, "sterilize the clippers. Prepare for the rabbi's haircut." Gerd had never seen his boss so respectful. For the next few minutes, they fussed over the rabbi's hair, always under the careful watch of his students, who collected all the clippings in a paper bag.

Gerd was now considered a man. He'd had his bar mitzvah at the Tabarin restaurant in February 1942—a few weeks after the adventure in the Marble Hall—and conducted the service under the watchful eyes of his great uncle, Rabbi Silberstein, who had instructed him for eighteen months. Gerd wore his brother Benno's gray pants, patched with a new bottom, and his father's blue sport coat, turned inside out and taken in. There were more than one-hundred guests.

Gerd's parents were struggling to provide a normal life for their sons. They had sold their wedding rings to pay for Gerd's bar mitzvah reception. Gustav and Benno made very little income from their window washing and the cost of living continued to rise. The Heimanns had been forced to sell their three houses on Chaoufoong Road and buy two smaller houses, first on Dalny Road then on Seward Road in January 1943. (Luckily for the Heimanns, the Seward Road houses were inside the designated area. The proclamation was issued three weeks after they moved in.) Gerd, Benno, and his parents lived in one house and Uncle Sally lived in the other. Their new houses didn't have the luxury of illegal toilets—the cart now stopped at their houses to empty their buckets—and they no longer received income from their rents. Gerd's mother Julie seemed to eat only rarely, saving her food for Gerd and Benno.

Gerd seemed like a typical boy. Before he graduated from school, he began to develop an interest in the opposite sex. He had a steady girlfriend, Evelina, a dentist's daughter who lived on Chusan Road. He took her to school dances and cowboy movies, but there wasn't much opportunity for romance. Evelina's mother watched them closely and never let her daughter stay out late. Gerd was curious about sex, but not yet ready to join his friends on their late-night adventures. Their rendezvous with bar girls and prostitutes intrigued him, but their painful visits to Dr. Didner made him wary.

In the summer of 1943, Gerd graduated from the new Kadoorie School. There were no colleges inside the designated area, so his parents encouraged him to learn a trade. His mother, Julie, wanted him to be a tailor. But Gerd thought tailors worked too hard; he looked for the easiest trade he could find. Barbers, he decided, kept their hands clean and spent most of their time talking. His father knew Fritz Abraham, who owned one of the best shops in Hongkew, and he volunteered to ask him about hiring Gerd.

Gerd started work that summer as an apprentice for Abraham and Mosberg in their shop on Muirhead Road.

Abraham owned the barber shop and his partner, Kurt
Mosberg, ran the beauty parlor. Gerd's father was proud his
son had a trade that promised a steady income. People would
always need their hair cut. Gerd was now able to contribute
something to the household income and he gave all of his
salary to his father. Few of Gerd's former classmates—and few
of the refugees who had been forced to move into the ghetto—
were doing as well as he.

By the time the proclamation took effect in May 1943,
dozens of refugees who had shops and restaurants in the
International Settlement and French Concession had moved
their businesses into Hongkew. Some factories outside the
ghetto, particularly those owned by the Japanese, continued to
produce goods for the war effort and employ some refugees.
Hans Becher, a Viennese, worked with his father at a
European paper mill in the Yangtzepoo area when they first
came to Shanghai early in 1939. They kept their jobs when the
Japanese took over the factory after Pearl Harbor. The plant
initially manufactured cardboard boxes, but the Japanese
converted it to produce cardboard cigarette packs and then
paper ones as conditions worsened. The Bechers were forced
to move from the French Concession to Hongkew after the
proclamation, but had no difficulty getting permission to leave
the ghetto to work for the Japanese.[1]

But more than three-hundred refugee businesses outside of
the designated area were forced to close; most received little in
return for the sale of their businesses.[2] Many were able to
relocate in Hongkew, but hundreds of refugees lost their jobs
as competition increased in a shrinking market. Tradespeople
and hawkers suffered the biggest loss of income, particularly
those who were unable to secure passes to sell outside the
ghetto during the day.[3] Some of the poorest refugees, wearing
flour sacks for clothing, worked at a peanut butter factory,
pulling on bamboo poles to turn a huge millstone that crushed
the peanuts.[4]

The conditions remained the most difficult for professionals,
such as academics and lawyers. A few academics were able to
keep their teaching jobs at local universities, including the
respected St. John's University near Jessfield Park; several

lawyers made some income working for the Arbitration Court run by the Jüdische Gemeinde. (The court had been established in 1939 by the Komor Committee and settled civil cases involving Jewish merchants.[5]) But many others could not or would not adapt. F. Goldenring, a tall, elegant-looking German academic who had spent his life studying and traveling and who spoke a half dozen languages, arrived in Shanghai aboard the *Conte Verde* in June 1939 at age 36. He briefly tried to make a living as a tutor, but several clients accused him of stealing from their homes and he was imprisoned. By 1944, he had sold his clothes and was wearing a flour sack. He lived for a short time in a SACRA camp on Chusan Road with other former convicts and died there, apparently of starvation.[6]

Other refugees continued to adjust, as they had so often since they first arrived in Shanghai. Fred Gunsberger, trained as an industrial chemist and chemical engineer in Vienna, first worked as a tutor and then as an inspector in a Japanese dairy. When he lost his job just before the Pacific war started, he sold most of his clothes and goods to pay for food. But in 1942, Gunsberger developed a process and built machinery to manufacture margarine. He opened a factory on East Seward Road and employed as many as fifteen refugee workers. The factory, just outside the designated area, remained in operation throughout the ghetto period. Gunsberger sold his Three Spot margarine to the Kitchen Fund, bakeries, and restaurants.[7]

The famous Fiaker restaurant, run by two Viennese refugees in the French Concession, also managed to remain open after the proclamation took effect. Two days before the owners planned to close, two Japanese police officials ate dinner there and were so impressed with the food that they secretly agreed to take over ownership with a Russian partner. It reopened late in 1943 after about seven months of negotiations. The new owners acquired passes for the refugee employees and purchased the best veal, filets, and wines through Chinese suppliers. Throughout the war, nearly anything was available in Shanghai for the right price. The restaurant continued to serve elegant, expensive food—the Fiaker's *sacher torte* was reputed to be the best outside Vienna. Most of the customers were leading Japanese businessmen and German and Japanese military officials.[8]

Other businesses readily made the adjustment to moving into Hongkew. Bruno and Lisbeth Loewenberg, who had run a bookstore in the International Settlement until the proclamation, opened a lending library in the ghetto, the Lion Bibliothek. They charged a daily rate for loaning books, which changed almost every day as inflation soared. The Loewenbergs marked each book with a letter and posted a list of letters with each day's rates.[9]

Some businesses already based in Hongkew didn't seem to suffer from the proclamation. Heinz Frankenstein, from East Prussia, had trained as an apprentice baker in Cologne and Essen. He worked as a baker in Shanghai for several years before he opened his own bakery, the Vienna Cake Factory, on Wayside Road. With enough money and a few connections, he always was able to purchase the finest butter and flour throughout the war years and ghetto period. Frankenstein's best customers were the Austrian refugees. Some would walk by his store three or four times, looking longingly at the pastries displayed in the window, before coming in. "No dinner tonight," they would often say, as they handed him the money for a luscious pastry.[10]

Abraham and Mosberg had sold their first shop on East Broadway after the proclamation and opened the new shop inside the ghetto just before they hired Gerd. They had lost some of their regular customers, the Japanese who wanted permanents and never argued about prices. The Japanese usually paid at least twice as much as the refugees. But many of the wealthier Japanese had left Hongkew, moving into the nice homes and apartments outside the district the refugees had been forced to give up. Now Abraham and Mosberg had to rely mostly on refugee customers. The competition among the shops was fierce and threatened to drive some of them out of business.

Other merchants in the ghetto were facing similar competitive pressures. To deal with the problem, the hairdressers and other craftsmen decided to form guilds, based on the European model, in the summer of 1943. The guilds could control wages and prices in the shrinking market as well as establish standards for training and licensing. Mosberg became head of the guild of hairdressers.[11]

Gerd had been working as an apprentice only a few weeks when he came down with tropical sprue, a mysterious disease apparently caused by improper nutrition, along with parasites or food toxins.[12] As the disease spread, Gerd grew weaker and was unable to walk or get out of bed. He had anemia and severe diarrhea, and he lost a lot of weight—he dropped thirty or forty pounds from his small, five-foot body.

Dr. Mannheim at the Ward Road Hospital gave Gerd charcoal pills for his diarrhea and advised his parents to try to send him out of Hongkew for a few months to recover. Gerd's friends from Betar made arrangements to send him to the Schwartzbergs, a Russian Jewish family who lived in the King Albert apartments in the French Concession. Gerd missed his family while he was away, but he thrived on the hearty, plentiful food. He also enjoyed the freedom of living outside the ghetto; as he got better, the Schwartzbergs took him out to the dog races and jai alai. He was gone for two months and came home that fall, healthy and back to his normal weight.

Shortly after Gerd returned to work, the guilds began to offer training classes for the apprentices. They began in November 1943 at the ORT Training Center at 475 Jansen Road. The center offered classes in gardening and agriculture, machine knitting, a special class to train young people in mechanics, and the "complementary school" for apprentices, which Gerd attended. The complementary school included young people being trained as tailors, hairdressers, locksmiths, confectioners, leather makers, furriers, radio repairers, goldsmiths, carpenters, and dental technicians. The youngest students were Gerd's age, fourteen, and the oldest were twenty-one. The courses included theoretical and practical schooling in their chosen fields as well as general knowledge classes.[13] Gerd took courses there once a week with Kurt Mosberg as his teacher.

At Abraham and Mosberg's shop, Gerd was an eager and

hard-working apprentice. He swept the floors, washed the towels, and soaped and shampooed the customers. He carefully observed the barbers at work and practiced by shaving and cutting his father's and brother's hair and beards while the masters watched and criticized. Gerd also learned about some of the tricks of doing business in Shanghai. Every three months, an electric meter reader came by to make sure Mosberg wasn't using more than the five kilowatts per month permitted by the Japanese. But the beauty parlor, which used electric curlers and dryers, always consumed far more than its quota. There was a simple Shanghai solution to the problem. Whenever the meter man came to the shop, Mosberg paid him a bribe (*kamsha*) to ignore the infraction and sign a sheet showing he had used less than five kilowatts.[14]

Gerd had heard about *kamsha* from his cousin Hans at the Cathay Hotel and learned the system a little too well. One of his duties as an apprentice was to order supplies, including the coal that was used to heat the towels. Gerd thought it was only natural to ask for a bribe from the coal dealer who delivered to the shop. But the dealer refused to pay—there was a severe coal shortage at the time and he was insulted by Gerd's demand. When the dealer complained to the owners, Abraham lost his temper and fired Gerd immediately.

It took Gerd only a day, however, to find another apprenticeship. Friedrich Szuran was a bit older than Abraham and Mosberg, but he had more business than he could handle. He was happy to have the help of a well-trained apprentice who was nearly ready for his own customers.

16

The Monkey

The Japanese proclamation ordering the refugees to move into the ghetto had not worked as planned. By the May 18, 1943, deadline, more than 1,500 refugees remained outside the designated area. Physicians and relief workers were granted three-month extensions; 1,100 others were put on a waiting list for housing.[1] SACRA, the Japanese-controlled organization of Russian Jews that supervised the relocation, had taken over and renovated only a handful of houses and apartment buildings. There were few private apartments available in the overcrowded ghetto, and real estate agents demanded excessive rents. A Japanese named Kano, who served as secretary to SACRA, had bought a number of buildings in Hongkew and collected huge sums for reselling them.[2]

As late as the winter of 1943–1944, there were still hundreds of refugees living outside Hongkew. Some of them, including many of the Polish Jews and yeshiva students, had declined to comply with the proclamation and actively resisted the Japanese order. The Poles, with the help of the Russian Jews, had rented some of the best housing when they first arrived in

Shanghai, mostly in the French Concession. Most of them were well-clothed and fed and had been receiving support from the local Russians and from abroad, even after Pearl Harbor.*

The Polish Jews had refused to recognize SACRA or to name representatives to its board. They claimed they were Polish citizens of the Polish government-in-exile rather than stateless refugees and therefore were exempt from the proclamation.[3] The Poles generated little sympathy from SACRA and even less from the Hongkew refugees, who resented the Poles' comfortable living conditions and their refusal to assist, or even acknowledge, the non-Orthodox German and Austrian Jews, many of whom were suffering from poverty and malnutrition.[4] The Japanese rejected the Polish appeals.

But the Polish Jews continued to resist. Mir Yeshiva students staged a riot in the SACRA office when they were ordered to move to a Salvation Army compound owned by SACRA, smashing furniture and throwing it out the window. The police arrested thirty-three of them until Rabbi Ashkenazi intervened, rescuing them from jail sentences. The Japanese eventually agreed to let them rent their own private housing.[5]

Other Poles simply refused to move. By the end of 1943, Japanese officials had begun to lose patience. They had established a Stateless Refugees Affairs Bureau, headed by T. Kubota, to oversee the relocation and threatened to arrest anyone violating the order. The arrests began the following March.

Three refugees, two Poles and a German, were arrested on March 3, one for being outside the ghetto without a pass and two others for living outside the designated area. They were sentenced to one or two days in the Wayside Police Station and held in a cell that had been used to detain Chinese beggars. Over the next two months, eighty-seven more refugees were

* Meyer Birman complained in 1944 to a Jewish organization in Lisbon about several Polish rabbis and yeshivas who "specialized in drawing money" from abroad with appeals that were exaggerated or false. He singled out the Mir Yeshiva as one group that lived under favorable conditions but was "always sending alarming reports to the various personalitiess abroad and try to drag money from them." (Birman to Seccao de Emigracao de Communidado Israelita, Lisbon, July 11, 1944, YIVO files.)

arrested, most of them Poles. The sentences were normally one or two days, but several were held for as long as thirty days.[6]

Subinspector Okura was in charge of enforcing the order. He often beat prisoners before throwing them into the cell. The cell was filled with typhus-infected lice. In April, one of the Polish refugees who had been held in the police station contracted typhus and died.[7]

Word spread that a sentence in the Wayside Police Station meant almost certain death. Okura continued to send violators to the so-called "death cell." Seven more refugees who had been jailed there died in May; eight others contracted typhus but survived.[8] The Japanese had accomplished their goal. By the spring of 1944, only about 250 refugees were living outside the ghetto.[9]

The Stateless Refugees Affairs Bureau had another function. As of August 10, 1943, any refugee who wished to leave the ghetto would have to apply for a pass. Those with jobs or businesses outside the designated area could ask the bureau for authorization to leave Hongkew during the day. The passes were limited to specified areas outside the district; signs were posted on the border reading: "STATELESS REFUGEES ARE PROHIBITED TO PASS HERE WITHOUT PERMISSION."

The man in charge of issuing most of the passes was less vicious, but far more unpredictable, than Okura. He was a short, schizophrenic Japanese named Ghoya who liked to call himself the King of the Jews. The refugees called him The Monkey.

Few refugees knew much about Kanoh Ghoya's past. He had been a police chief in a district of Kyushu before coming to Shanghai. He was an aficionado of Western culture, particularly classical music, and spoke English well. Before the proclamation, he had lived on Chaoufoong Road in Hongkew with his wife and two children. They had shared the house with the Simons, Jewish refugees from Germany who arrived in Shanghai in March 1939. Ghoya often would visit the Simons when young Ruth practiced her violin or when he heard Beethoven on their radio. They considered him a kind and friendly neighbor.[10]

Ghoya's wife had been quite ill and died before the Pacific war started. He later remarried and moved with his new wife to 810 East Seward Road, just outside the ghetto. When the Japanese appointed him to supervise the pass system in August 1943, he gradually became a different man.[11]

At first, Ghoya granted most requests for passes from the refugees who lined up daily at the Stateless Refugees Affairs Bureau at 171 Muirhead Road. (Ghoya had the authority to issue passes valid for one to three months. Okura was responsible for issuing daily passes, valid for less than two weeks.) Most passes were restricted to the International Settlement, French Concession, Western District, or Hongkew and Yangtzepoo. All pass holders were required to wear a round blue and white badge, inscribed with the Chinese character for "pass," on their right lapel when they were outside the ghetto area.[12]

But after a few months, Ghoya appeared to grow increasingly suspicious and even paranoid. He screamed at some of the refugees and accused them of being spies or liars. Often, he demanded that applicants bring him proof of their employment. "Bring me a list of customers," he would say. (Refugees joked that he once demanded such a list from an undertaker.) He accused some women applicants of being prostitutes.[13] Ghoya, only four feet tall, particularly hated tall men and would sometimes jump up on his desk and beat a taller refugee who applied for a pass.[14] During some of his fits of rage, Ghoya would drag a refugee to an office window and threaten to throw him off the second-floor balcony. Several Jewish refugees worked in the outer office and tried to warn applicants if Ghoya was in a particularly bad mood. "Does he beat today?" people in line would ask.[15]

Ghoya made some refugees wait in line all day and then come back each day for two or three weeks before making a decision. His moods swung wildly—on rare occasions he granted nearly every request for a pass.[16] He used his power to abuse and intimidate the refugees, many of whom were dependent on the passes for their daily survival.

He was equally unpredictable outside of his office. Ghoya would occasionally disappear for an entire day and no one was able to get a pass. Sometimes, he beat refugees on the street or in cafes if they were not wearing their badges. (The regulations only required that they wear badges outside the ghetto.[17]) On other days, he played with refugee children and posed for pictures in front of the line of people waiting for passes.[18] He often showed up at refugee soccer matches and concerts and plays performed by the refugees, yet he sometimes prohibited a performance for no apparent reason.[19] He loved to talk with refugees about classical music and often visited a refugee doctor's home to play violin while the doctor's wife accompanied him on the piano.[20] Yet when Ghoya's harmony once clashed with one of the virtuoso refugee violinists, Alfred Wittenberg, he yelled at him: "You play as I direct, or I kill you."[21]

Ghoya was not the most brutal of the Japanese, but, for many refugees, he was their most visible oppressor. Refugee artists, like Fritz Melchior, drew caricatures of him and comedians told jokes about him. Ghoya became a symbol of the refugees' oppression, a tyrant whose deeds were compared to the evil Haman of the Book of Esther.

There were other forms of oppression as well. The Japanese used both paid informers and a self-policing force to control the ghetto. The best-known—and most obvious—refugee informer was Ewald Drucker, who was believed to be working for the *kempetai*, the refugee bureau, and possibly the Nazis. Robert Peritz continued to work as an informer and advised the Japanese to jail refugees who complained about the quality of bread or other relief services of the Kitchen Fund he headed.[22]

The self-policing force, known as the *pao chia*, was assigned the task of patrolling the ghetto to enforce the pass system. The Japanese had used the *pao chia*, a traditional Chinese mutual surveillance system,[23] in Manchuria and other cities in occupied China; it was established in the Chinese community in Shanghai in the spring of 1942. The refugee *pao chia* was founded well before the proclamation, in September, 1942, and commanded by Felix Kardegg, president of the Jüdische Gemeinde. All refugees between the ages of twenty and forty-five were required to volunteer for duty. When the proclamation took effect, the *pao chia* became a border patrol. Men stood along the boundaries in three-hour shifts to make sure no one left or returned to the ghetto without a proper pass.[24] They also checked that refugees were carrying their resident certificates—the German refugee certificate had a sinister yellow stripe across the top.[25] Shanghai Municipal Police supervisors on bicycles watched over the patrols. The *pao chia* brought out the worst German militarism in some refugees, who eagerly reported violators to the authorities. Others took their duty half-seriously and let fellow refugees sneak in and out of the ghetto. A few paid bribes to avoid *pao chia* duty.

One of the most enthusiastic *pao chia* officers was an Austrian refugee named Fred Schrantz, who was in charge of one sector of the ghetto. In the summer of 1943, while Schrantz was patrolling Chusan Road on bicycle, a passing Japanese army truck struck his bicycle and knocked him to the ground. As a crowd gathered, Schrantz yelled furiously at the truck driver, pointing at the stripes on his arm that showed his rank in the *pao chia*. He demanded payment for his ruined bicycle. The driver agreed to take care of it and took Schrantz with him. He was never heard from again.[26]

Schrantz's family learned later that the operators of the truck were Korean staff for the Japanese army who had taken the truck without permission. They had murdered Schrantz and thrown his body in the river to cover up their mistake. The Japanese forced the Koreans to confess and later compensated Schrantz's widow by delivering a huge load of coal—a precious commodity at the time—to her home.[27]

The ghetto years were the low point for the Hongkew refugees. Malnutrition and disease were widespread as more families lost their sources of income and sold off what remaining valuables and household goods they still owned. Theft became more common, too—refugees would sometimes return home to find nearly everything they owned had been stolen. Rampant inflation magnified the problems. Prices sometimes doubled in a matter of hours.

By the spring of 1944, eggs cost more than $1 (U.S.) apiece, pork nearly $20 a pound, a loaf of bread $2.50, and milk nearly $10 a quart.[28] Refugees adapted to the inflation by hoarding commodities, such as flints and kerosene, since cash had become almost worthless. The commodities themselves sometimes proved to have little value. One refugee bought several tins of kerosene from a Chinese friend as a hedge against inflation, but decided to splurge during a cold winter week and use one tin as fuel. He opened it to find it filled with water. The refugee returned the tin to his friend and demanded an explanation. "I thought you wanted this as a commodity, not to use," his friend said. "If you wanted kerosene for heating, you should have told me."[29]

An increasing number of refugees depended on the limited resources of the Kitchen Fund—little was left from the funds Margolis and Siegel had arranged to borrow before they were interned—and the reluctant assistance of SACRA. (SACRA had taken over control of the Kitchen Fund in September 1943.[30]) The quality and quantity of the food deteriorated steadily as funds ran out. After the JDC had cut off funds in May 1942, no outside money—except those funds sent to the yeshivas—had reached the Shanghai refugees.

Margolis was repatriated in September 1943. On her return to the United States, she filed an extensive report on the events from Pearl Harbor until her release. She remained critical of the local Jewish community. "We have in Shanghai, and have always had," she wrote, "a group of Jews who have no social consciousness and no feeling of responsibility towards the community."[31] Margolis concluded on a pessimistic—and somewhat ominous—note:

> We have a group of refugees who are underfed and undernourished and terribly discouraged. I doubt that fifty

percent of the group will be material for rehabilitation if this war lasts another two years. And no one can ever know what the attitude of the Japanese will be towards this defenseless element of the Shanghai population once they start losing the war. Knowing the Japanese, I would venture to say that "anything might happen at any time." The only hope for these people, as for all peoples, lies in the victory of the United Nations.[32]

The Japanese maintained firm control over Shanghai and east China, but there were some small victories. When Italy fell in the summer of 1943, the crew of the *Conte Verde* scuttled the ship to avoid its capture by the Japanese. (The *Conte Verde* had been the first ship to bring European refugees to Shanghai in 1934 and had brought 1,500 more refugees on six voyages from 1938–1940. It had been stranded in Shanghai since early in the Pacific war by the British blockade.) But the Japanese tied a massive chain and pulley around one of the large buildings on the Bund, refloated the ship, and converted it into a troop ship. It was sunk by U.S. planes in December 1944.[33]

A few months after Margolis's departure, some financial assistance arrived for the refugees when the International Red Cross transferred 30,000 Swiss francs (about $40,000) from Zurich, donated by unnamed Jewish sources. Another 100,000 francs arrived in January. Disputes continued between the yeshivas and the other refugees over the allocation of the funds.[34] By May 1944, the JDC was again sending funds directly to Shanghai.[35]

V

EXODUS

(1945–1950)

17

Didner

The droning engines 10,000 feet overhead brought a smile to
Sam Didner's face as he ate lunch in his office on East
Seward Road. It was a familiar sound, a squadron of U.S.
bombers flying over Shanghai. By July 1945, the attacks were
coming almost every day, usually about noon. The warnings
always came too late. The hum of the planes came first, then
the high-pitched howl of the air raid sirens.

Didner had little reason to fear for his safety—the bombers
usually dropped their weapons on the airfields outside the city
or on warehouses near the waterfront. But the frequent attacks
were reassuring proof that the Americans were winning the
war in the Pacific. Didner had long ago concluded there was
no future for him and the other refugees in Hongkew,
particularly in the ghetto. Their only hope was the defeat of the
Japanese.

The droning grew louder as the bombers seemed to be flying
almost directly overhead. It sounded as if there were twenty or
thirty planes; it was unusual for them to come so close. Didner
walked outside his office to look up. But the thick clouds on

this hot, sticky July day blocked out even the sun. He turned to hear another familiar sound—the popping blasts of Japanese antiaircraft guns, firing from their concealed batteries on nearby roofs. The flak was falling far short of the bombers, but the shrapnel was showering the ghetto.

The next sounds surprised him: Bombs were whistling down toward Hongkew. A deafening blast shook the ground around him, nearly knocking him over. Seconds later, Didner could hear the screams and smell the smoke. A bomb had hit the ghetto, only a few blocks from where he was standing. He grabbed his medical bag from his office, joined two other doctors, and ran toward the site of the explosion.

In the two years since Didner had carried Herman Natowic from the Bridge House to Shanghai General Hospital, little had changed for the Jewish refugees in Hongkew. The only good news—other than reports from the war front—came early in 1945, when Ghoya and Okura were removed from their positions under pressure from the Japanese consulate. The new Japanese officials in charge of the ghetto were almost nonchalant. They gave Morris Feder, a refugee who had worked for Ghoya, authority to renew the passes. Requests to go outside during the day now were rarely denied.[1] But inflation had brought business life to a standstill; malnutrition and disease remained widespread.

Didner and the other refugee doctors had struggled to treat one epidemic after another. There had been a virulent dysentery epidemic in the winter of 1943–1944, followed by a year-long spinal meningitis epidemic that began the next spring and afflicted his girlfriend Grete and her two sisters. He treated them with the same sulfa drug that had saved their brother Albert five years earlier. More than 1,000 cases of meningitis were reported. Nearly all of the refugees suffered from roundworms, eye infections, and skin diseases.[2] Most were thin and undernourished. The influx of JDC funds over the past year had helped reduce malnutrition among the poorest refugees, but few were receiving even half the nutrition and vitamins they needed to build resistance to disease.[3]

Didner continued to earn a small income from the Finnish sailors trapped in Shanghai. He almost had lost that source of support a year earlier when Ghoya called him in and accused him of being a spy. But Didner remained calm, as he had when faced by Nazi accusers in Austria. He explained to Ghoya that he was simply doing his job and could not turn away people who needed care. Ghoya was apparently in a relatively good mood—he seemed satisfied and let Didner go. (Ghoya had been less rational earlier when he limited most doctors to spending twelve to fourteen hours a day outside the designated area; at one point, he even refused to issue passes to doctors who had patients in two hospitals outside the ghetto, one in Hongkew and the other in the Western District.[4])

The refugees were still cut off from the outside world, but news from the war fronts reached most of them. There were maps with pins marking troop locations in nearly every household. Didner spent many late nights on Chusan Road listening to news of the Russian victories in Eastern Europe on his friend Werner Braunsberg's shortwave radio. When the Russians took Kharkov in August 1943, Didner, Braunsberg, and Grete celebrated with a pheasant dinner and a bottle of wine. (The Japanese had declared a prohibition against shortwave radios early in the war, but it was widely ignored. Siegfried Haase even posted daily war news on his shop window on MacGregor Road.[5]) Several refugees, recruited to work for what they were told was an Allied underground network, listened to shortwave broadcasts and spread favorable war news among the refugees. They also passed on information about Japanese troop movements and reported on the damage from the American air raids. Some refugees reportedly assisted in the escape of American soldiers, including some of the Doolittle fliers, from the Ward Road jail in October 1944.[6]

Russian newspapers and radio stations in Shanghai also published and broadcast stories from the war front, although most refugees were skeptical of Soviet propaganda and their exaggerated reports of major victories. But the stories were not censored by local Japanese authorities, who seemed far more concerned with placating the Russians and keeping them out of the Pacific war than with concealing reports of Nazi defeats.

As the Soviets swept to the west in the summer of 1944, capturing eastern Poland, refugees who had lost touch with their families in Europe eagerly awaited some news of their fate. Didner hadn't heard from his mother and the rest of his family in Austria for more than two years.

The first reports appeared in *The Shanghai Jewish Chronicle* that fall. In a series titled "Treblinka," the paper published Russian accounts of their discovery of the Nazi death camp. Soldiers had found thousands of bodies piled in ditches, the paper reported, and evidence that thousands more had been gassed and cremated as part of a Nazi mass extermination campaign.

Didner and many others were skeptical. The Russians had used false atrocity stories in the past to justify their own brutality. And Ossi Lewin's *Chronicle* had little credibility in Hongkew—some refugees felt Lewin had cooperated too readily with the Japanese in order to keep his newspaper publishing during the war.[7]

The skepticism disappeared that spring. Throughout the war, the Russians had been showing war propaganda newsreels. When word spread that the latest Russian newsreels included scenes from the liberation of concentration camps, hundreds of refugees flocked to see them. The first reports had been beyond belief, but they could not deny what they saw with their own eyes.

They saw the ditches piled with twisted bodies, starved into skin-covered skeletons; the awful mountains of shoes, eyeglasses, pacifiers; the gas chambers and ovens still filled with ashes and half-burned corpses; the vacant stares from the faces of those few victims who had survived. Several refugees ran outside to vomit. During one showing, a man near the front row leaped to his feet when the newsreel showed a pale, thin man in a prisoner's uniform escorting Russian soldiers through the camp.

"Mein bruder! Mein bruder!" the man screamed, pointing at the picture. His shadow covered the screen as he continued to yell, half in joy and half in terror, at the sight of his lost brother. Two or three refugees tried to calm him and led him out of the theater.[8]

The film also had a profound effect on Gerd Heimann's sixty-eight-year-old uncle, Adolf Keibel. He and his wife Thekla—an older sister of Gerd's father, Gustav—had been the last Heimann relatives to leave Germany, coming on the Trans-Siberian railway. Gustav had insisted they come to Shanghai and had obtained Japanese permits for them. Adolf had complained bitterly throughout the war about conditions in Shanghai and had refused even to speak with Gustav since his arrival. When he learned about the concentration camps, however, he broke down in tears and begged Gustav to forgive him.

Yet the film from could not reveal—and no one in Shanghai could imagine—the vastness and efficiency of the Nazi extermination campaign. Levin remained optimistic that he would see his mother Betty and sister Ruth again soon; the Kantorowskys prayed that Hans was still alive; and Didner hoped that his mother, brother Isak, and sister Mitzi had survived the war, along with his other brothers and sisters in Israel and England.

In some ways, the refugees were even more cut off from the war in the Pacific than from the events in Europe. The Japanese had celebrated victories during the Ichigo offensive in China in the spring of 1944 as Chiang Kai-shek's armies continued to collapse and withdraw. Most of eastern China remained firmly under Japanese control. But there was little news about the continuing American assaults across the Pacific islands.

At the beginning of 1944, the Japanese authorities in Shanghai began preparations for the expected American air raids. A blackout was put into effect from sunset to sunrise in January, forcing many restaurants and taverns to close in the evenings. Air raid sirens were sounded nearly every night, months before the first attacks. The Japanese organized fire brigades, and refugees were ordered to dig trenches in the street to serve as shelters. With Shanghai's high water table, the trenches quickly filled up with water, and passersby often splashed into them at night.

In the summer and fall of 1944, Shanghai was only a secondary target for American bombers based in Burma and Chengtu. The first attacks came in June; the bombing grew heavier and more frequent in the fall and winter. The planes bombed docks, warehouses, and shipping. By the beginning of 1945, most of the bombing raids came during the day.[9]

Thousands of Chinese moved from Shanghai into the countryside to escape the attacks, and many of the Japanese still living in Hongkew moved into the French Concession, where they believed they would be safe from the bombing.[10] The Japanese had located munitions depots and communications equipment throughout Hongkew. They also had placed a radio station near one of the SACRA apartment buildings—also the site of a refugee kindergarten—at 826 East Yuhang Road.

By the end of June, U.S. forces had conquered Okinawa and were rapidly constructing air bases there. Shanghai was now an easily accessible target. The Seventh Air Force began to launch daily attacks.

On July 17, 1945, twenty-five new twin-engine A-26 bombers from the 319th Bomb Group took off from the Kadena airfield on Okinawa, a little more than five-hundred miles from Shanghai, at 9:49 A.M.(Shanghai time), carrying one-hundred-pound bombs. Their mission was to attack the Chiangwan Airdrome, just north of Shanghai. The 319th had just been redeployed from Italy and had flown its first mission in the Pacific, an attack on an airfield on Kyushu, a day earlier. Twenty-three bombers (two had returned after losing contact with the formation) reached Shanghai at 12:09 P.M., flying between 9,600 and 10,600 feet. There was a solid overcast at 6,000 feet and it was impossible to see the Chiangwan field. Bombardier Robert C. Roberts, flying in the lead plane, could only estimate the site of the target based on their flying time from Okinawa; the other planes released their bombs by following his lead. They dropped 263 bombs.[11]

A few of the bombs had been dropped too early; Hongkew had been hit. Dozens of buildings had collapsed, some solely from the air pressure of the explosions. Refugees and Chinese were wandering in the streets with bloody ears and noses, disoriented by the blast. At the Chinese market on Chusan Road, just past the intersection of Ward Road, there were dozens of limbs and bodies scattered in the street. Bloodied corpses had been tossed awkwardly against the walls and atop the stalls of fish and fruit. A few blocks east, the SACRA building on East Yuhang Road apparently had taken a direct hit. (Some refugees mistakenly assumed the bombers had targeted the Japanese radio station.) Refugees were beginning to dig bodies out of the rubble. Mothers who had children in the kindergarten in the same building had run to the site, but the *pao chia* held them back. A few mothers climbed to the roof of a nearby building and began to cry and scream; they could see that the roof had collapsed and most of the building was leveled.[12]

Didner had joined a team of refugee doctors. Prison guards had opened the gates of the Ward Road jail, and the refugee doctors set up a makeshift operating room in the yard. The hospital in the Ward Road camp already was filled to capacity. First-aid trucks and refugees with stretchers were collecting the wounded Chinese and fellow refugees and delivering them to the prison yard.

The nurses and doctors quickly organized a triage system. Most of the victims were in shock. Doctors first sutured the wounds and amputated the limbs of victims with the most serious injuries. Didner saw one fourteen-year-old Chinese boy covered with blood; his wounded intestines and liver were dangling outside his stomach. Didner couldn't stand the sight; he knew the boy couldn't be saved. He quickly filled a syringe with morphine and injected it in the boy's arm. He died peacefully from the a fatal dose.

The doctors had only a limited amount of ether for anesthesia and quickly ran out of bandages and dressing. Camp residents brought linens and clothing to the yard and ripped them up for use as bandages. Women refugees prepared tea and coffee for the wounded and brought blankets and pillows for them to rest on. The refugees organized a guard service to prevent looting.[13]

By sundown, all of the wounded had been treated. Didner's clothes were covered in blood as he headed back to his office. More than two hundred Chinese and thirty-one refugees had been killed, including Felix Kardegg, the head of the Jüdische Gemeinde and organizer of the refugee *pao chia*. There were more than five-hundred wounded, half of them refugees, and hundreds more were homeless.[14] But the kindergarten students had been saved. Their teacher had decided to let the children out early that day, and they had left the SACRA building just minutes before it was hit.[15]

The next day, the Chinese residents of Hongkew came to show their gratitude to the refugees. They wheeled dozens of rickshaws loaded with food for the homeless, donated money to the camps, and brought cakes for everyone.[16] The tragedy had momentarily bridged the gulf that had long separated the Chinese from the foreigners.

The American air raids continued over the next few weeks, including an attack on July 22 by more than 250 planes from the Fifth Air Force.[17] Heavy bombers regularly struck military targets into the first week of August. But although many of the planes flew overhead, no more bombs landed on Hongkew.

On August 6, soon after an American atomic bomb destroyed Hiroshima, Didner received word that the war was over. Grete's father had heard the news from a friend at the French consulate and she had called Didner. Grete was afraid to speak freely on the telephone, so she used a code: "I hear father and mother have stopped fighting," she said. When Didner figured out what she was saying, he called the Swedish consulate to check. Yes, a friend at the consulate told him, the Japanese have surrendered.

By that time, the rumors had spread throughout Hongkew and nearly one-hundred people had gathered outside Didner's house, knowing of his connections with the Swedes. "Is it true, Dr. Didner?" one of them yelled. "Is the war over?" Didner stepped outside on his second-floor balcony and confirmed the story, setting loose a celebration in the ghetto. A gang of boys began running through the streets yelling: "Dr. Didner says the war is over!"

A few hours later, fifty members of Betar, including Gerd Heimann, marched to the Japanese police station on Muirhead Road and announced they were taking it over. The Japanese didn't resist—they simply gathered up their goods and left. The Betar members proudly raised the blue and white Zionist flag over the police station. But the Japanese returned later that day and politely informed the refugees that they had been a bit premature—the war wasn't over yet. Just as peacefully as they had first switched places, the Betar members took down their flag and left as the Japanese returned to their posts.

18

Levin

It had taken him a few months, but by the end of 1945 Horst Levin had established himself once again in the Shanghai business community. His first job after the war was short-lived, selling books and antiques to American soldiers on their way home from the Pacific war. But his new position, as a manager for China United Chemical Corporation (CUCC), offered him a real chance to profit from Shanghai's postwar economic boom.

CUCC imported dyestuffs and chemicals from the United States to supply textile mills throughout China. In the early months of China's revival, the firm did well. It employed 250 Chinese and 2 Jewish refugees. The company's main office was on Avenue Edward VII in the French Concession, only a few blocks from the XMHA studio where, four years earlier, Levin had broadcast his last program for the refugee community.

Levin got the CUCC job because of Tiger Chang. Tiger was a well-educated and Westernized young Chinese man who had been a reporter for the American-owned *Shanghai Evening Post and Mercury* and several Chinese newspapers. Before the war, Levin and Tiger had spent many long evenings dining, drinking, and talking about sports and politics. In December 1941, when the Japanese took over all of Shanghai and began arresting journalists—including Horst—Levin lost touch with Tiger. He didn't see him again for nearly a year. Then, late in 1942, he saw Tiger at Jimmy's Kitchen, a popular and inexpensive Chinese restaurant not far from the Cathay Hotel. Tiger joined Levin for lunch and told him he had been living in Kunming, near the Burma border, and working with Chiang Kai-shek's army. He said he came to Shanghai two or three times a year to smuggle out goods.

Levin still lived in Hongkew, in the house with the terrace where he had been arrested just after Pearl Harbor. His landlords were Berlin Jews named Rosskamm. After the Japanese took over the radio station and the refugee radio program was discontinued, Levin spent a few hours each week keeping inventory for the Rosskamms' business. They sold toiletries and pharmaceuticals from an office in Sassoon House, across the street from Jimmy's Kitchen. Business had been slow since the war began. When Levin told him about his new job, Tiger seemed more than casually interested. He said the Nationalist army badly needed pharmaceuticals and he might want to buy all of the Rosskamms' stock. Tiger promised Levin a ten percent commission; Levin said he would prepare a list of goods and meet with him again the next day.

Levin had learned the Shanghai way of doing business in his days selling advertising for *Shanghai Woche* and XMHA. He typed up a list that doubled, tripled, or even quadrupled some prices. Rosskamm had priced drugs to treat venereal disease, for example, at ten dollars; Levin listed them at thirty or forty dollars. Over the next few days, Levin, Tiger, and Tiger's brother met for lunch at Jimmy's Kitchen. They talked about soccer, Chinese festivals, and the war. It was, Levin recognized, the Chinese way of doing business, slowly working toward making a deal. Eventually, Tiger and his brother agreed to buy everything Rosskamm had, paying about twenty-five percent less than Levin had asked and taking their own cut as well. That still would leave Levin with a remarkable profit. There was only one catch—all the goods would have to be transported to warehouses in the old Chinese city before they would pay for them.

That night over dinner, Levin talked to Rosskamm about the deal. His boss was quite eager to get rid of his merchandise but skeptical about the conditions. When Levin promised to oversee the delivery himself, Mrs. Rosskamm threw in her support and Rosskamm reluctantly agreed to sell.

Two days later, at about 10 A.M., Levin picked up Rosskamm's signed authorizations and went to his warehouse on North Szechuen Road. Levin and Tiger supervised as coolies carried the goods on shoulder poles to the street, where Tiger had about twenty rickshaws waiting. They loaded the goods and began to lead the procession of rickshaws along the banks of the Whangpoo River toward the Chinese city. But Tiger told Levin it was too dangerous for him to come with them—the Japanese troops certainly would stop them if they were accompanied by a Westerner—so he scrawled out an IOU and said he would meet him with the money at Jimmy's Kitchen by 1 P.M. Levin would have to trust his Chinese friend; he took a rickshaw downtown.

Time passed slowly at Jimmy's as Levin read the newspapers and had some tea. Tiger hadn't appeared by one o'clock, so Levin ordered lunch. He wasn't particularly worried because Tiger was invariably late. But by 2 P.M., Levin started to get nervous. His waiter seemed nervous, too—in the excitement of the day's events, Levin had forgotten his wallet and couldn't pay his bill until Tiger arrived. He continued to order cakes and coffee to keep the waiter occupied. He also telephoned Rosskamm, who was waiting at his office across the street, to tell him everything was going smoothly and that he would be there in an hour. Rosskamm seemed reassured, but said he couldn't wait any longer and was going home for the day.

By 3 P.M., Levin had read every newspaper he could find— even the Chinese ones—and had sampled almost every pastry Jimmy's had to offer. He began to have serious doubts that he would ever see Tiger again. He had thought of himself as a clever businessman. Now he realized he had been naive and stupid, blinded by greed and duped by someone he trusted. How would he break the news to Rosskamm? How could he explain that everything his boss owned was gone? How many years—how many lifetimes—would it take to pay him back? After all his successes in Shanghai, Levin had hit bottom. His future would be ruined.

Then Levin saw a rickshaw pull up outside the restaurant. It was Tiger, carrying two large suitcases. Levin exhaled slowly. His heart was still beating rapidly; it was cool in the restaurant, but his shirt was soaked with sweat. Tiger came inside and apologized profusely, then opened the suitcases. They were stuffed with thousands of Shanghai dollars. He asked Levin for his cut. But Horst was too agitated to accommodate him. He grabbed a few bills from one of the suitcases to pay the waiter, brusquely told Tiger he would pay him the next day, and carried the suitcases across the street.

There were still a few people at work in Rosskamm's office, so Levin unlocked the men's room down the hall and brought the suitcases into one of the stalls. He counted the money—it was all there—and took out Rosskamm's share. He left the suitcases with the remaining money on top of the toilet tank, locked the stall door, and crawled under it. Then he wrapped Rosskamm's money in some newspapers and telephoned him to say the deal was completed and he had his money. Rosskamm had been as nervous as Levin.

"Thank God," Rosskamm said. "We had already given up on you." He told Levin to bring the money to his house in Hongkew. Rosskamm and his wife greeted him with wine and cakes—they didn't know Horst had been eating pastry all afternoon—and toasted him to celebrate the sale. Rosskamm also gave Levin a ten percent commission, unaware that Levin had made at least two or three times as much as he had from the transaction.

Levin returned to the office before six the next morning, retrieved the suitcases, and deposited the money in a nearby bank. He paid Tiger his share later that day. The money was enough to allow Levin live comfortably throughout the remainder of the war. He established a partnership with his friend Mario Herbst and negotiated a few more deals between Tiger and other refugee businessmen that spring, but on a much smaller scale. And he always insisted on payment on delivery. All of Levin's business dealings came to an end in August when Ghoya took charge of the pass system.

While most other refugees were destitute in the ghetto, Levin lived a life of leisure. He had moved into a small apartment on Wayside Road with two other refugees and spent his time hanging out at the relocated Cafe Louis and Zum Weissen Roessl (The White Horse) on Ward Road. He also spent many afternoons drinking tea and discussing current events at the Roof Garden, the popular refugee cafe on the roof of the Broadway Theatre, or under the umbrellas at the outdoor cafe at Wayside and Chusan roads. Levin also joined a literary group and gave lectures, including one on the 1936 Berlin Olympics. He played cards and dice in the evenings and occasionally took his Austrian girlfriend to a movie or dinner at the Delikat on Chusan Road. Yet he was careful never to show off his wealth. He even went to the Kitchen Fund for a few free meals, but the thin soup and moldy bread tasted too terrible to eat.

Levin saw his Chinese friend only once more before the end of the war. Tiger came into the ghetto looking for Levin in the spring of 1944 and took him out to dinner. He told Levin it was no longer safe for him to come to Shanghai and he was leaving for Kunming for the last time. He offered to take Levin with him. Horst appreciated Tiger's concern, but declined the offer. Kunming seemed too far away, and life in Shanghai was relatively pleasant.

Levin began to doubt the wisdom of his decision when the bombing raids began to strike the city. But by August 1945, he was hearing about imminent landings by U.S. troops and watching the Japanese prepare for the defense of the city. The daily rumors spurred hope for the end of the war as well as fear that conditions could become worse. Levin wrote later:

> Suddenly, no one can say how or from where, people are getting peaceful. First it is an excited whispering and muttering among some, the curious then close in, everywhere collections of people build up, it gets more and more lively, one hears shouts of joy and bits of conversation above the humming. . . . "I

have it first hand, it's really true . . . ";"I was there when Mr. X was called out of the city . . . ";"In town everyone is up and about . . . "; "Cease fire . . . peace . . . liberation."

The excitement is getting greater and greater, one is trying to learn details by telephone calls to town, reports of celebrations in the city pour in, the careful and the thoughtful warn everyone to be quiet, for Japanese patrols crisscross the streets as usual, but the swelling joy cannot be kept down any longer, like an elemental volcanic eruption, flowing over everything and making its own pathway.

People lie in each other's arms, they rejoice; the Chinese, at first uncomprehendingly looking on, begin to express their joy in their own way. Is the improbable, shortly before the last catastrophe, now supposed to be true anyway? No more war, no more bomb attacks, no District, reunion with loved ones throughout the world. The brain cannot comprehend all this at once, it's too much, what so unexpectedly rushes in on these people, who for years had gotten used to just bad news.

Everywhere improvised celebrations are taking place, forgotten are the bomb attacks and the unbearable heat, illness and other bad things; from the windows, music and song ring out in the middle of the night, one hears *"Hatikvah"*; "God Bless America" is being sung. . . . There is hardly anyone this night in the District who will go to bed.

From street to street, joyful, laughing people are wandering, animated by new hope. One group of high-spirited people are going along the border of the District and are tearing down the front signs on which had been written "Stateless Refugees Are Prohibited to Pass Here Without Permission." The signs are being shown around like trophies, the Japanese patrols have disappeared from the streets, there is no more doubt: The war is over.[1]

In the months after the war ended, there were many reasons for optimism among the Jewish refugees in Shanghai. The Japanese and *pao chia* were gone; the ghetto had ceased to exist. Refugees could leave Hongkew to work, shop, or simply enjoy the freedom of walking Shanghai's once-more noisy and crowded streets. A few refugees re-opened their businesses and found apartments outside of Hongkew.[2]

The arrival of Americans further transformed their lives. The first small group of American soldiers flew into Shanghai at the end of August on a goodwill mission to visit former American and British prisoners at the Japanese internment camps. They toured Hongkew on August 29 and refugees filled the streets to greet them as liberators. At each of the camps, they were met with flags, cheering crowds, and children carrying flowers.[3]

In mid-September, thousands of American soldiers began arriving by ship. Shanghai was a processing center for American troops leaving the Pacific, and the soldiers and sailors brought money, jobs, and a free, almost carnival-like, spirit to the city. The Americans drew large crowds of Chinese when they hired rickshaws and pulled them through the streets while befuddled rickshaw drivers sat in the carriages. The soldiers handed out gum and candy to children and wooed refugee women with nylons and cigarettes. The only complaints came from the young Jewish men who lost their girlfriends to American soldiers.[4]

American culture also began to entice the refugees. Willy Tonn changed his Asia Seminar to the American Seminar and offered lectures and courses about American life and customs.[5] Interest in German music and operettas waned as refugees flocked to American movies in the French Concession. Refugee children found role models in Errol Flynn and Paul Muni and formed clubs to collect and trade Captain Marvel, Batman, and Superman comics.[6]

Restaurants, cafes, shops, and clubs thrived with the influx of new customers. The army and navy hired nearly 1,500 refugees to work as clerks in the newly-opened PXs or as carpenters, locksmiths, mechanics, drivers, and office staff.[7] The Americans paid salaries as high as two hundred dollars a month.[8] The JDC also hired more than two-hundred refugees as craftsmen, watchmen, hospital staff, and drivers. ORT expanded its course offerings and helped train more than a thousand refugees for technical jobs.[9]

But despite the economic revival, most refugees recognized that Shanghai remained a temporary refuge. It gradually became a less desirable one. Anti-Semitic articles appeared in

Chinese and English-language newspapers. (A November 1945 *Shanghai Herald* editorial questioned the loyalty of German and Austrian refugees who had formed residents' associations. "If the refugees are to constitute themselves as a separate community, working for private interests at the expense of the welfare of China," the editorial stated, "then they will alike forfeit any claim to Chinese goodwill and become *persona non grata* with the Chinese."[10]) Four months after the Japanese surrender, Chiang Kai-shek issued a promulgation calling for the deportation of all German and Austrian Jewish refugees in Shanghai. It was never enforced.[11]

A few months after the end of the war, Levin received a letter from his uncle in Chicago confirming his fears. His mother Betty and sister Ruth had been deported to Lwow and murdered by the Einsatzgruppen in 1941. Perhaps Betty had welcomed death after her years of mental anguish. Horst grieved for Ruth, his vibrant, lovely sister who had sacrificed her own life to care for their ailing parents and free him from Sachsenhausen. It was she who had made it possible for him to escape to Shanghai. He would always regret that he was never able to rescue her from Germany.

One other reminder of the Nazis haunted Levin and other refugees in Shanghai. Just after the American soldiers arrived, rumors spread that the site of a German extermination camp had been discovered in Shanghai. That fall, Levin met some American soldiers at the bookstore who showed him a report and later drove him to the site. He didn't see much, just some barracks and blockhouse buildings. But other refugees saw more. Curt Fuchs, Herman Natowic's nephew, rode with some soldiers on amphibious vehicles to Putong, the isolated peninsula across the Whangpoo River from Hongkew. Inside a cavernous brick building, Fuchs saw a dozen rounded, white, eight-foot high structures that appeared to be ovens. They apparently had never been used.[12]

The refugee *bonkes* (rumors) multiplied. Some said the camp was north of Hongkew Park or near the Chiangwan Airdrome. Others said it had been bombed and destroyed earlier by

American planes.[13] It was widely believed that the Nazis were responsible. Meisinger reportedly had sent German engineers to Shanghai early in the war to supervise the construction, although the Japanese resisted any plans to use them.

There appears to be no remaining evidence, either documentary or photographic, of the Shanghai death camp. Some have suggested that the rumor spread as a way to assuage the refugees of their guilt for having survived. But Curt Fuchs, a reliable witness for so much else from Shanghai, has no doubts about what he saw.

In the summer of 1946, Levin was married. His bride was his partner Mario Herbst's former wife, Thea. Herbst had left Thea for a Russian-American woman who refused to let him go, and Levin's Austrian girlfriend had jilted him. The uncertainty of the times was a boon to matrimony. Horst and Thea—and 125 other refugee couples, including Sam and Grete Didner—were married that year.[14] (There were even a few marriages between refugees and Chinese, performed by Rabbi Silberstein.) Horst and Thea moved into a nice apartment in Hongkew, next door to a noisy rubber factory.

There seemed to be little future for them in Shanghai. Tiger's friends had hired Levin to work for China United Chemical Company and he enjoyed his job, but Horst was being paid every two months in increasingly larger bundles of Chinese dollars. The currency was worth less every month. Shortly after the wedding, Levin wrote to his two uncles in the United States—his mother's brothers—to send emigration affidavits for him and Thea. CUCC urged him to stay, but offered to let him set up a branch office in New York.

It took about a year to get the necessary papers and visas. By the time they left for the United States, Thea was pregnant. If it was a girl, they decided, they would name her Ruth.

19

The Redeemer

In December 1945, Manny Siegel, the JDC's representative in Shanghai, prepared to leave for the United States. He had come in November 1941 to assist Laura Margolis, but had spent nearly three of his four years in Shanghai interned by the Japanese on Putong. Siegel had resumed his work for the JDC after he was released in August, but he was clearly exhausted and ready to return home. In his last report from Shanghai, he wrote:

> I do not see much hope for the refugees leaving China in any large numbers in the course of the next years. Their outlook for remaining in China seems to be increasingly dark, based on the Chinese nationalistic point of view and the increasing evidence of antisemitism.[1]

Siegel asked the JDC to replace him with a "Jewish personality of some renown" who could help develop more friendly attitudes toward the refugees.

The JDC selected Charles Jordan to take over in the Far

East. Jordan, thirty-seven, had been trained as a social worker in Philadelphia and New York and had studied at Berlin University. He joined the JDC in 1941 as director for the Caribbean area, enlisted in the navy from 1943–1945, then rejoined the JDC after the war.[2] Jordan was a dynamic, compassionate administrator who quickly won the respect of the Shanghai refugees.

Under Jordan's leadership, the JDC repaired and renovated the camps that housed 3,500 refugees and provided cash relief for 5,600, supplementing the United Nations assistance.[3] (Beginning in November 1945, UNRRA—the UN Relief and Rehabilitation Administration—each month shipped the refugees 9,000 bags of flour, 35,000 cases of food, and thousands of items of clothing, although the food was primarily U.S. Army rations and the clothing mostly of poor quality. After a few months, most of it was being sold on the black market.)

Jordan also established a nursery, children's home, a modern Joint House for 120 elderly persons, and a library stocked with nearly 3,000 books. He opened a new Jewish Community Center on the grounds of the Kadoorie School, directed by Mr. and Mrs. Aaron Grodsky, that offered handicrafts, lectures, music, dances, and religious activities.[4] The center also hosted several youth clubs, including one called Tikveh that published a newsletter and produced a play commemorating the Warsaw ghetto uprising.[5] Gerd Heimann was one of the actors.

Improved nutrition, as well as the availability of new drugs and expanded hospital care, contributed to a rapid decrease in illness and death. Other than tuberculosis, which affected thousands of the refugees, the only serious postwar health problem was liver leeches. Nearly half the refugees contracted them after eating raw herring sold by vendors on the street.[6]

The Jewish Recreation Club, run by the Russian Jewish community, revived the adult sports leagues that had been suspended by the Japanese. Refugee boxers once again fought American sailors, as they had before the war, and won most of their matches. The JRC also sponsored chess, tennis, handball, and ping-pong teams. The Jewish soccer league resumed competition and a JRC team vied for the city championship. Herman Natowic directed the referee section. The annual "Press versus Artists" soccer matches also reappeared after a five-year absence, featuring Gerhard Gottschalk's hilarious goaltending.[7]

Despite the improvements, Jordan, like Siegel, saw few reasons for optimism. The civil war and the Nationalist's mismanagement of the economy seemed to augur that the good times would be short-lived. Prices in Shanghai quintupled in the five months after the end of the Pacific war; they increased thirtyfold by the beginning of 1947. There were 1,716 strikes and labor disputes in the city in 1946, fed by communist infiltration of the unions.[8] Dozens of foreign firms closed their factories and offices and, by the middle of 1946, most of the American soldiers had left, putting an end to hundreds of jobs.[9]

The wave of Chinese anti-Semitism, which Siegel had reported before he left, had reached Hongkew. Mobs of Chinese, angry over the postwar housing shortage, broke into apartments and tried to throw out refugees and take over their living quarters. For two weeks in May, hundreds of Chinese squatters set up tents in the lanes surrounding the Ward Road camp and threatened to remain until the refugees moved out. The squatters strung up anti-Semitic banners, proclaiming "The Japs and the Jews are our enemies." Chinese also staged street demonstrations in the city, carrying anti-Jewish slogans and caricatures of bearded and hook-nosed Jews, chillingly similar, Jordan observed, to the cartoons he had seen in *Der Sturmer* in the 1930s when he was a student in Germany.[10]

The hostility was not directed solely toward Jews. It was part of a resurgence of nationalism that fanned hatred toward all foreigners. There were anti-American demonstrations and riots throughout China, including an ambush of American marines in Anping.[11] The Chinese had been liberated from a century of foreign domination and nearly fifteen years of brutal Japanese occupation. The foreign powers had exploited the Chinese people and enslaved them with opium; the Japanese had killed or wounded more than 20 million Chinese and ruined the nation's economy. The Nationalist government, as well as their increasingly powerful enemies, the Chinese Communists, each manipulated the postwar xenophobia for their own ends. These portents were not lost on the Jews who had escaped from Europe and who were uniquely sensitive to signs that they were no longer welcome by their hosts.

On April 23, 1946, Jordan wrote the JDC:

> We are now convinced that there is absolutely no place for the large majority of our people in either Shanghai or the rest of China. We are convinced that the solution to the problem here is emigration, and we are convinced furthermore that it requires speed.[12]

The JDC completed a survey at the end of March 1946 to determine where the refugees wished to emigrate. There were 13,475 European refugees remaining in Shanghai, all but 1,000 of them Jews. There were 7,498 Germans, 4,337 Austrians, 654 Poles, 181 Czechs, and 805 from other countries. More than 60 percent were over age 35, and 56 percent were male.[13]

Some of older refugees applied to return to their homelands. More than 2,200, mostly Austrians, had listed repatriation as their first choice, and about 800 of them were able to emigrate by the beginning of 1947.[14] They returned to a devastated postwar economy and, for some, years of court battles to win back their homes and businesses.[15] A few even searched for some of their valuables that had been stolen in the 1930s and tried to buy them back.[16] But for most of the refugees, the extermination of European Jewry made returning to Germany or Austria unimaginable.[17]

The refugees had come to Shanghai because there was no other place in the world that would take them. Not much had changed since the end of the war. They were faced once again with quotas, immigration restrictions, and discrimination. The refugees had survived six years of war, poverty, and isolation in Shanghai; now it would take some of them six more years to leave. Jordan led the fight to find them new homes:

These, our people, still have dignity, faith and hope, as well as a good sense of humor. And the youth is through and through sterling quality which, I must say, speaks well for their upbringing and for those who brought them up, considering conditions under which it was done.

I have no patience with people in countries of immigration who are always ready to find fault with the newcomers. Some of these critics, I am sure, would have been unable to survive the degradation, the humiliation and the plain physical sufferings of those they are so ready to condemn. I think that these, our people, will still, after all these deprivations and degradations, be able to make a good, new start somewhere else where economic and social conditions are more favourable to the integration and adjustment of newcomers and that every ounce of energy, and every penny spent on behalf of keeping them alive and helping them to get to other places, will certainly not be spent in vain.[18]

The United States—the nation that had liberated them from the Japanese, with its noble history as the *goldene medine*, the land of opportunity for the homeless and distressed—was the first choice of destination for more than 5,300 refugees.[19] At the beginning of January 1946, the U.S. consulate in Shanghai began accepting applications for quota numbers.[20] But the process was slow. It took three to four weeks for the consulate to investigate an applicant and another three or four weeks to issue a quota number. With its small and inexperienced staff, the consulate could handle only four or five quota immigration cases a day.[21] By the end of January 1947, a year after the consulate began its work, only 868 refugees had left Shanghai for the United States.[22]

Nearly half of those who emigrated to the United States in the first year were rabbis, students, and family members connected with the Mir Yeshiva. They and their representatives in the United States put enormous pressure on the State Department, UNRRA, and other agencies, demanding that they reach the United States before the September 1946 High Holidays. They monopolized the consulate, which was forced to focus on their cases and delay action on others. Jordan wrote in July:

I do not and cannot have objections to rabbis and rabbinical students being given the opportunity to go to the United States, but I do object to their taking up all the time and all the facilities the American consulate has for the processing of prospective immigrants, so that a large number of equally deserving, if not more urgent, cases cannot be taken care of.[23]

The emigration of the Polish Yeshivas further aggravated the problems for refugees who fell under the tiny Polish quota. That included 1,800 people—including Georg Kantorowsky, Bob Angress and his parents, and Gustav and Julie Heimann— who were born in parts of Germany that were now considered part of Poland. Sam Didner, whose mother had gone back to her native Poland to give birth to him, also was on that quota. Only sixty-eight Polish quota numbers were allocated to Shanghai in the first two years after the war.

Rabbi Kantorowsky formed an "Executive Committee of Polish Quota D.P.'s" to appeal to authorities and organizations in the United States for help. He wrote in 1947:

Once the war ended, we were full of hope that our sufferings were over and liberty in sight. We expected that after nine years of misery and hardships we would not encounter so many obstacles on our way to America. Our early hope, however, has given way to despair! We feel abandoned and forgotten. We cannot stand it very much longer! We have lost so much precious irretrievable time: years in concentration-camps, years of wandering, years in the Shanghai Ghetto, and now the post-war years of fruitless waiting. . . How much longer shall we have to endure the agonies of a dragging transitory period?[24]

The rabbi's daughter, Eva, like many children of the Polish quota refugees, was born in what was still Germany and would have been able to emigrate on the German quota. But it never occurred to her that she might leave her husband behind.

Eva had been out of work for much of her two years in the ghetto after Peritz fired her based on his unwarranted suspicion that she was reporting on his affairs to his wife. But in the fall of 1944, Meyer Birman, the grouchy and penurious manager of the Far Eastern Jewish Information Bureau who had been her boss for three months late in 1941, rehired her. Because she couldn't get a pass to leave the ghetto, Birman put her to work in the bureau's Hongkew office. Eva worked mostly with yeshiva students, sending messages for them and collecting money when they paid back loans they had received from HIAS. This time, the job was less stressful—she rarely had to deal directly with Birman—and she worked there for a little more than a year. Shortly after the war ended, Eva took a job with the American Red Cross.

She worked for the Red Cross Field Director's office, helping American servicemen contact their relatives. She was paid ninety dollars a month. Bob was working as an accountant for a British firm, and their combined income seemed like a fortune compared with their wartime poverty. Freed from the confines of the ghetto, they traveled around Shanghai, saw the new American movies, went out to eat in Chinese restaurants, like Sun Ya on Nanking Road, and went to tea dances at the luxurious Senet in the French Concession. (Italian sailors from the *Conte Verde*, stuck in Shanghai after they scuttled their ship in the summer of 1943, reportedly furnished the Senet with equipment they had stolen during the war.) But Bob and Eva tried to save most of their money. At first, they continued to live with Bob's aunt in their tiny room in her lane house, but soon they moved to a nicer lane house— with a toilet—on Kungping Road. Later they moved into Hamilton House, a high-rise apartment building downtown, where they shared an apartment with another couple.

After most of the American troops had left Shanghai, Eva took a position as secretary to the manager of Ekman's, a Swedish import-export and shipping agency. In her spare time, she continued to write letters to synagogues and her father's relatives in the United States—some of his family had emigrated to Arkansas in the late 1800s—to secure affidavits for her father and Bob and to find sponsors for Bob's parents.

The fate of the Shanghai refugees who wished to come to the United States was tied into a larger issue. President Truman and Congress were locked in a four-year-long battle over immigration, centered on the one million refugees, about twenty percent of them Jews,[25] in postwar displaced persons' camps in Europe. The fight kindled the worst of American isolationism and anti-Semitism. It left the refugees—including thousands in Shanghai—stranded for years.

In December 1945, Truman had issued a directive that maintained the existing limits on immigration, but shifted the restrictive quotas to provide preferential treatment for displaced persons, particularly orphans. It also granted social service agencies, such as the JDC, the authority to sponsor refugees. The directive would have allowed for more than 150,000 immigrants a year to enter the country.[26] But the process was slow, as the refugees in Shanghai discovered. Security screening, medical examinations, and dozens of bureaucratic procedures, as well as the shortage of ship transportation, limited emigration.[27]

By the middle of 1947, however, the U.S. consulate in Shanghai was processing about 250 visa cases a month.[28] Hundreds of refugees were sailing to the United States on the SS *General Meiggs* and other President Line ships. Jewish refugees had begun to benefit from Truman's humanitarian gesture—they made up two-thirds of the 41,379 refugees admitted under his 1945 directive.[29] By the time Jordan left Shanghai in April 1948, more than 5,000 Shanghai refugees had been admitted to the United States.

But the slow immigration process had convinced American Jews that it was necessary to fund a campaign for congressional legislation. Their humanitarian efforts, however, produced a result much different from what they had hoped for. The act that emerged from the Republican-controlled Congress, led by anticommunist and anti-Semitic reactionaries, blatantly discriminated against Jewish refugees, giving preference to farmers, refugees from the Baltic states, and, incredibly, to ethnic Germans, some of them Nazi collaborators.[30] Truman reluctantly signed the bill in June 1948, saying it "discriminates in callous fashion against displaced persons of the Jewish faith."[31] The new law drastically reduced opportunities for Jews remaining in displaced person camps—and in Shanghai. Most found that their emigration to the United States was blocked by the restrictive legislation.

Australia, with its two large Jewish communities and proximity to China, offered another opportunity for the Shanghai refugees. Australia's minister of immigration in August 1945 had proposed a program to accept Holocaust survivors who had relatives in the country. It was the first choice for about 2,500 refugees[32] and nearly 800 of them had left for Australia by the end of January 1947, almost as many as the number approved for emigration to the United States.

But the migration to Australia did not go smoothly. A group of 299 refugees from Shanghai was stranded for up to six months in two unfurnished ballrooms in Hong Kong's Peninsula Hotel awaiting transport to Australia. The government feared that a large influx of refugees would take away apartments needed for returning servicemen and refused to send empty troopships for them. Jordan intervened and chartered dozens of ships and planes.[33]

Another three hundred Jewish refugees traveled to Australia on the *Hwa Lien*, a forty-year-old ferry boat that was dirty, had no facilities for feeding large numbers of people, and was barely seaworthy. It was caught in a cyclone before it safely reached Sydney. The JDC paid about $165 for each passenger.[34]

The arrival of the refugees in Australia set off hostile reactions in the press and Parliament, similar to those in the U.S. Congress. Right-wing leaders accused the refugees of illegally importing large sums of money and gold bars; monopolizing transportation and housing needed by former servicemen; and threatening the nation's security as communist spies. The immigration minister responded by limiting to twenty-five percent the number of Jewish refugees permitted to travel on any one ship. That prevented the JDC from chartering boats for the refugees.[35]

Early in 1947, the Australian government sent an unofficial representative, Alec Masel, to Shanghai. His assignment was to prepare a list of young and skilled refugees, and he met with Jordan and representatives of other organizations, including the ORT. Many refugees saw him as a kind of Messiah, although Masel emphasized he could not issue permits. He drew up a list recommending 1,865 people, most of them European refugees, for immigration to Australia. That summer, Jordan visited Australia to help clear the way.[36]

But in the meantime, the Australian consul general in Shanghai had forwarded a secret report to the government about the danger of accepting Shanghai refugees. They had been influenced by the immorality of the city, he reported, and reduced "to the lowest levels of depravity and despair." He claimed that many of them, particularly the Russians, had collaborated with the Japanese. A migration officer sent to Shanghai filed a report referring to the refugees as "human flotsam and jetsam," criminals, and communists. He recommended complete cessation of immigration. Despite Jordan's pleas, Australia was nearly closed off to the Shanghai refugees. Only three hundred were granted permits in 1947–1948.[37]

Another possible destination was Palestine. It was the first choice for about 1,100 people, less than ten percent of the European refugees in Shanghai. There were a number of Zionists among the German and Austrian Jews, but few who wished to join the fight for Israeli statehood. Most of those who went to Palestine were Russian Jews.

The International Refugee Organization, the successor to UNRRA, had made it nearly impossible for Jewish refugees to travel to Palestine legally. The IRO was controlled by British officials, who used it to implement British policy. Even after the state of Israel was established on May 14, 1948, the IRO refused to assist Jewish refugees who wished to go there.[38] But as the United States, Australia, and other countries closed their doors—and as the political and economic situation in Shanghai deteriorated —Israel became the only choice for more and more refugees.

In the spring of 1948, Jordan prepared to leave Shanghai. He had spent two and a half years working to improve living conditions and assist the emigration of the Jewish refugees. Only 6,100 refugees remained, and Jordan expected at least 1,000 of them to leave by the end of the year. But the opportunities for the remaining refugees, many of them elderly or ill, were increasingly limited.

20

Heimann

It was an informal May wedding, held in a crowded harbor customs house in San Francisco, California. Gerhard Heimann, twenty-one, and his bride, Irine Stollman, twenty, had been married in a civil ceremony six months earlier, but this wedding was for the benefit of Gerd's parents, Gustav and Julie. It was officiated by Georg Kantorowsky, who by that time had become the rabbi of a San Francisco synagogue founded by Gerd and other Shanghai refugees. The customs house was divided by temporary wooden fencing for the ceremony. Immigration officials wanted to make certain that Gustav and Julie, and 104 other refugees who had just arrived from Shanghai, wouldn't enter the United States illegally.

Gerd had arranged for a small wedding with the President Line, the owners of the ship that had brought his parents from Shanghai. He had planned for eight people, including his parents, Aunt Thekla and Uncle Adolf and Uncle Sally from the ship, and his brother Benno, who had come from Bakersfield. But Rabbi Kantorowsky had called the newspapers and told them about the wedding. The arrival of the last refugees from what was now known as Red China had become a major news event. The customs house was crowded with reporters and photographers as well as dozens of former Shanghai refugees who had brought food and gifts for their compatriots.

Irine held a prayer shawl over her head as Rabbi Kantorowsky recited the blessings. The rabbi handed the kiddush cup to Gerd, but all the commotion had made the rabbi nervous—he spilled wine all over their marriage contract. Julie and Gustav hugged the new daughter-in-law they had met minutes earlier, handed her their wedding gifts, and introduced her to Uncle Sally and Aunt Thekla and Uncle Adolf. But there wasn't much time. The 106 refugees from Shanghai were scheduled to board a train for Ellis Island the next day.

Gerd had been in the United States for nearly two years. He had met his bride at a dance sponsored by some of the Shanghai refugees not long after he had arrived, and they were soon engaged to be married. After a few miserable months as a delivery boy, Gerd had taken the required courses and was now licensed to work as a barber in Culver City. It was a long way from Szuran's and Shanghai.

Five years earlier, a few months after the end of the war, the barber's guild had placed Gerd and Szuran in a shop owned by the U.S. armed services, not far from the Chiangwan Airdrome. A battalion of military police was based nearby, and Gerd, who had completed his apprenticeship, was making more than thirty-five dollars a month cutting hair and shaving beards. He didn't get to spend much of it—Gerd still gave all his earnings to his father and got a small allowance. When Szuran moved back into Hongkew the next year, Gerd earned even more money working for his former teacher, Kurt Mosberg, who had a shop in a prize location right on the air base. That summer, in 1946, Gerd also found an American friend.

Word had spread around the air base that a B-29 from Okinawa was having engine trouble and was going to try an emergency landing on the small Chiangwan airstrip. The plane landed successfully and about twenty scruffy American airmen, with long hair and beards, piled out. (It was rumored that the soldiers had been so desperate to get away from the isolation of Okinawa that they had sabotaged the plane when they flew near Shanghai.) The airmen asked to be directed to the nearest barbershop. The PX agreed to pay, because none of the soldiers had any American money.

Gerd and Mosberg spent hours cleaning them up. After Gerd gave one of the airmen a haircut, he opened his shirt to shave him and noticed he was wearing a *mezzuzah* around his neck. Gerd introduced himself to the airman, who was named Irving Raeder, and invited him to his parent's house for Shabbat dinner that evening. After dinner, Gerd treated Raeder to a tour of some Shanghai nightclubs and a brothel in the French Concession. (By then, Gerd knew his way around Shanghai's brothels. After the war, he'd had his first sexual experience in a house off Bubbling Well Road. But, like a few of his friends, he had his own Chinese girlfriend now and no longer frequented brothels. He was happy, however, to serve as Raeder's tour guide.) At 2 A.M., Gerd put Raeder on an army truck that took him back to the air base. After Raeder returned to Okinawa, he sent Gerd a box of *mezzuzahs*. They exchanged letters until Raeder was discharged later that year and returned to the United States.

Early in 1947, the Heimanns met to discuss leaving China. Benno, who was an ardent socialist, wanted to go back to Germany; Gerd wanted to go to Palestine. But Gustav wanted the family to go to the United States together.

Gerd and his father argued for weeks, but Gerd finally agreed to write to Raeder and ask him for an affidavit. Because Gerd was born in Germany, was young, and had a trade, he would have little trouble getting a quota number. But he didn't hear from Raeder for months; he assumed Raeder thought his request was preposterous. In the meantime, the airbase had closed and Gerd had opened his own shop in his family's home on Alcock Road.

Gerd was impatient and still not sure he wanted to go to the United States, even after Raeder's affidavit arrived on the first day of Rosh Hashanah in 1947. His years with Betar had convinced him that he really should be in Palestine, helping his people fight for statehood against the British and the Arabs. Two Betar members already had traveled illegally to Palestine and returned to form the Etzel contingent, an underground unit associated with the Irgun. They planned to raise money for arms and to send trained Betar members back to Palestine.[1]

The United Nations vote in November to create a Jewish state set off a two-day celebration in the Shanghai Jewish community. There was free food and liquor in all the Hongkew restaurants and dancing in the streets. Betar members marched in a parade from Wayside Park to the new Kadoorie School, and Rabbi Kantorowsky led a religious service for all the members of the Hongkew Jewish community. A few days later, Gerd and a few of his friends decided they had to go to Israel. Without telling their parents, they stowed away on a British ship. But they got only as far as Hong Kong, where they were caught and sent back to Shanghai.

When he returned, Gerd got a stern lecture from his father. They had escaped together from the Nazis, Gustav said, and he had struggled to bring nearly all of his relatives to China. They had survived ten difficult years in Shanghai. Gustav and Julie, Uncle Sally, Uncle Adolf, and Aunt Thekla all had applied for U.S. visas; several other relatives were expecting to get U.S. visas soon. Gustav insisted that the family stay together once again. The United States, he said, was the only place for all of them.

Gerd acceded to his father's wishes. He filed his affidavit with the consulate and, in the spring of 1948, just as Charles Jordan was preparing to leave Shanghai, he received his visa for the United States. He left at the end of March 1948 on the SS *General Meiggs* with four of his friends. Jordan promised Gerd that Benno would join him in the United States within three months.

On the day they departed, Gustav divided up the money the family had saved and gave Gerd fifteen dollars to take with him. Gerd and his friends stood on the deck like soldiers, waving goodbye and holding back their tears. As soon as the ship headed up the Whangpoo, they all began to cry for what seemed like hours. But the rest of the trip went smoothly. A friend had told them to bring bottles of vodka along to bribe the crew, and the boys were able to gorge themselves on meat and desserts for the entire voyage. It reminded Gerd of his trip from Italy to Shanghai ten years earlier, when crew member Enrico Lupe took care of him so well. But on this passage, he had left his family behind. His parents, the Keibels, and Uncle Sally would be stuck in Shanghai for two more years.

Jordan's successor at the JDC in Shanghai was Adolph C. Glassgold. In his first quarterly report, Glassgold described what he called "a kind of dry rot that has infected the refugee community." Many of the remaining 5,342 refugees were bitterly disappointed by the restrictive new U.S. immigration act, he said, because it apparently would slow emigration to the United States to "a mere trickle." It was particularly hard on the more than 500 refugees who had been cleared for corporate affidavits from the JDC and were about to obtain U.S. visas until the act made them ineligible.[2]

The Stratton Bill that President Truman reluctantly signed in June 1948 virtually prevented displaced persons from receiving visas. Less than 2,500 immigrants worldwide entered the United States in the first six months under the act.[3] Some refugees were encouraged when Representative Emmanuel Celler of Brooklyn proposed new legislation to liberalize the law and admit an additional 179,000 displaced persons. The bill included a special provision for 4,000 European refugees from Shanghai. But that legislation was held up for more than a year and came too late for the Shanghai refugees. Senator Pat McCarran of Nevada, chairman of the Senate Judiciary Committee, led the effort to stall the bill, claiming it would allow large numbers of Jews and communists into the country.[4]

Glassgold wrote in July 1948:

But for the few hundreds that will be admitted to Australia, it may be said that our population is now pretty much down to rock bottom. This brings with it the urgent necessity to introduce as quickly as possible a constructive work program to counter-act the psychological and cultural deterioration that may follow in the wake of frustrated hopes for migration, and is already noticeable because of the long years of complete

financial dependence upon the relief grants distributed by the
JDC. Unfortunately, a large part of the population is afflicted
with a passivity and negativism that may prove to be serious
obstacles.[5]

About half the refugees were on cash relief, he noted.

As the population shrinks, work opportunities shrivel and many
who were hitherto self-supporting find themselves forced to
apply for cash assistance. To this must be added the rapidly
deteriorating economic situation in Shanghai and the run-away
inflation.[6]

By the summer of 1948, shopkeepers were increasing prices
several times a day. Cash transactions were becoming nearly
impossible, even with bills in ridiculously large denominations.
A large bag of flour, for example, which had sold for 42 Chinese
yuan in 1937, cost 1.95 million yuan in June 1948; by August, it
sold for 21.8 million yuan. The cost of living increased by nearly
6,000 times between July 1947 and July 1948.[7]

"What was once a fairly well-paying job may now be just
enough to keep one above the barest margin of existence,"
Glassgold wrote. Those still employed by the U.S. military, he
wrote, found their pay raises could not keep up with the
increasing cost of living; most were better off quitting their
jobs and accepting JDC relief. The economic situation would
only get worse.[8]

That August, the collapsing Nationalist government issued a
new currency, the gold yuan—one gold yuan was equal to
three million of the old yuan. Chiang Kai-shek used his
emergency powers to ban wage and price increases, strikes,
and demonstrations. He appointed his eldest son, Chiang
Ching-kuo, to oversee the reforms. Chiang Ching-kuo focused
his efforts on Shanghai, where prices temporarily stabilized.
But farmers and businessmen began to take their goods
outside the city where they could get higher prices, leading to
severe shortages of food and other items in Shanghai. By
October, the reforms had failed and inflation again soared out
of control. In February 1949, the cost of living was 52,000
times higher than it was in August 1948.[9]

The Nationalists were equally inept on the battlefield, as the communists continued to control the countryside and encircle Chiang Kai-shek's armies. The communists captured strongholds in Manchuria in the fall and won a major battle near Hsuchou at the end of 1948. Tientsin fell in January 1949, and the Communists closed in on the ancient capital, Peking.[10]

As the communists advanced, most foreigners remaining in China were desperate to get out. American citizens had priority at the U.S. consulate, making it even more difficult for the Jewish refugees to get visas. Sam Didner was eager to join his wife and two-year-old daughter in the United States. Grete was on the German quota and had left in the spring of 1948. But Didner, still stuck on the Polish quota, encountered the same delays and rejections he had faced more than ten years earlier when he tried to get out of Austria. It would take months to qualify for a U.S. visa, so he went from consulate to consulate, looking for a way out of Shanghai. Early in 1949, he got a visa from the Canadians. It permitted him to visit San Francisco and be with Grete when their second daughter was born in February. After he arrived in the United States, Didner received official word that his mother, oldest brother, oldest sister, and two nephews had been murdered in Theresienstadt.

The Kantorowskys and Bob and Eva Angress, who by then were expecting their first child, also received their U.S. visas early in 1949. They had been waiting for more than three years. In April, as the communists neared Shanghai, Georg, Frieda, Bob, and Eva left for San Francisco on the SS *President Wilson*. On the voyage to the United States, they received word that Shanghai had fallen. Eva later learned that her brother Hans had died in Auschwitz in September 1943, just a few months after she received her last letter from him.

For other refugees, Israel remained the only certain escape. As the war of independence came to an end and conditions worsened in Shanghai, more refugees considered emigrating there, even temporarily. Representatives of the Jewish Agency for Palestine freely issued thousands of visas to the remaining Russian, Sephardic, and European Jews in Harbin, Tientsin, and Shanghai. By the spring of 1949, more than 2,000 European refugees had left for Israel.[11]

The communists took Shanghai without a fight late in May; they assumed control of the rest of the country by the end of the year. The communists quickly made dramatic improvements, controlling inflation, cleaning up the cities, repairing public works, and eliminating privilege and corruption.[12] Some refugees volunteered to assist the new government. Bauhaus architect Richard Paulick, who had fled to China in 1933, helped design a city plan for Shanghai before returning to communist Germany and directing the reconstruction of the Stalinallee and the city of Dresden.[13] Violinist and teacher Alfred Wittenberg, at age seventy, turned down invitations to teach in the United States, preferring to remain with his pupils in Shanghai until his death in 1952.[14]

But most foreigners felt unwelcome and were eager to get out. The communists limited their travel and refused to let them leave the country. The JDC negotiated with the new government for four months and obtained exit permits for three hundred refugees, most of them without visas, who left in September for the United States.[15] The U.S. consulate in Shanghai closed a few weeks later. The IRO continued to evacuate anyone who had a permit to leave, bringing most of them to displaced persons camps in Europe. At the end of one long voyage in December 1949, 420 passengers on the *Wooster Victory* telegraphed an appeal to be taken to Israel rather than the camps in Italy. The IRO refused, so the JDC took over and financed the rest of the trip.[16]

By 1950, there were less than 1,000 European Jewish refugees left in China, most of them still hoping for visas to the United States. Many were inadmissable because they had criminal records or suffered from tuberculosis, syphilis, or insanity. Some were handicapped by age or lack of a sponsor. But most of them were on the small Polish or Austrian quotas.[17]

After another year of negotiations, the JDC and IRO in May 1950 arranged for one last voyage to the United States on the SS *General Gordon*. There would be 106 passengers. At least 7 had been rejected previously by the U.S. consulate because of criminal records or collaboration with the Japanese; 6 had tuberculosis, and several others had serious health problems. Others had been waiting for visas for as long as four years. The oldest were two sisters from Bremen, Rosa Cohn, seventy-four, and Isabella Samuel, seventy-six. The youngest was Jerry Mahrer, born in Shanghai two years earlier. The group included cellist Walter Joachimsthal, noted journalist and teacher Herbert Karo, and Hugo Lewisohn, the chief physician of the Jewish Hospital. Gerhard Heimann's parents, Gustav and Julie, Uncle Sally and Uncle Adolf, and Aunt Thekla also were scheduled to be part of the group.[18]

The communists refused to let the *General Gordon* inside China's coastal waters. It anchored off Tientsin and UNRRA sent a train to take the refugees on the long trip up the coast. They were joined by some Americans and other foreigners who had been trapped in Shanghai, including a Catholic Italian seaman from the *Conte Verde*, Giuseppe Romanelli. In Tientsin, they were towed on barges out to the ship. But one of the barges didn't make it before nightfall and, unable to dock with the *General Gordon*, circled in the choppy waters all night without food or blankets.

The passengers completed boarding the ship the next morning and sailed for Hong Kong, where the *General Gordon* dropped off most of its non-refugee passengers and picked up new ones. It then sailed to Manila and Yokohama to pick up more passengers en route to the United States. The refugees spent three weeks on the ship, a crowded troop transport with no amenities, but there were few complaints. They finally had left China and were headed for the United States.[19]

Most of the refugees on the *General Gordon* did not have visas and had little hope of entering the United States. Many of their dossiers had been lost when the U.S. consulate closed. But Congress was about to pass the new immigration bill and some of the refugees hoped it would make them eligible for visas. The ship arrived in San Francisco on May 23.

Immediately after Gerd and Irine's wedding, the 106 refugees were ordered to leave San Francisco. They were put on Pullman cars and sent across the United States to Ellis Island. A representative of the U.S. Justice Department rode on each coach, making sure the refugees did not try to get off. A few of the refugees on the train urged the group to stay together when they reached New York and began telegramming appeals to Representative Celler and Senator Jacob Javits.[20] But their compatriots, the refugees who already had settled in the United States, had not forgotten them. At each train stop along the way, dozens of refugees came to greet the train and bring gifts to the passengers.

By the time the refugees reached Ellis Island, they were virtually national celebrities. Celler and Javits were campaigning for them and they were front-page news. Immigration officials, however, planned to deport them the day they arrived, May 28. A navy troopship, the *C.C. Ballou*, was to take them to a displaced persons camp in Europe. That day, more than five hundred friends and relatives came to send them off and brought them packages of food and clothing. But minutes before they were scheduled to sail, the U.S. Attorney General, J. Howard McGrath, ordered a delay, setting off a celebration among the refugees. McGrath agreed to review their status under the new immigration bill, which had been approved by both houses and was awaiting action by a conference committee.[21]

The act was approved two weeks later and signed by President Truman on June 16.[22] McGrath extended the delay and permitted the refugees to stay in the Great Hall on Ellis Island for more than three weeks, where Jewish organizations paid for their care. On June 18, McGrath announced that he had completed his review. The new immigration law, he said, would not permit them to be admitted without visas. The refugees could not enter the United States, he said, because they were already here. They would have to be deported and then apply to re-enter the country.[23]

"It seems most tragic," Representative Celler said at the time, "that these victims of Nazi sadism should be deported because of some technicalities."[24] President Truman showed his sympathy by directing that they be treated as temporary residents, rather than displaced persons, when they arrived in Germany.[25]

On June 21, the 106 refugees boarded the *S.D. Sturgis* to sail for a camp in Bremerhaven, Germany. "We're going back to a country where our people were gassed after we fled from persecution," one of the refugees, Ernst Elguther, told *The New York Times*. "We'd go back to nothing but graves and bitter memories."[26]

Some were confident of returning to the United States soon, but most of them, including the Heimanns, would remain bitter. After fleeing the Nazis and enduring more than ten years in Shanghai, they were still unwanted refugees.

Coda

Gustav and Julie Heimann spent more than a year in displaced persons camps before they returned to the United States and were reunited with their sons. Gary (Gerhard) used German restitution money* set aside for scholarships to complete college and attend law school. He is now an attorney in Los Angeles, where he lives with his wife, Irine. They have three children.

Sam Didner, his wife, and two daughters moved to New York where he worked in area hospitals for two years. After he qualified for citizenship, Didner received his medical license and opened a practice in Long Island City, Queens. He still works there today.

Eva Kantorowsky Angress and her husband Bob settled in San Francisco. They had two children. Bob graduated from college and worked as an accountant; Eva worked as a secretary and office manager. Bob died in 1960. Rabbi Kantorowsky headed B'nai Emunah, the congregation he

---

* The German government eventually paid restitution to European Jewish refugees who lived in the Hongkew ghetto. They all received 5,000 deutschemarks; those who continued their education received an additional 5,000 marks. Germany recently agreed to pay claims to survivors who should have been compensated by the former East Germany.

founded with a group of Shanghai refugees, until his death in 1972.

Horst (Howard) Levin continued to work in the import-export business in New York City. He had one daughter with his first wife and was divorced and remarried three times. He died on New Year's eve 1992.

The evacuation of most of the remaining Jews in China was completed in November 1950, when two IRO ships took 714 immigrants to Israel. Most were Russian Jews and all of them were considered hard-core cases—the elderly or people with serious medical or mental problems. Only a few were originally from the Hongkew community. But a handful of Jews remained in Shanghai, Tientsin, and Harbin. Max Leibovich, a Russian with Parkinson's disease who was living with a Chinese woman, was believed to be the last Jewish refugee in Shanghai when he died in January 1982 at seventy-five.

Epilogue

In September 1992, after two years of studying the story of the Jewish refugees, I returned to Shanghai to look for the remnants of their community. Despite the economic development in much of the city, change has come slowly to Hongkou* (Hongkew). Isolated by Suzhou (Soochow) Creek, it has only one new luxury hotel. It remains one of the poorest areas of the city, and there are no tourist attractions—except for those tourists who once lived there as refugees.

My Chinese guide and I went first to the "new" Russian synagogue on Xiang Yang Nan Road (formerly Rue de la Tour in the French Concession), consecrated in 1941. The original building still stands and it is now used as an auditorium for the Shanghai Education College. Chen Weng Zhang, the former doorkeeper for the synagogue, still works there. He told us the interior of the synagogue was destroyed in a fire in the early 1950s. But the outside—with round windows over the entrance and long, narrow windows along the side of the building—remains the same. Chen was never allowed inside the synagogue, but he remembers that there were some tablets (memorial tablets) in the front lobby. The *youtairen* (Jews)

* The modern pinyin system of Chinese romanization is used in this epilogue to reflect current usage.

257

burned candles or incense there, he said, much like the Buddhists.

We found some other former Jewish sites in Shanghai only slightly altered. The Kadoorie mansion, the Marble Hall, is now a school where gifted children go for classes in art, ballet, and music. The changes are at the entrance of the building, where two young Greek figures have been replaced by statues of patriotic Chinese youths blowing trumpets; a yellow star, topped by a red flame, sits above the portico.

The Sephardic synagogue and the nearby Shanghai Jewish School on Shanxi Bei (Seymour) Road remain intact, although renovations have removed any sign that these were once Jewish sites. The buildings are now occupied by the Shanghai Education Bureau, which is reluctant to permit visitors beyond its locked gates. The other Sephardic synagogue, Beth Aharon, was demolished in 1985. Through the efforts of a visiting Jewish refugee, one of the two large granite menorahs that flanked the synagogue's entrance is being preserved at the Shanghai Museum.

Many of Sir Victor Sassoon's edifices also remain, including Hamilton House and the Metropolitan Building on Fuzhou (Foochow) Road. Sassoon's grandest achievement, the Cathay Hotel/Sassoon House, is now the Peace Hotel, a fading monument to the wealth of Shanghai's Sephardic community. The top floors, where Sassoon had his penthouse and which Japanese officers took over during the war, are now closed, used to house water tanks. The Embankment Building on North Suzhou (Soochow) Road, where hundreds of refugees first lived in Shanghai, is only slightly modified. A few blocks away, the once-notorious Bridge House on North Sichuan (Szechuen) Road is now the Da Feng Garment Company.

In Hongkou, we found several older Chinese residents who remember the Jewish refugees fondly. Mr. Yu at 33 Zhoushan (Chusan) Road was fourteen when the refugees arrived. Now white-haired and bespectacled, but with a ready smile and a lively step, he was happy to show us his neighborhood. Several refugees once lived in the building he and several other Chinese families now occupy, and he took us on a tour of the three-story house. In one of the Zhoushan Road lanes, he pointed out a building where some of the first Jewish refugees lived. Yu remembers well the day the American bombs hit Hongkou, not far, he said, from the new twenty-seven-story Ocean Hotel with its revolving restaurant on the top floor. After the war, Yu said, all the refugees left and "went to Hong Kong."

At Zhoushan and Changyang (Ward) roads, the three-story Ward Road camp, where many refugees lived among lice and bedbugs and where thousands came for their meals, still stands. Much of the black paint has chipped off. It is now an apartment building. Bamboo sticks draped with laundry hang out nearly every window. The Ward Road jail, where Sam Didner operated on victims of the bombing, looks much the same, but it is no longer a jail. Some of the surrounding walls are gone and the courtyard is crowded with apartment buildings.

The southern end of Zhoushan Road, where it meets Huishan (Wayside) Road, was once called "Little Vienna." Refugees gathered under umbrellas at the corner to drink sodas and eat pastries in front of Alfred Flatow's store. There are still umbrellas at the corner, but now Chinese residents congregate to eat dumplings and drink tea. All along Zhoushan Road, there are booths covering the sidewalk where Chinese salesmen, instead of Jewish refugees, sell watermelons and oranges, pants and jewelry. A store on Huishan, near the corner, provides a hint of the past. It is called "Vienna Shoes Shop."

The two nearby cinemas, the Broadway on Wayside and the Wayside on Broadway, still show movies, but the modern Hong Kong variety with kung fu and romance instead of Nelson Eddy and Jeanette MacDonald. The roof of the Broadway is closed now, but, from the top of the Ocean Hotel, it is possible to look down and imagine the days when it was called the Roof Garden and was filled with tables of Jewish refugees drinking their afternoon tea.

Throughout Hongkou, along Tangshan (Tongshan), Kunming (Kwenming), and Jingzhou (Kinchow) roads, the lane houses still line every alleyway and dozens of people are crowded into tiny rooms. In the warm weather, families still cook, eat, talk, and sleep on streets and sidewalks. But the residents are all Chinese now.

Much else has changed. There are new apartment buildings and businesses on nearly every block; landmarks such as the Kadoorie School and MacGregor Synagogue on East Yuhang (Dong Yuhan) Road have been demolished. All the Jewish cemeteries—on Mohawk (Huangbe Bei), Baikal (Huiming), Columbia (Fanyu), and Point (Liping) roads—are gone. The Point Road cemetery was moved to the western suburbs in the late 1950s, but all the cemeteries were demolished during the Cultural Revolution.

Now that China is again reaching out to foreigners, and China and Israel have established diplomatic relations, there is a new interest in Jewish studies and Jewish tourists. Local officials say that the original grave records for the Jewish cemeteries have been recovered and reburials are planned. With El Al flying regularly from Tel Aviv to Beijing, there is even talk of restoring one of the old synagogues as a museum for an exhibition on the Jews in China. Such talk has been heard before.

One memento is in place. Ohel Moishe at 62 Changyang (Ward) Road, the old Russian synagogue that at one time was a meeting place for Betar, has been almost completely demolished and replaced by a mental hospital. But a small plaque has been placed near the gate. It reads: "Site of Ashkenazi synagogue built by the Russian Jewish community." For now, it may be the only evidence that Jews once lived and found refuge in Shanghai.

Notes

Prologue

1. John King Fairbank, *The Great Chinese Revolution, 1800–1895*, Harper & Row, New York, 1986, p. 85.
2. Ibid., pp. 91–92.
3. Ernest O. Hauser, *Shanghai: City for Sale*, Harcourt, Brace and Co., New York, 1940.
4. Fairbank, p. 49.
5. Harriet Sergeant, *Shanghai: Collision Point of Culture 1918/1939*, Crown Publishers, Inc., New York, 1990, p. 23; Fairbank, pp. 118–119
6. Sergeant, p. 18.
7. Marie-Claire Bergere, "Shanghai, or 'The Other China,'" in *Shanghai: Revolution and Development in an Asian Metropolis*, Christopher Howe, ed., Cambridge University Press, New York, 1981, p. 7.
8. Albert Feuerwerker, "The Foreign Presence in China," in *The Cambridge History of China*, vol. 12, John K. Fairbank, ed., Cambridge University Press, New York, 1983, p. 132.
9. Ibid., pp. 70–71.
10. Wesley R. Fishel, *The End of Extraterritoriality in China*, University of California Press. Berkeley and Los Angeles, 1952, pp. 173–74, 192.

11. Jonathan D. Spence, *The Search for Modern China*, W.W. Norton & Co., New York, 1990, p. 393.
12. Ibid., p. 447.
13. Ibid., p. 448.
14. Sergeant, p. 310.
15. Ibid., p. 314.

Chapter 1. Didner

1. Lists of voyages, dates, and passenger numbers compiled from Shanghai Municipal Police, Joint Distribution Committee, and HIAS files.
2. Merkblatt. A copy was provided by Kurt Maimann of Tel Aviv, Israel and reprinted and translated in the Igud Yotzei Sin Bulletin, no. 322, April 1992, p. 26.
3. Karl Baedeker, *Baedeker's Austria-Hungary*, Charles Scribner's Sons, New York, 1911, pp. 236–42.
4. Bruce F. Pauley, *From Prejudice to Persecution: A History of Austrian Anti-Semitism*, University of North Carolina Press, Chapel Hill, 1992, p. 13.
5. Mosche Karl Schwarz, "The Jews of Styria," in *The Jews of Austria*, Josef Frankel, ed., Vallentine, Mitchell & Co., London, 1970, p. 391.
6. Pauley, p. 25.
7. Ibid., p. 59
8. Baedeker, p. 241.
9. Pauley, p. 89.
10. Ibid., p. 91.
11. William M. Johnston, *The Austrian Mind: An Intellectual and Social History, 1848–1938*, University of California Press, Berkeley, 1972, pp. 226–27.
12. Steven Beller, *Vienna and the Jews, 1867–1938. A Cultural History*, Cambridge University Press, New York, 1989, pp. 14–32.
13. Ibid., p. 36.
14. Pauley, p. xv.
15. Beller, p. 120.
16. This image was suggested in an interview by Paul Grosz, president of the Austrian Jewish Community, September 5, 1991.
17. Pauley, pp. 260–63.
18. Ibid., p. 273.
19. Ibid., p. 270.
20. Ibid., p. 279.
21. Herbert Rosenkranz, "The Anschluss and the Tragedy of Austrian Jewry 1938–1945," in Frankel, op. cit., p. 483.

22. *The New York Times*, March 24, 1938, p. 7.
23. Pauley, p. 280.
24. Ibid., p. 282.
25. Ibid., p. 283–4.
26. Ibid., p. 285.
27. Ibid., p. 282–3.
28. Rosenkranz, p. 489.
29. David S. Wyman, *Paper Walls: America and the Refugee Crisis 1938–1941*, The University of Massachusetts Press, Amherst, 1968, p. 49.
30. Ibid., pp. 233–34.
31. Rosenkranz, p. 491.
32. Pauley, p. 287; Rosenkranz, pp. 496–97.

Chapter 2. Levin

1. Betty Peh-T'i Wei, *Shanghai: Crucible of Modern China*, Oxford University Press, New York, 1987, p. 104.
2. Ibid., pp. 110, 120.
3. Ibid., p. 110.
4. Rabbi Louis M. Levitsky, "Fading Footprints of a Wandering People," December 26, 1930, report to the Jewish Tribune, Central Zionist Archives, file KKL5, 3933; Wei, pp. 105-06.
5. Shanghai Municipal Police, "Germans of the Jewish Faith Who Have Recently Arrived in Shanghai," D.S. Pitts, Special Branch, November 11, 1933, National Archives, RG 263.
6. "Drei Jahre Immigration," Shanghai Modern Times Publishing, Shanghai, 1942, pp. 30–38.
7. Robert B. Asprey, *The German High Command at War*, William Morrow & Co., New York, 1991, pp. 89–91.
8. Lucy S. Dawidowicz, *The War Against the Jews*, Bantam Books, New York, 1986, p. 58.
9. Julius Guttman, "The Jews of Berlin," Jewish Frontier, April 1945, pp. 14–16.
10. Avraham Barkai, *From Boycott to Annihilation, the Economic Struggle of German Jews*, University Press of New England, Hanover, N.H., 1990, pp. 95–96.
11. Ibid., pp. 111, 116–17.
12. Ibid., p. 133.
13. Interview with Rabbi Theodore Alexander, Congregation B'nai Emunah, San Francisco, April 1991.
14. Monika Richarz, ed., *Jewish Life in Germany*, Leo Baeck Institute, New York, 1991, p. 36.
15. Barkai, p. 153.

Chapter 3. Heimann

1. Barkai, p. 115.
2. The checks were issued by HICEM, the European acronym for Hebrew Immigration Aid Society and Jewish Colonization Society, to German refugees who had registered before they left the country.

Chapter 4. The Philanthropists

1. Ships, dates, and numbers of passengers compiled from Joint Distribution Committee, Shanghai Municipal Police, and HIAS files.
2. JDC file no. 456, letter from J.C. Hyman to Maurice Bisgyer, December 27, 1938.
3. JDC file no. 457, letter from Franz Bischofswerder, Arthur Prinz, and Victor Loewenstein to JDC in Paris, February 10, 1939.
4. JDC file no. 457, report from M. Speelman to JDC, Annex I, June 22, 1939.
5. JDC file no. 456, letter from H. Gensburger, M. Brown, and E. Kelen to J.C. Hyman, October 28, 1938.
6. Stanley Jackson, *The Sassoons, Portrait of a Dynasty*, William Heinemann, Ltd., London, 1989.
7. Ibid.
8. *The Jewish Encyclopedia*, vol XI, Funk & Wagnalls, New York, 1925.
9. Ibid.
10. Interview with Jacob Alkow, Herzlia, Israel, August 19, 1991.
11. Interviews with Danny Moalem and Lea and Ellis Jacobs, Sydney, Australia, July 10 and 11, 1991.
12. Ibid.
13. Sergeant, p. 127.
14. Ibid.
15. Moalem and Jacobs interviews.
16. Jackson, p. 229.
17. Ibid., pp. 151-3.
18. Ibid., p. 229-34.
19. Ibid., p. 235.
20. Ibid., p. 211.
21. Levitsky.
22. Sir Horace Kadoorie, "Shanghai Jewish Youth Association: Its Foundation and a Short History," 1940. From JDC file no. 458.
23. Ibid.

24. Paul Komor, "Report of the International Committee," February 28, 1939. From Shanghai Municipal Police files.

25. Ibid. and Shanghai Municipal Police report by D.S. Pitts, March 15, 1939. SMP files.

26. Speelman report, Annex I.

27. "Jewish Refugee Camps on 8/4/39," SMP files.

28. Memorandum from Herbert Katzki, June 6, 1939. JDC file no. 457.

29. SMP report, March 15, 1939.

30. From the "Russian Voice," A. Antononoff, ed., January 7, 1939, translated by Shanghai Municipal Police. SMP files.

31. John Ahlers, "Economic Threat Caused by Jewish Refugees," *Shanghai Evening Post and Mercury*, April 17, 1939. SMP files.

32. Ibid.

33. David Kranzler, *Japanese, Nazis & Jews*, Yeshiva University Press, New York, 1976, pp. 268–69.

34. Speelman report, June 21, 1939.

35. "Japanese to Restrict Jewish Immigration into Hongkew," *North China Daily News*, August 12, 1939. SMP files.

36. "Shanghai Municipal Council to Ban Jewish Refugees," *North China Daily News*, August 15, 1939. SMP files.

37. "850 Refugees May Not Land Here," *North China Daily News*, August 16, 1939. SMP files.

Chapter 5. Didner

1. Annual Report of Committee for Assistance of Jewish Refugees Medical Board, 1939–1940, Joint Distribution Committee Archives, file 458; *The China Press*, March 26, 1939, p. 2.

2. *North China Daily News*, May 2 and May 6, 1939; Minutes of meetings in the medical library of the Public Health Department, May 11, May 25, and June 22, 1939, concerning arrival of central European Jews, Shanghai Municipal Police files.

3. Annual Report of CAEJR Medical Board.

4. *The Columbia University College of Physicians and Surgeons Complete Home Medical Guide*, Montague Books, New York, 1985, pp. 387–88.

5. Helmuth M. Bottcher, *Wonder Drugs: A History of Antibiotics*, J.B. Lippincott Co., New York, 1964, p. 135.

6. *North China Daily News*, August 16, 1939.

7. "Drei Jahre Immigration," pp. 33–37.

8. Ibid.

9. Interview with Paul and Eva Engel, Sydney, Australia, July 13, 1991.

10. Felix Gruenberger, "The Jewish Refugees in Shanghai," *Jewish Social Studies*, vol. 12, 1950, p. 334.
11. Interview with Eve Rumjanek Perkel, Boynton Beach, Fla., December 23, 1991.
12. "Drei Jahre Immigration," pp. 98–102.
13. Ibid.

Chapter 6. Levin

1. *North China Daily News*, October 14, 1939.
2. Inaugural broadcast transcript, May 2, 1939. From the papers of Howard Levin held by Professor Irene Eber, Hebrew University, Jerusalem.
3. *The New York Times*, May 1 and 2, 1939.
4. "Drei Jahre Immigration," pp. 93–97.
5. Xu Buzeng, "Jewish Influence on the Musical Life of Shanghai," Shanghai Judaic Studies Association, paper presented at Harvard University symposium on Jewish Diasporas in China, August 1992.
6. Ibid. Interviews with Gerhard Heimann, Curt Fuchs, and others.
7. "Drei Jahre" and photographs courtesy of G. Heimann.
8. Shanghai Municipal Police files, Special Branch reports, September 2 and November 13 and 19, 1940.
9. Ibid. and *Shanghai Evening Post and Chronicle*, November 14 and 18, 1940.
10. "Drei Jahre," pp. 73–79.
11. Ibid.
12. *The China Press*, February 20, 1940.
13. *North China Daily News*, August 21 and 27, 1940.
14. Levin files, Hebrew University.
15. Levin files, transcript of broadcast, October 1, 1940.

Chapter 7. Kantorowsky

1. I.A. Richards, *Basic English and Its Uses*, William Norton & Co., New York, 1943, p. 44.
2. Dawidowicz, p. 67n.
3. List of voyages compiled from JDC, SMP, and HIAS files.
4. *Shanghai Times*, October 22, 1939; *The China Press*, October 27, 1939; Shanghai Municipal Police files, Special Branch report 5422, May 2, 1940.
5. Eduard Kann, letter, January 4, 1940, Joint Distribution Committee files.
6. SMP report, May 2, 1940.

7. JDC file no. 459.
8. SMP report.
9. Ibid.
10. Fishel, pp. 198–99.
11. Bergere, p. 23.
12. Michel Speelman, letter to M.C. Troper, April 6, 1940, JDC files.
13. *Shanghai Evening Post*, April 5, 1940.
14. Speelman to Troper.
15. Shanghai Municipal Police, Special Branch report, April 15, 1942.
16. SMP report, May 2, 1940.
17. Kann letter.
18. Speelman letter.
19. *North China Daily News*, April 12, 1940.
20. Bergere, p. 23; *North China Daily News*, January 24, 1941, p. 1.

Chapter 8. The Administrator

1. Yehuda Bauer, *American Jewry and the Holocaust*, Wayne State University Press, Detroit, 1981, pp. 21–22.
2. United Jewish Appeal, interview with Mrs. Laura Margolis Jarblum by Menahem Kaufman, Tel Aviv, April 26, 1976.
3. Ibid.
4. Author's interview with Laura Margolis Jarblum, October, 1992.
5. Laura Margolis, "Race Against Time in Shanghai," *Survey Graphic*, March 1944, p. 168.
6. Ibid.
7. Bauer, p. 315.
8. Annual Report of the Committee for the Assistance of European Refugees in Shanghai, 1940, Joint Distribution Committee files.
9. UJA interview.
10. JDC files. Letter from Ellis Hayim to Paul Komor, October 11, 1939; Komor to Hayim, October 12, 1939; E. Kann to Hayim, November 20, 1939; memorandum from Sir Victor Sassoon, December 20, 1939; M. Speelman to M. Troper, January 12, 1940; Speelman to Sassoon, January 12, 1940; Sassoon to Speelman, January 15, 1940.
11. UJA interview.
12. Letter no. 19 from Margolis to Robert Pilpel, JDC, August 2, 1941.
13. Margolis interview, October 1992.
14. Margolis to Pilpel, letters no. 4 (May 29, 1941), no. 10 (June 18, 1941).
15. Margolis to Pilpel, letter no. 11 (July 2, 1941).

16. Margolis to Pilpel, letter no. 20 (August 11, 1941).
17. Ibid.
18. Margolis interview, October 1992.
19. August 11, 1941, letter.
20. Efraim Zuroff, "Attempts to Obtain Shanghai Permits in 1941," *Yad Vashem Studies*, vol. 13, 1979, 323–24.
21. Joseph R. Fiszman, "The Quest for Status: Polish-Jewish Refugees in Shanghai, 1941–49," paper delivered at Harvard University symposium on Jewish Diasporas in China, August 1992.
22. Ibid. and Zorach Warhaftig, *Refugee and Survivor*, Yad Vashem, Jerusalem, 1988, pp. 107–11, 156.
23. Zuroff.
24. Warhaftig.
25. Memorandum from Inuzuka to Captain Herzberg, September 17, 1941.
26. Herman Dicker, *Wanderers and Settlers in the Far East*, Twayne Publishers, Inc., New York, 1962, p. 102.
27. Margolis to Pilpel, Letter no. 27 (October 26, 1941).
28. Ibid.; Margolis to Pilpel, letter no. 30 (November 5, 1941).
29. Dicker, pp. 69–73; Kranzler, pp.57–65.
30. Ibid.
31. Ibid. and Pan Guang, "Jewish Sites in Shanghai," courtesy of Tess Johnston, U.S. consulate, Shanghai.
32. Interview with Lieselotte Kwiat Salant, Jerusalem, August 1991.
33. Kurt Redlich to Henry L. Tischler, November 27, 1974. Appendix L, unpublished Tischler Ph.D. thesis, Northeastern University, Department of Sociology, Boston, May 1976.
34. Interview with Karl and Sylvia Marishel, Sydney, Australia, July 14, 1991.
35. Translation in JDC files. From *Jewish Daily Forward*, November 15, 1941.
36. *Asiana*, September 1941, JDC archive.
37. Margolis, letter no. 27.
38. Ibid.
39. Ibid.
40. Ibid.
41. Ibid.
42. Margolis letter no. 30.
43. Ibid.
44. Margolis letter no. 27.
45. Bauer, pp. 126–27.
46. Margolis letters no. 27 and no. 30.

47. Margolis, Report of Activities in Shanghai, China, from December 8, 1941 to September 1943, JDC files.

Chapter 9. Kantorowsky

1. Kranzler, pp. 97–99.
2. Margolis to Pilpel, October 26, 1941.
3. Redlich to Tischler, April 9, 1974. Appendix M, unpublished Tischler Ph.D. thesis.
4. "Drei Jahre," pp. 47–54; *Almananc—Shanghai, 1946/47*, Ossi Lewin, ed., Shanghai Echo Publishing Co., Shanghai, 1947, p. 49.
5. "Drei Jahre," pp. 47–54.
6. Ibid.
7. Ibid., and *Almanac—Shanghai, 1946/1947*, p. 58.
8. Kranzler, p. 415.
9. SMP files, Special Branch report, August 6, 1941.
10. "Drei Jahre," pp. 47–54; Pan Guang, "Jewish Sites in Shanghai."
11. "The Labour Conditions of the Jewish Immigrants in Shanghai," JDC files, undated.
12. Ibid.
13. Ibid.
14. Eleanor M. Hinder, *Life and Labour in Shanghai*, Institute of Pacific Relations, New York, 1944, p. 77.
15. Henri Lewin, *Be a Mensch*, Vector Press, Mt. Royal, N.J., 1990, p. 34.
16. "Labour Conditions," JDC files.

Chapter 10. Levin

1. Kranzler, pp. 175, 215–16.
2. Naoki Maruyama, "The Shanghai Zionist Association and Japan," paper delivered at Harvard University symposium on Jewish Diasporas in China, August, 1992.
3. Dicker, pp. 162–70.
4. Kranzler, pp. 177–8, 195.
5. Ibid., pp. 212–13.
6. Maruyama.
7. Ibid., and Kranzler, pp. 220–41.
8. Kranzler, p. 174.
9. *North China Daily News*, February 24, 1940.
10. *North China Daily News*, February 27, 1940.

11. Kranzler, pp. 172–73.
12. Letter from Michael Speelman to Joint Distribution Committee, New York, September 9, 1940, JDC files.
13. Ibid.
14. Letter from K. Inuzuka to M. Speelman, August 27, 1940, JDC files.
15. *Shanghai Evening Post*, February 2, 1941, p. 1, JDC files.
16. Memorandum from Inuzuka to Captain Herzberg, September 17, 1941, JDC files.
17. Barbara W. Tuchman, *Stilwell and the American Experience in China*, Bantam Books, New York, 1972, p. 294.
18. Arch Carey, *The War Years at Shanghai*, Vantage Press, New York, 1967, pp. 28–29.
19. Ibid.
20. "Shortage of Food in Shanghai Grave," *The New York Times*, January 6, 1942.
21. Ibid.
22. Lloyd E. Eastman, "Facets of an Ambivalent Relationship: Smuggling, Puppets and Atrocities During the War, 1937–45," in *The Chinese and the Japanese*, Akira Iriye, ed., Princeton University Press, Princeton, N.J., 1980, pp. 279–83.

Chapter 11. Heimann

1. Dennis A. Leventhal, *Sino-Judaic Studies: Whence and Whither*, (Appendixed by the Kadoorie memoir), Jewish Historical Society of Hong Kong, 1985; and Sergeant, pp. 124–26.
2. Interviews with Yedida Kohn Gottfried, Haifa, August 1991; Kurt Maimann, Tel Aviv, August 1991; Leo Meyer, Riverdale, N.Y., November 1991; and H.P. Witting, Melbourne, Australia, July 1991.
3. Ibid.
4. Ibid.; "Drei Jahre," pp. 67–72; and *Almanac—Shanghai, 1946/1947*, p. 62.
5. Kranzler, pp. 427–29.
6. Letter from Shanghai Municipal Council to Ellis Hayim, May 30, 1940, JDC files.
7. "Drei Jahre," pp. 67–72.
8. Shanghai Municipal Police report, "Further re Educational Establishments Conducted by Jewish Refugees in the Wayside Area," June 23, 1942, National Archives.
9. Interview with Erika Jeretzky Wilhoit, Haifa, Israel, August 1991.
10. Kranzler, p. 397.
11. Hinder, p. 16.

Chapter 12. The Rosh Hashanah Plot

1. Bernard Wasserstein, *The Secret Lives of Trebitsch Lincoln*, Yale University Press, New Haven, Conn., 1988, pp. 276–77; War Department Office of Assistant Secretary of War, headquarters, Strategic Services Unit, China Theater, Summary Report on German Intelligence Activities in China, X-2 Branch, 1946, pp. 71–85, RG 226, Entry 182, Box 28, Folder 152, U.S. National Archives.
2. Wasserstein, pp. 277–78, and Richard Hughes, *Foreign Devil: Thirty Years of Reporting from the Far East*, Century Press, London, 1984, pp. 34–35.
3. Headquarters, United States Forces European Theater, Military Intelligence Service Center, AOP 757, CI Preliminary Intelligence Report, no. 93, Joseph Albert Meisinger. U.S. National Archives microfilm.
4. Wasserstein, pp. 276–77
5. Bernard Wasserstein, "Ambiguities of Occupation: European Jewish Refugees in Japanese-Occupied Shanghai, 1941–45," paper delivered to Study Group on the Jews in Modern Europe, Harvard Center for European Studies, February 10, 1992.
6. Margolis, "Report of Activities in Shanghai, China From December 8, 1941 to September, 1943, JDC files; Special Branch reports on meetings of Committee for Assistance of European Jewish Refugees in Shanghai, May 26 to September 2, 1942, Shanghai Municipal Police files; Fritz Kauffmann, "The Jews in Shanghai During World War II," a speech before the Shanghai Tiffin Club of New York, February 12, 1963, published in *Bulletin des Leo Baeck Instituts*, vol. 73, 1986, pp. 13–23.
7. Kauffmann.
8. Ibid.
9. Ibid.
10. Ibid.
11. Margolis report.
12. Ibid.
13. *Shanghai Jewish Chronicle*, January 12, 1942. SMP files.
14. Margolis report.
15. Ibid.
16. Ibid.
17. Martin Domke, *Trading with the Enemy in World War II*, New York, Central Book Co., 1943, appendixes B-G, pp. 430–450.
18. Kranzler, pp. 461–62.
19. Margolis report.
20. Gruenberger, "The Jewish Refugees in Shanghai," JSS, p. 338.

21. Catalogue of the Exhibition, Jewish Life in Shanghai, September 1948–January 1949, Yiddish Scientific Institute-YIVO, p. 9.
22. Margolis report.
23. Kiyoko Inuzuka, *Yudaya Mondai to Nihon no Kosaku* (The Jewish Problem and Japan's Policy), Nihon Kogyo Shinbunsha, Tokyo, 1982, Passage translated for the author by Naoki Maruyama.
24. Ibid.
25. Kauffmann.
26. Kauffmann, Margolis report.
27. Kauffmann.
28. Ibid.
29. Ibid.; Office of Naval Intelligence, report by L.K. Little, January 29, 1943, RG 226, OSS files, Folder 27989, U.S. National Archives.
30. Kauffmann.
31. China Theater, X-2 Branch Report, November 6, 1945, "B. Topaz: Treatment of Subject by Japanese," War Crimes, RG 226, Entry 182, Box 18, Folder 102, U.S. National Archives.
32. Ibid.
33. Margolis report.
34. Ibid.
35. Office of Naval Intelligence report.

Chapter 13. Kantorowsky

1. Interview with Curt Fuchs, Jackson Heights, N.Y., October, 1991.
2. "Re performance of Mr. Herbert Zerbert [sic], German Jewish Refugee," April 12, 1943. SMP files.
3. Gruenberger, JSS, p. 340.
4. YIVO files, Kranzler, pp. 489–91.
5. Ibid.
6. Ibid.
7. Ibid.
8. Wasserstein, "Ambiguities of Occupation."
9. Redlich to Tischler, November 27, 1974.
10. *SACRA Bulletin* no. 3, YIVO.
11. Redlich to Tischler, April 9, 1974.
12. Hinder, p. 89.
13. Charles Jordan, March 11, 1947 letter to JDC, New York, JDC archives.
14. Redlich to Tischler, November 27, 1974.
15. Kranzler, p. 491.
16. Margolis report; SACRA minutes, Feb. 28, 1943–July 16, 1945, YIVO.

17. Ibid., and Dicker, p. 120.
18. Meyer Birman to Commissao Portuguesa de Assistancia sos Judeus Refugiados, July 8, 1943, YIVO.

Chapter 14. Didner

1. Interviews with Herman Natowic, Melbourne, Australia, July 1991, and Curt Fuchs, Jackson Heights, N.Y., October 1991, February 1992, and August 1992.
2. Ibid.
3. Natowic, Leo Meyer interviews.
4. Shanghai Municipal Police Report, March 2, 1943, Misc. 72/43, "Re two German Jewish Refugees Reported to be Missing from Wayside District," SMP files, National Archives.
5. Carey, pp. 106–107.
6. SMP report, Natowic interviews.
7. Ibid.
8. Natowic interviews.
9. Ibid.
10. SMP report.
11. Ibid.
12. "Shanghai: Treatment of Allied Prisoners by the Japanese," Report YV-263, September 26, 1945, Z-Magpie Division, based on depositions by civilian British, American, and Belgian prisoners, War Crimes files, National Archives.
13. SMP report.
14. Carey, p. 104.
15. Report YV-263.
16. Report YV-263; Natowic interviews.
17. Ibid.
18. Ibid.
19. Natowic interviews.
20. Report YV-263; Natowic interviews.
21. Ibid.; Carey, p. 106.
22. Natowic interviews.
23. Fuchs interviews.

Chapter 15. Heimann

1. Interview with Hans Becher, Melbourne, Australia, July 1991.
2. *SACRA Bulletin*; Strategic Services Unit report.
3. Shanghai Municipal Police Report, "The Situation of Refugees After the Start of Segregation on 8/10/43," SMP files, National Archives, August 16, 1943.

4. Curt Fuchs interview.
5. Shanghai Municipal Police Report, "Arbitration Court for Central European Refugees," April 1, 1942, National Archives.
6. Interview with Fred Barry (formerly Baumgarten), Rickshaw Reunion, Philadelphia, Penn., October 1991.
7. Telephone interview with Fred Gunsberger, North Stratfield, New South Wales, Australia, July 1991.
8. Interviews with Heinz Fischl and Julius Rabin, Sydney and Melbourne, Australia, July 1991.
9. Interview with Lisbeth Loewenberg, San Francisco, November, 1991.
10. Interview with Heinz Frankenstein, San Francisco, California, May, 1991.
11. Interview with Kurt Mosberg, Sydney, Australia, July 1991.
12. *Complete Home Medical Guide*, p. 516.
13. *ORT in China, 1941–1947*, YIVO files.
14. Mosberg interview.

Chapter 16. The Monkey

1. M. Siegel to American Jewish Joint Distribution Committee, August 26, 1945, letter, JDC files.
2. Strategic Services Unit, War Department, "Shanghai—Conditions of German Jewish Refugees During the Occupation," October 29, 1945, National Archives, RG 153, Entry 143; Report YV-438; "Preliminary Report on the SACRA," G.L. Flatow, RG 226, 182, Box 2, Folder 11, National Archives.
3. SACRA minutes.
4. Sandor Ultmann, interview with Irene Eber, March 1976, Institute of Contemporary Jewry, Hebrew University, Jerusalem.
5. Kranzler, pp. 529–30.
6. "List of Detained Persons," YIVO files; "China—Jap Treatment of Jewish Refugees in Shanghai," Major Vaughn F. Meisling, JICA/China, October 15, 1945, RG 226 XL 23620, National Archives; and "Japanese Atrocity Case," Office of Strategic Services, November 3, 1945, RG 226, Entry 182, Box 18, Folder 102, National Archives.
7. Ibid., and YV-438.
8. Ibid., and SACRA minutes, YIVO.
9. Siegel letter.
10. Interview with Ruth Simon Zimmerman, Hadera, Israel, August 1991.
11. Ibid.

12. Strategic Services Unit report YV-438.
13. Interview with Paul Engel.
14. Interview with Joachim Flieg, Melbourne, Australia, and Peter Schattner, North Balwyn, Australia, July 1991.
15. Flieg interview.
16. YV-438.
17. Ibid.
18. Gruenberger, JSS.
19. Ibid., and Interview with Ruth Callmann, San Francisco, May 1991.
20. Interview with Trixie Braun Wachsner, Los Angeles, April 1991.
21. Kranzler, p. 499.
22. Preliminary Report on the SACRA and Stateless Refugees Affairs Bureau, RG 226, 182, Box 2, Folder 11, National Archives; YV-438, National Archives.
23. Fairbank, p. 297.
24. Strategic Services Unit report; "Statement on Foreign Pao Chia," August 29, 1945, YIVO.
25. Kranzler, p. 495.
26. Interview with Kurt Frey, Sydney, Australia, July 1991.
27. Ibid.
28. JICA Report #10.562, November 28, 1944, National Archives, RG 226, 108073.
29. Becher interview.
30. Margolis report.
31. Ibid.
32. Ibid.
33. Frederick Emmons, *The Atlantic Liners, 1925–70*, Drake Publishers, Inc., New York, 1972, p. 68.
34. Memorandum no. III, from Mr. Josef Bitker to Mr. Manuel Siegel, January 9, 1946, JDC files.
35. Siegel letter, August 26, 1945.

Chapter 17. Didner

1. Report YV-438, National Archives.
2. Interviews with Chinese doctors and former residents obtained July 6–August 21, 1945, XL 17699, National Archives.
3. "Condensed Report of the Development Concerning the Medical Care of the European Refugees in Shanghai, from Oct. 1942 Until Present Time," T. Kunfi, superintendent, S.R. Hospital, September 25, 1945, JDC files.
4. YV-438.

5. Curt Fuchs interview.
6. Interview with Alfred Zunterstein of Bellevue, Wash., at Rickshaw Reunion, Philadelphia, October 19, 1991.
7. Report YV-438.
8. Interview with Curt Fuchs; H.P. Eisfelder, "Chinese Exile: My Years in Shanghai and Nanking," unpublished manuscript provided by Fred Fields.
9. Kenn C. Rust, *Fifth Air Force Story . . . in World War II*, Historical Aviation Album, Temple City, Calif., 1973, p. 28; Wesley Frank Craven and James Lea Cate, eds., *The Army Air Forces in World War II, Volume Five*, The University of Chicago Press, Chicago, 1953.
10. "Conditions in the Shanghai Area," JICA/China, Report R-525-CH-45, June 25, 1945, RG 226, 137380, National Archives.
11. Craven and Cate, p. 693; "Operational Intelligence Summary no. 2," July 17, 1945, Headquarters 319th Bombardment Group (Light), Army Air Forces, Department of the Air Force, Historical Research Agency, Maxwell Air Force Base, Alabama; Kenn C. Rust, *Seventh Air Force Story . . . in World War II*, Historical Aviation Album, Temple City, Calif., 1973, pp. 33–34; Telephone interview with Robert C. Roberts, North Myrtle Beach, S.C., October 1991.
12. Interviews with Curt Fuchs; Herta Mosberg, Sydney, Australia, July 1991; Kurt Nussbaum, Tel Aviv, August 1991; Inge Kaufman Frankenstein, San Francisco, April 1991; Ruth Callmann, San Francisco, May 1991; Gruenberger, JSS, pp. 344–45.
13. Gruenberger.
14. "Report on Air Raid July 17th," July 18, 1945, YIVO; Kranzler, pp. 553–55.
15. Inge Frankenstein interview.
16. Gruenberger.
17. "History of the Fifth Air Force, 15 June 1944–2 September 1945, Vol. 2," Air Force Historical Research Agency, Maxwell Air Force Base, Alabama.

Chapter 18. Levin

1. Howard Levin, "From Someone Who Was There: How the End of the War Came for the Hongkew Ghetto in Shanghai," *Aufbau*, August 2, 1985.
2. Gruenberger, JSS, pp. 345–46.
3. Manuel Siegel, September 25, 1945, letter to American Jewish Joint Distribution Committee, New York, JDC archives.

4. Interviews with Jacob Lomranz, Tel Aviv, August 1991; Curt Fuchs.
5. *Almanac—Shanghai, 1946/47*, p. 63.
6. Lomranz interview.
7. Gruenberger, p. 346.
8. Siegel to JDC, November 4, 1945, JDC archives.
9. *Almanac—Shanghai*, pp. 39,46.
10. Letter from Manuel Siegel to American Jewish Joint Distribution Committee, New York, November 4, 1945, JDC archives.
11. Letter from Charles Jordan to American Jewish Joint Distribution Committee, New York, January 21, 1946, JDC archives.
12. Curt Fuchs interview.
13. Interview with Ernst Sloan (Solomon), Hallandale, Fla., December 1991.
14. "Catalogue of the Exhibition, Jewish Life in Shanghai, September 1948–January 1949," YIVO archives.

Chapter 19. The Redeemer

1. Siegel to JDC, December 4, 1945, JDC archives.
2. Suzanne D. Rutland, "'Waiting Room Shanghai': Australian Reactions to the Plight of the Jews in Shanghai after the Second World War," *Leo Baeck Institute Yearbook*, vol. 32, 1987, p. 411, n. 16.
3. *Almanac—Shanghai, 1946/47*, pp. 38–42
4. Ibid., and interview with Kurt Maimann, Tel Aviv, August 1991.
5. Interviews with Fritz Gottfried, Haifa, Israel, August 1991, and Peter Schattner, Melbourne, Australia, July 1991.
6. *Almanac—Shanghai*, p. 77, Didner interview.
7. *Almanac—Shanghai*, pp. 70–75.
8. Spence, pp. 498–99.
9. Jordan to JDC, May 28, 1946, JDC archives.
10. Siegel to JDC, November 4, 1945, and Jordan to JDC January 21, April 23, and May 28, 1946, JDC archives.
11. Spence, p. 489.
12. Jordan to JDC, April 23, 1946, JDC archives.
13. "Abstract of a Statistical Analysis of 13,475 Refugees in Shanghai, China as of March 31, 1946," memo to JDC, November 25, 1946, JDC archives.
14. "Statistical Analysis" and "Statement of Refugees Who Left Shanghai from March 1st to January 31st, 1947," JDC archives.

15. Interview with Gertrude Laufer, Vienna, September 1991.
16. Interview with Erika Kesten Schlesinger, Haifa, August 1991.
17. Gruenberger, pp. 346–47.
18. Jordan letter, December 30, 1946, JDC archives.
19. "Statistical Analysis."
20. Jordan, January 21, 1946.
21. Jordan, May 28, 1946.
22. "Statement of Refugees."
23. Jordan to JDC, July 27, 1946.
24. Letter from Dr. G. Kantorowsky, Executive Committee of Polish Quota D.P.'s, Shanghai, November 1947. Courtesy of Eva Angress.
25. Leonard Dinnerstein, *America and the Survivors of the Holocaust*, Columbia University Press, New York, 1982, p. 164.
26. Ibid., pp. 112–14.
27. *The New York Times*, March 31, 1946, p. 4.
28. Jordan, "Final Summary of the Shanghai Situation as of the Date of My Departure, April 10, 1948," April 21, 1948, JDC archives.
29. Dinnerstein, p. 182.
30. Ibid., pp. 172–74.
31. *The New York Times*, June 26, 1948, p. 1
32. "Statistical analysis."
33. Rutland, pp. 412–23.
34. Ibid., pp. 413–14.
35. Ibid., pp. 415–18.
36. Ibid., pp. 419–21.
37. Ibid., pp. 422–31.
38. Dinnerstein, p. 200.

Chapter 20. Heimann

1. Yaacov S. Liberman. "The Boys from China," *Igud Yotzei Sin*, no. 303, February–March 1989.
2. Adolph C. Glassgold, Letter no. 224, July 12, 1948, to JDC, JDC archives.
3. *The New York Times*, February 2, 1949, p. 1.
4. Dinnerstein, pp. 224–26, p. 233.
5. Ibid.
6. Ibid.
7. Spence, p. 502.
8. Glassgold, Letter 224.
9. Spence, pp. 502–04.
10. Ibid., pp. 505–08.

11. "Report of Activities of the Far Eastern Palestine Office Covering the Period from January 1948 to March 1949," (unsigned), March 11, 1949, Central Zionist Archives, Jerusalem.
12. Fairbank, p. 279.
13. Herbert A. Strauss, ed., *International Biographical Dictionary of Central European Emigres, Vol. II*, K. G. Saur, New York, 1980–83, p. 891.
14. Xu Buzeng.
15. Glassgold, Report no. 434, September 23, 1949, JDC archives.
16. *The New York Times*, December 22, 1949, p. 18, and copy of telegram from "Stein, Israeli committee," December 18, 1949, Central Zionist Archives.
17. Glassgold, October 7, 1949, letter, JDC archives.
18. "Analysis of S.S. *General Gordon* Repatriates" and list of passengers, United Service for New Americans, June 2, 1950, JDC archives.
19. Telephone interview with Arnold Fuchs, South Casco, Maine, November 1992.
20. Ibid.
21. *The New York Times*, May 29, 1950, p. 1.
22. *The New York Times*, June 17, 1950, p. 1.
23. Ibid., June 19, 1950, p. 1.
24. Ibid.
25. Ibid., June 21, 1950, p. 15.
26. Ibid., June 20, 1950, p. 1.

Sources

Unless noted otherwise, the information in this book is based on interviews with the four major characters. Each was repeatedly interviewed during two-and-a-half years of research, with sessions ranging from two to eight hours. I spoke with Dr. Didner five times in his office in Queens, between October 1991 and November 1992. My four interviews with Levin took place in his apartment in Manhattan from February to June 1991. I interviewed Heimann over four weekends at his homes in Los Angeles and Rancho Mirage, California, between April 1991 and November 1992. Eva Kantorowsky Angress and I met twice in San Francisco, at B'nai Emunah in May 1991 and at her home and office over three days in November 1991. These visits were followed up with three lengthy telephone interviews.

I often went over the same events several times with each of the four major characters to check on apparent inconsistencies or memory lapses. Each of their accounts was checked against the stories of other refugees, documents, written accounts, and a variety of other sources. I have attempted to eliminate any accounts that seemed questionable and could not be independently verified with other sources. In the chapters on Didner, a 1939 Fox Movietonenews newsreel of the *Conte Biancamano* arriving in Shanghai, pictures of Didner at the

Emigrants' Hospital, a 1911 Baedeker on Austria-Hungary, and several medical texts helped me break loose some of his long-buried memories. Didner's wife, Grete, joined us several times and contributed valuable information. In the Levin chapters, his pictures of his boyhood home, articles he wrote, and transcripts of his radio broadcasts were particularly useful. I also was able to compare my interview with a 1988 interview he did in Jersualem. Frank Wachsner of Los Angeles also added information after Levin's death. Heimann had saved a wealth of photographs and other memorabilia that were useful. My interviews with some of his contemporaries in Shanghai, particularly Curt Fuchs, helped refresh some of his childhood memories. Heimann's brother Benno also contributed. Irine Heimann, as well as one of the surviving passengers from the 106 refugees on the *General Gordon*, Arnold Fuchs, assisted with the final chapter. Eva Angress helped translate some entries from her diaries, which added to her accounts. I also received help from interviews she conducted with Udo Goswald for his book on Jewish life in Neukölln (*Spuren Jüdischen Lebens in Neukölln*, Emil Fisher Museum, 1988). Finally, Dr. Didner, Heimann, and Mrs. Angress reviewed the chapters in my manuscript pertaining to them (Levin had died by the time they were completed) and made a number of helpful corrections and additions.

Other sources that helped verify accounts included the *Emigranten Adressbuch*, published by The New Star Group, Shanghai, November 1939; H.P. Eisfelder's unpublished *Chinese Exile: My Years in Shanghai and Nanking*; Horst Wartenberger's unpublished *My Shanghai Memories*, provided by Gary Heimann; two almanacs, *Drei Jahre Immigration in Shanghai* (1942) and *Almanac—Shanghai 1946/47*(1947); Shanghai city directories and other material provided by Tess Johnston of the U.S. consulate in Shanghai; and maps of Berlin, Vienna, and Shanghai, particularly one published with Alfred Kneucker's book. Arthur D. Holder, an instructor of German at Northeastern University, provided me with translations from the German, and David Arnold, a former journalism graduate student at Northeastern, did much of the research in the Shanghai Municipal Police files.

Acknowledgments

This book would not have been possible without the wise guidance of my friend Paul Wilkes and the assistance of my agent, Alison Bond. I also am deeply indebted to the four former refugees who are the major subjects of this book—Eva Kantorowsky Angress, Sam Didner, Gerhard Heimann, and the late Howard Levin. They were generous with their time, patient with my long hours of questioning, and open and honest about intimate details of their lives.

Dozens of other former refugees and their families also assisted me and hosted me in cities throughout the world including Kurt Mosberg in Sydney, Australia, and H.P. Eisfelder in Melbourne; Gertrude Laufer and Mary Steinhauser in Vienna; Kurt Maimann in Tel Aviv, Israel, and Fritz Gottfried in Haifa; and Gary Matzdorff in Ventura, California. I also owe special thanks to Curt Fuchs of Jackson Heights, New York, and Fred Fields of Hallandale, Florida.

I also received valuable assistance from a number of archivists and librarians, including John Taylor of the Military Reference Branch at the National Archives; Diane Spielman at the Leo Baeck Institute; Regina Chimberg at the Joint Distribution Committee Archives; Rachel Rubinstein at the Central Zionist Archives in Jerusalem; Esther M. Oyster of the

319th Bomb Group Reunion Association; and the staff of YIVO in New York and the Beth Hatefutsoth Photo Archive in Tel Aviv.

Several scholars also provided guidance, among them Bernard Wasserstein of Brandeis University, Danny Schwarz of Hebrew University in Jerusalem, and Naoki Murayama of Meiji Gakuin University in Tokyo.

I am also indebted to my colleagues in the School of Journalism at Northeastern University, particularly LaRue Gilleland and Nicholas Daniloff, for their support throughout this project. I received financial support for travel and research from the University's Research and Scholarship Development Fund, the University Honors Program, and from the Freedom Forum in Arlington, Virginia.

I also wish to thank my editors at The Free Press, Adam Bellow and Charles Hanson, for their careful and sensitive editing.

Finally, a few words of appreciation to my family My mother, Eleanor Ross, provided moral and financial support and has promoted this book far beyond the borders of the two states in which she lives. My wife, Irene Coletsos, traveled with me to Europe and China, commented insightfully on dozens of drafts and rewrites, patiently withstood my long absences, comforted me through difficult times, and joined me in celebrating moments of triumph. Her energy and enthusiasm sustained me throughout the two and a half years it took to bring this story to the printed page.

Index